G.G.Williamson.
Watts Hall — U.T.S
Richmond 1944

THE ESSENTIALS OF
BIBLICAL HEBREW

THE
ESSENTIALS OF
BIBLICAL HEBREW

by

KYLE M. YATES, Ph.D.

NEW AND REVISED EDITION

HARPER & BROTHERS
NEW YORK　　　　　　　　LONDON

TABLE OF CONTENTS

SYNTAX OF HEBREW VERBS

INTRODUCTION

President John R. Sampey

Doctor Kyle M. Yates has introduced many hundreds of theological students to the study of the Hebrew Scripture. Through his skill in presenting the "Essentials of Biblical Hebrew" he reduces the toil of the student to a minimum in acquiring sufficient mastery of the language to be able to read and interpret the Hebrew Old Testament.

By the time the student has completed the course of study required to master "Essentials of Biblical Hebrew" he is prepared to use to advantage a Hebrew lexicon like that of Brown, Driver and Briggs and a large grammar such as Cowley's English edition of Gesenius–Kautzsch. He can now understand the best critical commentaries on the Hebrew Old Testament.

I congratulate the hosts of young men who come to the class room of Doctor Yates to study Hebrew under his leadership, and I congratulate students of Biblical Hebrew in other institutions that they now have access to a textbook which will make attractive the study of the language in which the Hebrew historians, poets and prophets wrote. May the number of preachers who can make use of the Hebrew be greatly increased by this excellent manual.

PREFACE

Professor Ernest Sellin has given much encouragement to one who seeks to lead students to learn Hebrew. He asserts that a working knowledge of the language is obligatory unless the preacher is willing to become a helpless plaything in the hands of the unfair critics of the Old Testament. Surely we must do all that we can to stimulate a genuine interest in the study and then present the facts of grammar and syntax in a manner that men will be enabled to learn to be interpreters of the Word.

These lessons have been used in a class numbering one hundred and forty. The men have been led to learn and love the Hebrew Scriptures. The familiar words of the Bible are used over and over while the student masters the rules and laws of the language. The needs of the class of beginners have determined the method and order of presentation. The earlier grammar has been rewritten and enlarged. The exercises are completely new.

Lessons on syntax have been added so that the class may use this same book for two years. The author is aware of the fact that Hebrew syntax is best learned by reading the Old Testament in the original under the guidance of a wise teacher who directs the search for truth. It is hoped that these brief lessons will help both instructor and pupil in the task of interpretation.

It gives genuine joy to record my great debt to President John R. Sampey, D.D., LL.D., for years of guidance, counsel, instruction, encouragement and actual assistance. He taught me to love Hebrew and to seek to become an accurate scholar.

In the actual preparation of this volume several friends and associates have given of their time, energy, and counsel that we might have a useful book. A sincere word of thanks must go to each of them. Of these, Dr. J. Wash Watts, Dr. H. Cornell Goerner, Dr. J. Leo Green, Dr. Claude U. Broach, Dr. Verlin Kruschwitz, Dr. J. J. Owens, and Dr. Wm. T. Bruner have rendered exceptional help.

All the available grammars have been consulted and used freely in the preparation of this volume. The lexicon of Brown, Driver and Briggs has been used constantly. Grateful acknowledgment is hereby made for all the help received.

Kyle M. Yates

Louisville, Ky., February 22, 1938.

PREFACE TO THE SECOND EDITION

It has been a labor of love to revise this grammar in the light of the criticisms and suggestions of friends from all sections of our land. It humbles one to know that the grammar is so widely accepted. I take this occasion to salute with best wishes all toilers in the sphere of Hebrew exegesis.

Kyle M. Yates

Louisville, Ky., May 15, 1943.

THE ESSENTIALS OF
BIBLICAL HEBREW

LESSON I

THE ALPHABET

Form	Final form	Represented in transliteration by	Name	Pronounced as
א		'	'Ālĕph	(Silent)
ב (ב)		b (v)	Bêth	b in *boy*
ג (ג)		g (gh)	Gîmĕl	g in *go*
ד (ד)		d (dh)	Dālĕth	d in *day*
ה		h	Hê	h in *hat*
ו		w	Wāw	w in *way*
ז		z	Zăyĭn	z in *zeal*
ח		ḥ	Ḥêth	ch in "*loch*"
ט		ṭ	Ṭêth	t in *toy*
י		y	Yôdh	y in *yet*
כ (כ)	ך	k (kh)	Kăph	k in *keep*
ל		l	Lāmĕdh	l in *let*
מ	ם	m	Mêm	m in *met*
נ	ן	n	Nûn	n in *net*
ס		ṣ	Sāmĕkh	s in *set*
ע		'	'Ăyin	(Silent)
פ (פ)	ף	p (ph)	Pê	p in *put*
צ	ץ	ts	Tsādhê	ts in *hits*
ק		ḳ	Qôph	q in *oblique* (k)
ר		r	Rêsh	r in *run*
שׂ שׁ		{ s / sh	{ Sîn / Shîn	{ s in *so* / sh in *shell*
ת (ת)		t (th)	Tāw	t in *to*

3

Notes

1. Hebrew has twenty-two consonants. (The letters שׂ and שׁ are considered one).

2. These characters are always written separately and *from right to left*.

3. There are no special forms for capital letters.

4. Vowels points were invented and inserted in the text during the seventh century A. D.

5. Certain letters are similar in form. Examine the following characters, noting the differences:

ב (Bêth)   כ (Kăph)   פ (Pê)

ג (Gîmĕl)   נ (Nûn)

ד (Dālĕth)   ר (Rêsh)   ך (Kăph final)   ף (Pê final)

ה (Hê)   ח (Ḥêth)   ת (Tāw)

ו (Wāw)   ז (Zăyĭn)   ן (Nûn final)

ט (Ṭêth)   מ (Mêm)   ם (Mêm final)   ס (Sāmĕkh)

ע ('Ăyĭn)   צ (Tsādhê)   ץ (Tsādhê final)

שׂ (Sîn)   שׁ (Shîn)

6. At the end of a word the letters כ מ נ פ צ have different forms, called final letters.

כ — ך (Kăph)

מ — ם (Mêm)

נ — ן (Nûn)

פ — ף (Pê)

צ — ץ (Tsādhê).

7. Six letters (ב ג ד כ פ ת) have two sounds. When written with the dot (called dāghĕsh-lēne) in the bosom, they have the

hard pronunciation. When the dot is absent, the sound is soft. The dot is omitted after a vowel sound. In all other cases the hard pronunciation is found.

בּ = b		כּ = bh or v	
גּ = g		ג = gh	
דּ = d		ד = dh (as th in *this*)	
כּ = k		כ = kh	
פּ = p		פ = ph or f	
תּ = t		ת = th (as in *think*)	

8. Other letters

א ('Ălĕph) has no sound. (Do not confuse with English "A"). It is a scarcely audible breathing from the lungs, the *Spiritus lenis* of the Greek.

ע ('Ăyĭn) is a guttural consonant that should be pronounced with a slight movement of the uvula. It is represented in transliteration by the rough breathing (*Spiritus asper*).

Exercises

1. Practice writing these letters until it can be done accurately and rapidly.

2. Arrange them promiscuously and practice calling them by name and by the English equivalent.

3. Write in English characters (begin at right).

בּרא משׁלתּם כּרת לבשׁתּן רדף לא תּרצח ותּנאף גּדל

צדק ולא תּגנב לקח יכל זכר הארץ החדשׁ ענן:

4. Write in Hebrew characters.

mym, rgl, bḳr, tmm, zmn, ṭrm, dvr, drk͡h, sml, s͡hmr, 'nn, nts͡h, ksylym, t͡sdyḳ, mzbḥ, 'zḳ, 't.

LESSON II

THE VOWELS

Ancient Hebrew had no system of vowel notation. Finding only the consonants the reader supplied the proper vowel. In some cases help was given by the use of certain consonants (א and ה to denote *a*, י to denote *i* or *e*, and ו to denote *o* or *u*).

After Hebrew had ceased to be a living speech a system of vocalization was invented to preserve the proper pronunciation and meaning of the Sacred Writings.

The Palestinian system employs points and signs above, below, and in the bosom of consonantal letters. All vowels are sublinear except Ḥôlĕm and Shûrĕḳ.

TABLE OF VOWEL SIGNS

Sign	Name	English Equivalent	Sounded as	Illustration
ָ	Ḳāmĕts	ā (ä)	a in *father*	יָד yādh
ַ	Păthăḥ	ă	a in *hat*	עַם 'ăm
ֵ	Tsērê	ē	e in *they*	שֵׁם shēm
ֶ	Ṣᵉghôl	ĕ	e in *met*	אֶל- 'ĕl
ִי	Ḥîrĕḳ Yôdh	î	i in *machine*	שִׂים sîm
ִ	Ḥîrĕḳ	ĭ	i in *pin*	הִק hĭḳ
ֹו, ֹ	Ḥôlĕm	ô, ō	o in *roll*	קֹול ḳôl כֹּל kōl
ָ	Ḳāmĕts Ḥāṭûph	ŏ	o in *not*	כָּל- kŏl
ֹו	Shûrĕḳ	û	u in *true*	קֹום ḳûm
ֻ	Ḳĭbbûts	ŭ	u in *put*	הֻק hŭḳ

Vocal and Silent Sh^ewa

In addition to the vowels given above, Hebrew employs still another sign ־ָ called Sh^ewa. When it stands under a consonant closing a syllable it is not a vowel but a Silent Sh^ewa, or a Syllable-divider. When it is under a consonant at the beginning of the syllable it is a vocal Sh^ewa and is pronounced as a very short *e*. It is, however, only a half-vowel. The first vowel sign in the Bible is this Simple Sh^ewa בְּרֵאשִׁית b^erē'-shîth.

This Simple Sh^ewa may be combined with the three short vowels to form Compound Sh^ewas. These are also half-vowels.

־ֲ	Ḥāṭēph-Păthăḥ	very short *a* sound	חֲמוֹר (h^amôr)
־ֱ	Ḥāṭēph-S^eghôl	very short *e* sound	אֱלֹהִים ('^elôhîm)
־ֳ	Ḥāṭēph-Kāmĕts	very short *o* sound	חֳלִי (ḥ^olî)

Notes

1. Each syllable must begin with a consonant. (There is one exception. It is the conjunction וֹ).

2. When י (Yôdh) is preceded by an *i* or an *e* it combines with the vowel and loses its consonantal force. (יִם=yĭm, but שִׂים= sîm).

3. Ḥôlĕm and Shûrĕķ, when written fully, use the letter waw (וֹ). The point is placed over it for Ḥôlĕm and in the bosom for Shûrĕķ.

4. When the vowel sign Ḥôlĕm, ־ֹ, occurs in a syllable preceding the consonant שׁ, it coincides with the dot over the right hand tip of the consonant. מֹשֵׁל = mō-shēl. Similarly, when ־ֹ

occurs after שׁ, the dot does double service. שֹׁבֵע = sō-vă'. It is clear that the ִ must be read, otherwise there would be no vowel for that particular syllable.

5. Occasionally we find יֵ ê and יֶ é in addition to the signs given above.

6. It will be noted that the sign for long "*a*" and for short "*o*" are the same. The beginner must be content to wait for the full explanation until he has learned the laws of the syllable and the tone (accent).

7. Short vowels may be heightened.

    ַ ă to ָ ā
    ֶ ĭ to ֵ ē
    ָ ŭ to ֹ ō

8. Certain vowels are unchangeable. They are ָ â, יֶ é, יֵ ê, יִ î, וֹ ô and וּ û. (Note the circumflex marking). Apparently these vowels are characteristic of the forms in which they appear and these forms would lose their identity if the vowels were allowed to change.

EXERCISES

1. Practice writing, naming, and sounding the vowels.

2. Transliterate the following consonants and vowel signs:

דַּל כָּל שָׁת אֵם שִׂים עוֹד בֵּית אָדָם שָׁמַר קוֹטֵל בְּרִית אֲשֶׁר
מָשָׁל בְּדָלוּ שָׂנֵא אָמַר לָךְ כָּתַב מְשָׁלָם יַעֲלוּ סוּסִים קוֹלִי
הָאִישׁ כָּתוּב.

3. Write the following in pointed Hebrew (right to left): bēn, băth, dôr, lēv, măr, rîv, ḳôl, ḳûm, bêth, nûn, 'ᵉlôhîm, lô, lû, lî, yîm, yĭm.

LESSON III

THE SYLLABLE

Each syllable begins with a consonant and includes only one full vowel. It may include two or more consonants. It may include a half-vowel before the full vowel. Thus there is a syllable for each full vowel but never for a half-vowel alone.

When marking syllables, begin with the end of the word. Thus the last syllable, the ultima, in קָמַל is מַל. The pathaḥ must be included to give a full vowel and the מ must be included in order to begin with a consonant. Accordingly the penult is קָ. In בְּרִית (bᵉrîth) there is only one full vowel, so only one syllable. (The one exception to this rule will be presented on page 19).

KINDS OF SYLLABLES

1. **Open,** ending in a vowel בּוֹ bô, לְ lā. The vowel in the open syllable must be long unless accented. It may then be short. בּוֹ bô, an open syllable with a long vowel. מַיִם mă-yĭm, an accented open syllable with a short vowel.

NOTE: The mark ⊤ is the accent.

2. **Closed,** ending in a consonant. מַל tăl, קוֹל ḳôl. The vowel in the closed syllable must be short unless accented. It may then be long, נִקְטָל nĭḳ-tăl. Each of these two syllables is closed, and each vowel is short. שֵׁם shēm, is a closed syllable, but the accent makes it possible for the vowel to be long. א and ה do not close a syllable (except when ה bears mappiḳ סוּסָה sû-ṣāh; see page 11).

3. **Sharpened,** a closed syllable which ends in a consonant that is doubled. קִטֵּל kĭṭ-ṭēl.

NOTE: When a consonant would be repeated (as קִטְטֵל) instead of writing both of them, one is usually omitted and a point called *dāghĕsh-forte* is placed in the bosom of the one that remains. קִטֵּל kĭṭ-ṭēl.

The vowel of the sharpened syllable is short unless accented. הַקּוֹל hăk-ḳôl, אִמִּי 'ĭm-mî, הֵמָּה hēm-mā(h).

4. **Half-open,** an unaccented open syllable with a short vowel. עִבְדוּ 'ĭ-vᵉdhû, הַחֹשֶׁךְ hă-ḥō-shĕk. This violation of the rules for an open syllable is permitted because it is impossible to tell, when the word is pronounced normally, whether or not the letter following the vowel is repeated. The syllable sounds like a closed syllable and its vowel is allowed to stand like that of a closed syllable.

VOCABULARY

אָב	'āv	father	בֵּן	bēn	son	יוֹם	yôm	day
אָח	'āḥ	brother	בַּת	băth	daughter (f.)	קוֹל	ḳôl	voice
אֵם	'ēm	mother (f.)	טוֹב	ṭôv	good	שֵׁם	shēm	name

EXERCISES

1. Pronounce, transliterate, and divide into syllables. Indicate the kind of syllable.

לֹא אַתֶּם מַיִם אָדָם אֲשֶׁר בְּרִית טוֹב עִיר אֱלֹהִים הַחֶרֶב
שָׁנָה קוֹלוֹ בָּרָא בְּרֵאשִׁית קְטָלָתַם הַבֵּן הַשָּׁמַיִם הַסּוּסִים עִבְדוּ:

2. Write in pointed Hebrew:

way-yar' 'ᵉlô-hîm 'ĕth-kŏl-'ᵃshĕr 'ā-sā(h) wᵉhĭn-nē(h) ṭôv mᵉ'ôdh wă-yᵉhî 'ĕ-rĕv wă-yᵉhî vō-ḳĕr yôm hăsh-shîsh-shî.

NOTE: The consonants in parentheses represent letters tnat have lost their consonantal value and remain as vowel letters only.

LESSON IV
SOME TECHNICAL MATTERS

Dăghĕsh-lēne

The dot placed in the six letters, ב ג ד כ פ ת, when they do not immediately follow a vowel or a vocal shᵉwa, is called *dāghĕsh-lēne*. It serves to harden the pronunciation. כָּתַבְתָּ kā-thăv-tā.

Dāghĕsh-forte

Any letter, except א, ה, ח, ע, ר, may receive in its bosom a point called *dāghĕsh-forte*, indicating that it is doubled. It is always preceded by a vowel sound. הַמַּיִם hăm-mă-yĭm. הַקּוֹל hăḳ-ḳôl.

Măppîḳ

Măppîḳ is a point placed in final ה to indicate that it is to be treated as a consonant and not as a silent vowel letter. עָמָהּ 'ĭm-māh. גָּבַהּ gā-văh.

Syllable-divider

The syllable-divider is a silent shᵉwa which is used to mark the end of certain syllables. It is used with closed syllables only, and with them only in the following cases: (1) when they are not final, as in the penult of יִקְטֹל; (2) When they end in ךְ, as in לֵךְ (lēkh); (3) when they have two consonantal characters at the end, both receiving a syllable-divider and both conso-nants being pronounced, as in the ultima of קָטַלְתְּ. Only the first receives it when the second is silent, as in the ultima of וַיִּרְא.

The Gutturals

The letters א, ה, ח, ע, (and for some purposes ר) are called gutturals. א and ה do not close a syllable. They are usually silent at the end of a word and lose their consonantal character completely. This is always true of א at the end of a syllable within a word. However ה, when within a word, remains a guttural consonant and does so at the end when the dot (măppîk) is placed in its bosom.

The following peculiarities are to be noted:

1. They **refuse to be doubled.** Daghesh-forte cannot be placed in a guttural. When the dot is rejected the preceding vowel is usually heightened, ־ֱ to ־ָ, ־ֵ to ־ֵ, ־ִ to ־ֵ. Before ה and ח the vowel is not heightened. (Cf. note on the half-open syllable). יְקַטֵּל yᵉḳăṭ-ṭēl but יְקָאֵל yᵉḳā-'ēl, קַטֵּל ḳĭṭ-ṭēl but קָהֵל ḳĭ-hēl.

2. They **prefer compound shᵉwa under them** rather than simple shᵉwa. (Usually ־ֲ, but may be ־ֱ, especially with א). אֱלֹהִים ᵉlôhîm. יַעֲטֹל yă-'ᵃṭōl.

3. They have a decided **preference for the "a" class vowels around them.** (In most cases this is ־ַ. It may be ־ֶ). יִקְטֹל yĭḳ-ṭōl but יַעֲטֹל yă-'ᵃṭōl.

Maḳḳeph

The maḳḳeph is a small horizontal line like the English hyphen used to join words which are connected in thought or utterance. The words become one and the accent is on the last word. From two to four words may be united in this way. אֶת־כָּל־אֲשֶׁר־לוֹ 'ĕth-kŏl-ᵃshĕr-lô.

The Accents

In the Hebrew text one finds a large number of marks in addition to the regular vowel points. These marks of accentuation are placed above, below, and between the consonants. They are designed: (a) to mark the tone syllable of the word; (b) as punctuation marks; (c) as musical notations. There are about thirty of these signs in the Hebrew text. Since it will be impossible to treat them adequately here, we may give ourselves to a consideration of the more essential matters.

The main accent or tone falls generally upon the ultima, מָשַׁל mā-shăl. In certain nouns (מֶלֶךְ) and some verbal forms (מָשַׁלְתִּי mā-shăl-tî) it falls on the penult. The syllable that bears the main accent is known as the tone syllable. In this grammar words which are accented on the last syllable are not marked (קָטַל ḳā-ṭăl); those accented on the penult have ־ under the vowel of the accented syllable to call special attention to the accentuation, קָטַלְתִּי ḳā-ṭăl-tî.

Metheg

Metheg is a secondary accent used in the same word with the regular accent. The natural position for this secondary accent is on the second and fourth syllables before the tone,

הַכּוֹכָבִים hăk-kô-khā-vîm. The sign used is a small perpendicular stroke under the syllable to the left of the vowel to be accented, הָאָדָם hā-'ā-dhām.

The sign is used:

1. Usually on the second syllable before the tone if the vowel is long. In case that vowel is short it goes back to the third syllable, הָאִשָׁה hā-'ĭsh-shā(h), הָאַרְבָּעִים hā-'ăr-bā-'îm.

2. With all vowels before compound shᵉwa, וַאֲנִי wă-'ᵃnî.

3. With all long vowels before vocal shᵉwa pretonic, מָשְׁלוּ mā-shᵉlû.

4. With a long vowel in a closed syllable before maḳḳeph, שֵׁם־הַנָּהָר shēm-hăn-nā-hār.

Pause

In a Hebrew verse there are two natural pauses. The accents *silluḳ* (ⲧ) and *'Athnah* (ⲅ) mark these pause syllables. *Silluḳ* occurs on the last tone syllable and *'Athnah* on the principal syllable near the middle of the verse. A syllable bearing either of these marks is said to be *in pause*. The vowel so marked usually becomes long. מַיִם mă-yĭm, in pause, becomes מָיִם mā-yĭm.

VOCABULARY

אִישׁ	'îsh	*man*	יָד	yādh	*hand* (f.)	עֵץ 'ēts *tree*
אָדָם	'ā-dhām	*man*	סוּס	sûs	*horse*	עַם 'ăm *people*
לֵב	lēv	*heart*	עִיר	'îr	*city* (f.)	עַל 'ăl *upon*

LESSON V

THE ARTICLE

Hebrew has no indefinite article. Indefiniteness is generally indicated by the absence of the article, קוֹל ḳôl, *a voice,* שֵׁם shēm, *a name.*

The definite article is always a prefix. It is joined to the word so closely as to make one word in writing and pronunciation. It suffers no change for gender or number.

TABLE FOR WRITING THE ARTICLE

· הַ before non-gutturals הַקּוֹל hăḳ-ḳôl *the voice.*

הָ before א, ר (ע generally) הָאָב hā-'āv *the father.*

הַ before ה and ח הַחֹשֶׁךְ hă-ḥō-shĕk *the darkness.*

הֶ before ח and unaccented הָ, עָ הֶחָג hĕ-ḥāg *the festival.*

NOTES

1. The usual way of writing the article is to prefix הַ to the substantive and put daghesh-forte in the first consonant, הַשֵּׁם, הַגָּדוֹל, הַטּוֹב, הַבַּת.

2. Gutturals (א, ה, ח, ע) and ר refuse the daghesh-forte and hence the vowel changes noted above. The short vowel of the article is left in an open syllable, unaccented. The normal thing is to heighten the ־ַ to ־ָ.

3. When the substantive begins with א or ר (ע usually) the normal change of vowel takes place, הָעֵץ hā'ēts, *the tree.*

4. In the case of ה and ח the doubling is refused, but the

vowel is allowed to remain short. They are said to be doubled
by implication, הַחֲרֵב. (See note on half-open syllable, p. 10).

5. אֶרֶץ 'ĕ-rĕts, *earth*, with the article becomes הָאָרֶץ hā-'ā-
rĕts, *the earth*. עַם 'ăm, *people*, becomes הָעָם hā-'ām, *the people*.
הַר hăr, *mountain*, becomes הָהָר hā-hār, *the mountain*. (These
syllables are accented and the vowel is at liberty to change its
length for the sake of euphony).

6. The interrogative particle הַ is usually prefixed to the
first word of an interrogative sentence. It may be written הֲ,
הַ or הֶ; הֲיִקְטֹל *will he kill?;* הַאֶקְטֹל *shall I kill?;* הֶאָמַר *did
he say?*

VOCABULARY

דָּבָר dā-vār	*word, thing*	מָקוֹם mā-ḳôm	*place*
שָׁלוֹם shā-lôm	*peace*	שָׁנָה shā-nā(h)	*year* (f.)
נָבִיא nā-vî'	*prophet*	בֹּקֶר bō-ḳĕr	*morning*
רֹאשׁ rô'sh	*head*	בְּרִית bᵉrîth	*covenant* (f.)

EXERCISES

1. Prefix the article with the proper pointing:

סוּס, רֹאשׁ, שָׁלוֹם, אֵל, חָשֶׁךְ, אֵם, יֶלֶד, אוֹר, זָהָב, יָם,
הַר, מֶלֶךְ, עֵד, רֶגֶל, אָחָד, עֵת, פֶּה, חוּץ, נַעַר, יַיִן, חֶסֶד,
לָשׁוֹן, פְּרִי, עָנָן.

2. Write in Hebrew:

*The man, the father, the day, the voice, the head, the city, the
peace, the place, the morning, the covenant, the darkness, the prophet,
the heart, the horse.*

LESSON VI
PREPOSITIONS

The Inseparable Prepositions

בְּ *in, by, with*

כְּ *as, like, according to*   } always prefixes

לְ *to, for, at*

They are pointed as follows:

ְ usually {

בְּ   בְּשֵׁם   *in a name*

כְּ   כִּדְבָר   *according to a word*

לְ   לְקוֹל   *to a voice*

ְ (ǐ) before another shᵉwa {

בְּ   בִּדְבַר   *by word of*

כְּ   כִּבְרִית   *according to a covenant*

לְ   לִפְרִי   *to fruit*

ֲ (ă)   before compound shᵉwa

ֱ (ĕ)   corresponding short vowel:

ֳ (ŏ)   ֲ ֲ , ֱ ֱ , ֳ ֳ

בַ, בֶ, בָ

כַ, כֶ, כָ   כַּאֲשֶׁר

לַ, לֶ, לָ   *according as*

ַ (ă)   before the article,

ָ (ā)   with the vowel

ֶ (é)   of the article

בַּ   בַּיּוֹם   *in the day*

כָּ   כָּרֹאשׁ   *like the head*

לֶ   לֶחָג   *to the festival*

NOTES

1. Sometimes the preposition may receive ָ (ā) before the tone syllable. This is usually true before an "*a*" sound in a monosyllabic word, לָעַד *to eternity*.

2. When the preposition precedes the article the הַ of the article is lost, and the preposition takes the vowel of the article. Instead of בְּהַיּוֹם we find בַּיּוֹם. Instead of לְהַקּוֹל we find לַקּוֹל. Instead of בְּהַחֹשֶׁךְ we find בַּחֹשֶׁךְ. Instead of לְהָעִיר we find לָעִיר.

The Preposition מִן *from*

It may stand alone or be prefixed to the substantive.

It is pointed as follows:

מִן־	before the article (usually)	מִן־הַקּוֹל	*from the voice*
מִ·	before non-gutturals, with the nun assimilated	מִקּוֹל	*from a voice*
מֵ	before א, ע, and ר (usually)	מֵאִישׁ	*from a man*
מֵ	before ה and ח (usually)	מֵחוּץ	*from abroad (outside)*

VOCABULARY

אוֹר	'ôr	*light*	יָם	yām	*sea*
חֹשֶׁךְ	ḥō-shĕkh	*darkness*	זָהָב	zā-hāv	*gold*
סֵפֶר	ṣē-phĕr	*book*	מֶלֶךְ	mĕ-lĕkh	*king*
מְאֹד	mᵉ'ôdh	*exceedingly*	רֶגֶל	rĕ-ghĕl	*foot* (f.)

EXERCISES

1. Pronounce aloud, translate and transliterate.

מִבָּקָר, כַּדָּבָר, כִּדְבָר, מֵאִישׁ, בַּמָּקוֹם, לַבֵּן, בָּעִיר, מֵרֹאשׁ, לְיָד, לַבְּרִית, מִן־הַמֶּלֶךְ, מֵחֹשֶׁךְ, מֵאוֹר, מִן־הָרֶגֶל.

2. Write in Hebrew.

To the day, in a name, for the man, from the father to the mother,

according to the word, in the city, from day to day, for a man,
for a woman, from father to son, in the morning, in the light.

LESSON VII

The Conjunction and the Adjective

The Conjunction

The inseparable prefix וְ *and*, is written as follows:

וְ usually, וְשֵׁם wᵉshēm, *and a name.*

וּ before בּ, מ, פּ, and consonants with simple shᵉwa וּבֵן û-vēn,
and son, וּמָקוֹם û-mā-ḳôm, *and place*, וּדְמוּת û-dhᵉmûth, *and
likeness.*

וִ before the form יְ, וִיהִי wî-hî (instead of וְיְהִי), *and let it be.*

וַ, וֶ, וֵ before compound shᵉwa (the corresponding short vowel),
וַאֲנִי wă-ᵃnî, *and I.*

NOTE: It may be written וָ before a heavily accented syllable,
וָרָע wā-rāʿ, *and evil.*

The Adjective

In Hebrew the adjective may be used attributively or pred-
icatively.

1. When it **qualifies** (modifies) a substantive it stands after
the substantive and agrees with it in gender, number and definiteness, שֵׁם טוֹב shēm ṭôv, *a good name*, הַשֵּׁם הַטּוֹב hăsh-
shēm hăṭ-ṭôv, *the good name* (*the name, the good*), הַקּוֹל הַטּוֹב
וְהַגָּדוֹל hăḳ-ḳôl hăṭ-ṭôv wᵉhăg-gā-dhôl, *the voice, the good, and
the great* = *the good and the great voice.*

2. The **predicative** adjective agrees with the substantive in
gender and number, but it never takes the article. It usually

stands before the substantive, but may follow it, טוֹב הַקּוֹל
ṭôv hăḳ-ḳôl or הַקּוֹל טוֹב hăḳ-ḳôl ṭôv, *the voice (is) good,* טוֹב
וְגָדוֹל הַשֵּׁם ṭôv wᵉghā-dhôl hăsh-shēm, *the name (is) good and
great.*

VOCABULARY

תָּמִים	tā-mîm	*perfect*	קָדוֹשׁ	ḳā-dhôsh	*holy*
גִּבּוֹר	gĭb-bôr	*hero*	יֶלֶד	yĕ-lĕdh	*child*
אָדוֹן	'ā-dhôn	*lord*	עֵד	'ēdh	*witness*
חֶרֶב	ḥĕ-rĕv	*sword* (f.)	כּוֹכָב	kô-khāv	*star*

EXERCISES

1. Pronounce aloud, translate, and transliterate.

הַבֵּן הַטּוֹב וְהַבַּת, טוֹב הַיֶּלֶד, הַיֶּלֶד הַטּוֹב, תָּמִים הַבֹּקֶר,
הָעֵץ גָּדוֹל, קָדוֹשׁ הָאָדוֹן, הַיֶּלֶד וְהָאֵם בָּעִיר, הַגִּבּוֹר עֵד,
גָּדוֹל הַכּוֹכָב, הַחֹשֶׁךְ הַגָּדוֹל, הַמֶּלֶךְ קָדוֹשׁ:

2. Write in Hebrew.

*A great day, the good brother, in the great day, the great man
(is) good, mother and son, father and daughter, light and darkness
(are) in the day and in the book. The morning (is) perfect. The
hand and the heart (are) for the son.*

LESSON VIII

THE VERB

Hebrew has no "tenses." Tense indicates time. The time of
a Hebrew verb is indicated by its context.

The inflections of a Hebrew verb indicate state instead of

time. They present the condition as complete, incomplete, continuous or imperative. The completed states will be called perfects, the incomplete ones imperfects, the continuous ones participles and the imperative ones imperatives. Infinitives are not verbs but nouns or adverbs used to name the action of a verb or to modify a verb.

EXAMPLES

Perfect	קָטַל	ḳā-ṭăl *he killed, he has killed, he will have killed.*
Imperfect	יִקְטֹל	yĭḳ-ṭōl *he began to kill, he kills, he will kill.*
Participle	קוֹטֵל קָטֵל	ḳô-ṭēl *(he) was killing, (he) is killing, (he) will be killing.*
Imperative	קְטֹל	ḳᵉṭōl *kill thou.*
Infinitive	קָטוֹל קְטֹל	ḳā-tôl ḳᵉṭōl *killing.*

The Perfect

The fundamental part of any verb is the root. The simplest verb form is the third person masculine singular of the perfect. The consonants of this form, as a rule, constitute the root. The letters of the strong verb like קטל appear in all forms of the verb without change. The vowels of the 3rd masculine singular perfect continue in all other forms unchanged except as the laws of syllable and tone require a change when afformatives are added. Afformatives are remnants of personal pronouns, which are added to indicate variations in person, number and gender.

The afformatives for the perfect are:

Singular				Plural		
3 m.	—	*he*		3 c.	וֹ—	*they*
3 f.	הָ—	*she*		2 m.	תֶּם—	*you*
2 m.	תָּ—	*thou*		2 f.	תֶּן—	*you*
2 f.	תְּ—	*thou*		1 c.	נוּ—	*we*
1 c.	תִּי—	*I*				

When we start with the root קטל and add these afformatives we find the following forms:

Singular

3 m.	קָטַל	ḳā-ṭăl	*he killed*
3 f.	קָטְלָה	ḳā-ṭᵉlā(h)	*she killed*
2 m.	קָטַלְתָּ	ḳā-ṭăl-tā	*thou didst kill*
2 f.	קָטַלְתְּ	ḳā-ṭălt	*thou didst kill*
1 c.	קָטַלְתִּי	ḳā-ṭăl-tî	*I killed*

Plural

3 c.	קָטְלוּ	ḳā-ṭᵉlû	*they killed*
2 m.	קְטַלְתֶּם	ḳᵉṭăl-tĕm	*you killed*
2 f.	קְטַלְתֶּן	ḳᵉṭăl-tĕn	*you killed*
1 c.	קָטַלְנוּ	ḳā-ṭăl-nû	*we killed*

Explanation of Vowel Changes

1. With vowel afformatives

Two of these afformatives, הָ and ו, begin with a vowel and are called vowel afformatives. Since they begin with a vowel, they cannot form separate syllables and so attach themselves to the final consonant of the root. They draw the accent to themselves. Then the vowel of the original ultima, being left in an unaccented open syllable, must be either heightened or volatilized. It is usually volatilized. Thus the ultima of קָטַל becomes טָלָה or טָלוּ. The sh⁰wa of this syllable, being a volatilized vowel, is vocal. It is also pretonic. Therefore the vowel preceding it receives a metheg. Thus the penult of קָטַל becomes קָ (קָטְלָה, קָטְלוּ).

2. With consonant afformatives

The other afformatives begin with a consonant and are called consonant afformatives. When they include a full vowel, they form separate syllables which are not accented except in the case of the heavy suffixes, תֶּם and תֶּן. When these heavy afformatives draw the accent from the penult, the vowel of the antepenult, standing in an open syllable two places before the tone, must receive a metheg or volatilize. Usually it volatilizes (קְטַלְתֶּם).

In the case of the 2nd feminine singular the ת cannot form a separate syllable and so attaches itself to the ultima. Both the final consonants then receive a syllable divider (קָטַלְתְּ).

Vowel afformatives and תֶּם and תֶּן take the accent. The nearest vowel in an open syllable is shortened to sh⁰wa.

VOCABULARY

מָשַׁל	mā-shăl	he ruled	גָּדַל	gā-dhăl	he was great
נָתַן	nā-thăn	he gave	דָּבַר	dā-văr	he spoke
שָׁמַר	shā-măr	he kept	כָּרַת	kā-răth	he cut
לָבַשׁ	lā-văsh	he put on	פָּקַד	pā-ḳădh	he visited

EXERCISES

1. Write the perfect using מָשַׁל to rule and פָּקַד to visit.
2. Translate, pronounce aloud, and transliterate.

מָשַׁלְתִּי, לָבַשְׁתָּ, כָּרַתוּ, נָתְנָה, גְּדַלְתֶּם, שְׁמַרְתֶּן, פָּקַדְנוּ,

מָשְׁלָה, נָתַן אֶת הַסֵּפֶר לָאִישׁ הַטּוֹב, כָּרְתָה אֶת הַסֵּפֶר:

NOTE: The direct object (if definite) is usually marked by the placing of אֶת immediately before it. The אֶת is not to be translated. It may be written as a separate word (אֶת הַקוֹל) or joined by maḳḳeph to the following word (אֶת־הַקוֹל). When joined to the word the vowel is shortened.

The verb stands first in the sentence unless special emphasis is desired, שָׁמַר הָאִישׁ אֶת הָעֵץ *the man kept the tree.*

LESSON IX

THE IMPERFECT

The imperfect, expressing unfinished action, is formed from an abstract substantive, (*nomen actionis*) preceded by the fragments of the personal pronouns (י, ת, א, נ) which are called preformatives, תִּקְטֹל tĭḳ-ṭōl, *thou wilt kill* (lit. *thou (to) kill*).

In the perfect (complete action) we are more particularly interested in the fact, and the part denoting the person comes last קָטַלְתָּ. In the imperfect (action still incomplete) we are more interested in the person of the agent, and the pronoun stands before the root of the verb תִּקְטֹל. In some forms of the imperfect we have preformatives and afformatives.

Singular			Plural		
3 m.	– – – י	*he*	3 m.	י – – – וּ	*they*
3 f.	– – – תּ	*she*	3 f.	תּ – – – נָה	*they*
2 m.	– – – תּ	*thou*	2 m.	תּ – – – וּ	*you*

2 f.　תּ – – – ְ י　*thou*　　　2 f.　תּ – – – נָה　*you*

1 c.　– – – א　*I*　　　1 c.　– – – נ　*we*

Beginning with the root קטל and adding the afformatives and preformatives we have:

Singular

3 m.	יִקְטֹל	yĭḳ-ṭōl	*he will kill*
3 f.	תִּקְטֹל	tĭḳ-ṭōl	*she will kill*
2 m.	תִּקְטֹל	tĭḳ-ṭōl	*thou wilt kill*
2 f.	תִּקְטְלִי	tĭḳ-ṭᵉlî	*thou wilt kill*
1 c.	אֶקְטֹל	'ĕḳ-ṭōl	*I shall kill*

Plural

3 m.	יִקְטְלוּ	yĭḳ-ṭᵉlû	*they will kill*
3 f.	תִּקְטֹלְנָה	tĭḳ-ṭōl-nā(h)	*they will kill*
2 m.	תִּקְטְלוּ	tĭḳ-ṭᵉlû	*you will kill*
2 f.	תִּקְטֹלְנָה	tĭḳ-ṭōl-nā(h)	*you will kill*
1 c.	נִקְטֹל	nĭḳ-ṭōl	*we shall kill*

NOTES

1. The vowel of the preformative is ־ִ (ĭ) (thinned from an original ă), except under א which prefers ־ֶ (ĕ). (See rules for gutturals for this preference for the "*a*" class vowel).

2. The second vowel in most strong verbs is ֹ (ō). It is a tone long *o* heightened from an original ־ֻ (ŭ). This stem vowel

is volatilized before the vowel afformatives יִ and ־ֹ. (Instead
of יִקְטְלוּ we find יְקַטְלוּ).

3. The preformative syllable יִק is closed. Thus we know the
sh°wa under the first radical ק is a syllable-divider. Watch for
daghesh-lene following this closed syllable, יִקְדַּשׁ, יִשְׁבֹּר, יִכְתֹּב.

VOCABULARY

מָלַךְ	mā-lăkh	*he reigned*		סָפַר	ṣā-phăr	*he numbered*
כָּתַב	kā-thăv	*he wrote*		קָדַשׁ	ķā-dhăsh	*he was holy*
זָכַר	zā-khăr	*he remembered*		כָּשַׁל	kā-shăl	*he stumbled*
לָמַד	lā-mădh	*he learned*		רָדַף	rā-dhăph	*he pursued*

EXERCISES

1. Write the imperfect using מָשַׁל *to rule* and שָׁמַר *to keep*.
2. Translate and locate* fully:

יִמְלֹךְ, אֶלְמֹד, יִפְקֹד, תִּכְתֹּב, תִּזְכְּרִי, אָכְשַׁל, יִסְפְּרוּ,
תְּקַדֵּשְׁנָה, תִּכָשְׁלוּ, נִרְדֹּף, תִּזְכֹּרְנָה, תִּמְשְׁלִי, יִלְבְּשׁוּ, אֶשְׁמֹר,
תִּגְדַּלְנָה, נִכְרֹת:

3. Translate.

I shall write, you (m.) *will keep, we shall speak, they will remember the word. Thou wilt reign in the city. She will learn, we
shall remember. You will visit the son and the daughter.*

*NOTE: To locate the verb form מָשַׁלְתָּ let the student say:
"Perfect, 2nd, masculine, singular from מָשַׁל, to rule. Thou
didst rule." For the word שׁוֹמֵר let him say: "Active participle
from שָׁמַר, to keep. Keeping or a keeper."

LESSON X

IMPERATIVES, INFINITIVES AND PARTICIPLES

The Imperative, used only for affirmative commands, is identical with the imperfect except that it drops the preformative, תִּקְטֹל *thou wilt kill*, but קְטֹל *kill thou.*

	Singular			Plural		
2 m.	קְטֹל	ḳᵉṭōl	*kill thou*	קִטְלוּ	ḳĭ-ṭᵉlû	*kill ye*
2 f.	קִטְלִי	ḳĭ-ṭᵉlî	*kill thou*	קְטֹלְנָה	ḳᵉṭōl-nā(h)	*kill ye*

The Imperative is never used with a negative. Prohibitions are expressed either by לֹא (*not*) with the imperfect or by אַל with the jussive. (The jussive is usually an abbreviated form of the imperfect. It is employed in the second and third persons to express commands, wishes and prohibitions.)

The Infinitives appear in two forms.

The Absolute קָטוֹל is rare.

The Construct קְטֹל is more common.

The usual infinitive is the short form קְטֹל, being used frequently with prepositions prefixed, לִמְשֹׁל *to rule.* It is identical in form with the 2nd masculine singular imperative (except in Hiph'il).

The Absolute infinitive קָטוֹל does not admit of any prefix or suffix. It has the effect of throwing forward prominently the bare idea of the verb without defining it in any way. It merely paints an action, without regard to agent, time or circumstance. It usually accompanies a finite verb for added emphasis or to

28

THE ESSENTIALS OF

denote continuance of the action, שָׁמוֹר שָׁמַרְתִּי *keeping, I have kept,* מָלוֹךְ תִּמְלֹךְ *ruling, thou shalt rule (thou shalt verily be king).* (Do not confuse with the participle).

The Participle represents action as continuous. It is unbroken. The simple stem of the verb has two forms, an active participle (קֹטֵל) קוֹטֵל *killing* or *one who kills*, and a passive participle קָטוּל *killed* (dead).

By way of summary we have the simple verb as follows:

PERFECT

	Singular			Plural	
3 m.	מָשַׁל	*he ruled*	3 c.	מָשְׁלוּ	*they ruled*
3 f.	מָשְׁלָה	*she ruled*	2 m.	מְשַׁלְתֶּם	*you ruled*
2 m.	מָשַׁלְתָּ	*thou didst rule*	2 f.	מְשַׁלְתֶּן	*you ruled*
2 f.	מָשַׁלְתְּ	*thou didst rule*	1 c.	מָשַׁלְנוּ	*we ruled*
1 c.	מָשַׁלְתִּי	*I ruled*			

IMPERFECT

	Singular			Plural	
3 m.	יִמְשֹׁל	*he will rule*	3 m.	יִמְשְׁלוּ	*they will rule*
3 f.	תִּמְשֹׁל	*she will rule*	3 f.	תִּמְשֹׁלְנָה	*they will rule*
2 m.	תִּמְשֹׁל	*thou wilt rule*	2 m.	תִּמְשְׁלוּ	*you will rule*
2 f.	תִּמְשְׁלִי	*thou wilt rule*	2 f.	תִּמְשֹׁלְנָה	*you will rule*
1 c.	אֶמְשֹׁל	*I shall rule*	1 c.	נִמְשֹׁל	*we shall rule*

IMPERATIVE

	Singular			Plural	
2 m.	מְשֹׁל	*rule thou*	2 m.	מִשְׁלוּ	*rule ye*
2 f.	מִשְׁלִי	*rule thou*	2 f.	מְשֹׁלְנָה	*rule ye*

Infinitives

מָשׁוֹל *ruling*

מְשֹׁל *to rule*

Participles

מוֹשֵׁל (מֹשֵׁל) *ruling*, or *one who rules (a ruler)*

מָשׁוּל *ruled* (under complete subjection)

Vocabulary

דָּבַק *cleave, cling* קָבַר *bury*

לָכַד *capture* צָדֵק *be righteous*

שָׁכַן *dwell* שָׂכַל *be wise, prudent*

Exercises

1. Translate and locate the verb forms.

שָׁמְרוּ, אֶשְׁמֹר, מָשַׁל, קָבַר, צָדֵק, כָּתוֹב, לָמוֹד, נָתֵן,
סְפָרְנָה, זִכְרוּ אֶת הַדָּבָר, זָכוֹר תִּזְכֹּר לִשְׁמֹר אֶת הַבְּרִית,
מָשׁוּל, קָדַשְׁנוּ, נִשְׂכֹּל, מִשְׁלִי, דְּבֵק:

2. Write in pointed Hebrew.

Learn ye, rule thou in the city, we will learn to keep the head and the heart, thou wilt be great, I shall visit, they will stumble, number ye, remember thou, keeping thou shalt keep the covenant, we shall be righteous, they wrote in the morning.

LESSON XI

Personal Pronouns

In order to use the personal pronoun correctly one must know the separate forms and the abbreviated forms. The former are distinct words and are used to express the nominative case. They are unchangeable and indeclinable.

The abbreviated forms, called pronominal suffixes, are used to represent the oblique cases. Attached as suffixes to the verb or to the particle אֵת they stand as the direct object of the verb (Accusative). When attached to a noun they denote possession (Possessive). When they are joined to the inseparable prepositions they may stand as the object of the preposition.

אֲנִי אִישׁ   I (am) *a man* (separate form)

מְשָׁלַנִּי
מָשַׁל אֹתִי } *he ruled me* { suffix attached to verb
suffix attached to אֵת }

סוּסִי   *my horse* (suffix attached to a noun)

לִי   *to me* (suffix attached to a preposition)

SEPARATE FORMS

Singular			Plural		
אֲנִי	'ᵃnî	} *I*	נַחְנוּ	năḥ-nû	} *we*
אָנֹכִי	'ā-nō-khî		אֲנַחְנוּ	'ᵃnăḥ-nû	
אַתָּה	'ăt-tā(h)	*thou* (m.)	אַתֶּם	'ăt-těm	*you* (m.)
אַתְּ	'ătt	*thou* (f.)	אַתֵּנָה	'ăt-tē-nā(h)	*you* (f.)
הוּא	hû'	*he*	הֵם, הֵמָּה	hēm	*they* (m.)
הִיא	hî'	*she*	הֵנָּה, הֵן	hēn-nā(h)	*they* (f.)

These separate forms are rarely used to express the subject of the verb, except with the participle. The verb form contains the pronominal subject (מָשַׁל *he ruled*). Only when the writer wished to place special emphasis on the subject would he use

הוּא מָשַׁל *he ruled.*

The Pronominal Suffixes with a Preposition

Singular		Plural	
לִי	*to me*	לָנוּ	*to us*
לְךָ	*to thee* (m.)	לָכֶם	*to you* (m.)
לֵךְ (לָךְ)	*to thee* (f.)	לָכֶן	*to you* (f.)
לוֹ	*to him*	לָהֶם	*to them* (m.)
לָהּ	*to her*	לָהֶן	*to them* (f.)

The Pronominal Suffixes with אֵת (Direct Object)

Singular		Plural	
אֹתִי	*me*	אֹתָנוּ	*us*
אֹתְךָ	*thee* (m.)	אֶתְכֶם	*you* (m.)
אֹתָךְ	*thee* (f.)	(אֶתְכֶן)	*you* (f.)
אֹתוֹ	*him*	אֹתָם	*them* (m.)
אֹתָהּ	*her*	אֹתָן	*them* (f.)

The Pronominal Suffixes with a Noun

Singular		Plural	
סוּסִי	*my horse*	סוּסֵנוּ	*our horse*
סוּסְךָ	*thy* (m.) *horse*	סוּסְכֶם	*your* (m.) *horse*
סוּסֵךְ	*thy* (f.) *horse*	סוּסְכֶן	*your* (f.) *horse*
סוּסוֹ	*his horse*	סוּסָם	*their* (m.) *horse*
סוּסָה	*her horse*	סוּסָן	*their* (f.) *horse*

EXERCISES

1. Pronounce and translate.

אָנֹכִי אָב, אַתָּה הָאִישׁ, הוּא הַיֶּלֶד, מָשַׁל הַבֵּן אֶת סוּסוֹ,

קוֹלָהּ טוֹב, גָּדַל יוֹמָם, נָתַן אֶת הַסֵּפֶר לִי, הוּא הַנָּבִיא הַטּוֹב,

נָתְנוּ אֶת סוּסָם לַמֶּלֶךְ:

2. Translate into Hebrew.

The father gave the covenant to him. Her horse (is) *in the city. The king ruled the people. The mother kept him. Thou* (art) *the woman.*

LESSON XII

OTHER PRONOUNS

The Demonstratives

	Singular			Plural		
this	m.	זֶה	zĕ(h)	*these* c.	אֵלֶּה	'ēl-lĕ(h)
	f.	זֹאת	zô'th			
that	m.	הוּא	hû'	*those*	m. (הֵם) הֵמָּה	hēm-mā(h)
	f.	הִיא	hî'		f. (הֵן) הֵנָּה	hēn-nā(h)

These pronouns conform to the same rules as the **adjective** with regard to the article; i. e., they take the article when qualifying, but not when predicative.

זֶה אִישׁ טוֹב   *this* (is) *a good man.*

זֶה הָאִישׁ הַטּוֹב   *this* (is) *the good man.*

הָאִישׁ הַזֶּה   *this man.*

הָאִשָּׁה הַזֹּאת   *this woman.*

הָאִישׁ הַטּוֹב הַזֶּה   *this good man.*

The Relative

אֲשֶׁר who, which, what, is the one relative pronoun. It is invariable for all genders, numbers, and cases. (In later Hebrew שָׁ or שֶׁ followed by daghesh-forte is occasionally found for אֲשֶׁר).

The Interrogatives

מִי (mî) who, refers to persons,   מִי אַתָּה who (art) thou?

מָה (mā(h)) what, refers to things,   מַה־הִיא what (is) that?

The pointing of מָה varies according to the consonant which follows it. (cf. the pointing of the article).

מַה plus daghesh-forte, (usually)	מַה־לָּךְ	what to thee?
מַה before ה and ח	מַה־הִיא	what (is) that?
מָה before א, ע and ר	מָה־אֵלֶּה	what (are) these?
מֶה before gutturals with "a"	מֶה־עָשִׂיתִי	what have I done?

NOTE: אֵי (where) plus the demonstrative (אֵי־זֶה) may be used as an interrogative, אֵי־זֶה הַדֶּרֶךְ which way?

NOTE: The pronoun מִי stands alone while מָה is always joined to the following word by maḳḳeph.

VOCABULARY

מָכַר	mā-khăr	sell		שָׁבַת	shā-văth	rest
שָׁלֵם	shā-lēm	be whole		שָׁבַר	shā-văr	break
קָרַב	ḳā-răv	draw near		שָׁפַט	shā-phăṭ	judge

EXERCISES

1. Translate.

זֶה הַדָּבָר, הַדָּבָר הַזֶּה, הָאִישׁ אֲשֶׁר הָאָב, הַסּוּס הַהוּא,

הוּא הַסּוּס הַטּוֹב, מָה-אֵלֶּה, מִי הַנָּבִיא, הַשֵּׁם הַקָּדוֹשׁ הַזֶּה,
הָאִם הַזֹּאת:

2. Write into Hebrew.

Who gave the good book to the prophet? What (is) in the hand? This woman sold the horse. They rested in the light. Ye will draw near. We shall judge the child.

LESSON XIII

THE SUBSTANTIVE

Cases

Strictly speaking there are no cases in Hebrew. There is no clear set of case endings as we find in other languages. The old accusative ending הָ֫ is found occasionally at the end of nouns to denote *direction* or motion toward, הָהָ֫רָה *toward the mountain*. Usually, however, there is no ending to indicate the accusative. It is the case of the direct object and, if the word is definite, it is preceded by אֵת, *he kept the man* שָׁמַר אֶת הָאִישׁ (The pronominal suffix attached to the end of a verb expresses the accusative, מְשָׁלָם *he ruled them*).

The Genitive is clearly indicated by a combination of words which is called the **construct** relation. It is the use that corresponds to the expression "*of*" in English, סוּס הָאִישׁ *the horse of the man* (*the man's horse*). The substantive סוּס is said to be in the **construct** state, and the substantive אִישׁ is in the **absolute** state. The governing substantive always stands first, never takes the article, and must be followed immediately by the substantive in the absolute state. They form a compound word, since the accent has been lost from the word in the construct. When the accent is lost, the long vowels (unless unchangeable) are volatilized (shortened).

דָּבָר	word but	דְּבַר אִישׁ	a word of a man.
יָד	hand but	יַד הַבֵּן	the hand of the son.
כֹּל	all but	כָּל־הָאָרֶץ	all (of) the earth.
תּוֹרָה	law but	תּוֹרַת יַהְוֶה	law of Yahweh.

Gender and Number

Hebrew has two genders, masculine and feminine, and three numbers, singular, plural, and dual. The dual is confined to substantives. It is used in the names of objects that go in pairs (ears, eyes, feet, etc.). The following table gives the various endings for gender and number:

		Singular		Plural	
Masc.	Abs.	סוּס	horse	סוּסִים	horses
	Const.	סוּס	horse of	סוּסֵי	horses of
Fem.	Abs.	סוּסָה	mare	סוּסוֹת	mares
	Const.	סוּסַת	mare of	סוּסוֹת	mares of

Dual

Masc.			Fem.		
Abs.	סוּסַיִם	horses (a pair)	סוּסָתַיִם	mares (a pair)
Const.	סוּסֵי	horses of (a pair)	סוּסָתֵי	mares of (a pair)

NOTES:

1. The masculine singular has no separate ending.

סוּס horse, טוֹב good, קוֹל voice.

2. The masculine plural ending ‏ים ‎ is usually added to the masculine singular form.

‏סוּסִים‎ *horses*, ‏טוֹבִים‎ *good* (*ones*).

3. The feminine ending is ‏ָה‎, formed from the original ending ‏ָת‎. (Watch for the return of this old ending ‏ַת‎ before suffixes.)

‏שָׂרָה‎ *princess*, ‏טוֹבָה‎ *good*, ‏סוּסָה‎ *mare*.

4. The feminine plural ends in ‏וֹת‎.

‏דּוֹר‎ *generation*, ‏דּוֹרוֹת‎ *generations*, ‏שָׂרוֹת‎ *princesses*, ‏פָּרוֹת‎ *cows*, ‏טוֹבוֹת‎ *good* (*ones*).

5. The dual ending is the same for masculine and feminine ‏ַיִם‎.

‏יָדַיִם‎ *hands* (a pair), ‏אָזְנַיִם‎ *ears* (a pair)

6. Irregular plurals

(a) Some masculine nouns use the feminine plural ending.

‏שֵׁמוֹת, קוֹלוֹת, מְקוֹמוֹת, אוֹתוֹת, אָבוֹת‎.

(b) Some feminine nouns use the masculine plural ending.

‏יוֹנִים‎ (from ‏יוֹנָה‎ *dove*), ‏מִלִּים‎ (from ‏מִלָּה‎ *word*).

(c) Some substantives have two plurals, one in ‏ים‎ and one in ‏וֹת‎.

‏דּוֹר‎ *generation*, ‏שִׁיר‎ *song*, ‏שָׁנָה‎ *year*.

(d) Some substantives are found only in the plural.

‏שָׁמַיִם‎ *heavens*, ‏מַיִם‎ *waters*, ‏פָּנִים‎ *faces*.

VOCABULARY

‏אֵשׁ‎ *fire* (f.)	‏גֵּר‎ *sojourner*	‏לַיְלָה‎ *night*
‏גַּם‎ *also*	‏חַג‎ *feast*	‏כֹּל (כָּל־)‎ *all, every*
‏גַּן‎ *garden*	‏חֹק‎ *statute*	‏צוּר‎ *rock*

EXERCISES

1. Translate.

הַסּוּסִים הַטּוֹבִים, הָאוֹר הַגָּדוֹל, אִישׁ שָׁלוֹם, קוֹל הָאָב,
הַקּוֹלוֹת הַטּוֹבוֹת, הַסּוּסוֹת וְהַפָּרוֹת, חֶרֶב הַמֶּלֶךְ, מֶלֶךְ הָאָרֶץ
הַגָּדוֹל, קוֹלוֹת הָעָם, הַשָּׁמַיִם וְהָאָרֶץ, הָאָזְנַיִם וְהַיָּדָיִם:

2. Write in Hebrew.

He has kept the law of the covenant. They pursued the man toward the mountain. The word of God (is) perfect. They will write the book for the king.

LESSON XIV

PRONOMINAL SUFFIXES WITH SUBSTANTIVES

The possessive pronouns, *my*, *thy*, *his*, *her*, *our*, *your*, and *their*, are not found as separate words in Hebrew. As stated on page 29 they are represented by fragments of personal pronouns attached to the substantive. This is really another example of the *construct* state. The substantive is in the construct before a fragment of the pronoun. Instead of saying *my horse*, we are forced to say *the horse of me* סוּסִי. *Your word* = דְּבַרְכֶם, *the word of you.*

MASCULINE SUBSTANTIVES WITH PRONOMINAL SUFFIXES

	Singular	Plural
	סוּס *horse*	סוּסִים *horses*
	סוּס *horse of* (Const.)	סוּסֵי *horses of* (Const.)
1 c. sg.	סוּסִי *my horse*	סוּסַי *my horses*

2 m. sg.	סוּסְךָ	*thy horse*	סוּסֶיךָ	*thy horses*
2 f. sg.	סוּסֵךְ	*thy horse*	סוּסַיִךְ	*thy horses*
3 m. sg.	סוּסוֹ	*his horse*	סוּסָיו	*his horses*
3 f. sg.	סוּסָהּ	*her horse*	סוּסֶיהָ	*her horses*
1 c. pl.	סוּסֵנוּ	*our horse*	סוּסֵינוּ	*our horses*
2 m. pl.	סוּסְכֶם	*your horse*	סוּסֵיכֶם	*your horses*
2 f. pl.	סוּסְכֶן	*your horse*	סוּסֵיכֶן	*your horses*
3 m. pl.	סוּסָם	*their horse*	סוּסֵיהֶם	*their horses*
3 f. pl.	סוּסָן	*their horse*	סוּסֵיהֶן	*their horses*

This paradigm gives all the suffixes attached to substantives. Many words will present variations in vowels, due to the influence of the tone, but these endings remain the same after all substantives. We may recognize the ending ִי as "*my*," the the ending ךָ as "*thy*," the ending נוּ as "*our*," the ending כָ as "*your*." We see that instead of many "declensions," we really have none in Hebrew. We merely have substantives in the construct plus these suffixes. Let nothing hinder a complete mastery of these endings.

FEMININE SUBSTANTIVES WITH PRONOMINAL SUFFIXES

The same endings are used with feminine substantives. When the substantive does not have the ending ָה the suffixes are attached directly. When the ending is ָה the suffixes are added to the original form of the substantive ַת (the construct). סוּסָה becomes סוּסַת when suffixes are to be added.

	Singular			Plural	
	סוּסָה	*mare*		סוּסוֹת	*mares*
	סוּסַת	*mare of* (Const.)		סוּסוֹת	*mares of* (Const.)
1 c. sg.	סוּסָתִי	*my mare*		סוּסוֹתַי	*my mares*
2 m. sg.	סוּסָתְךָ	*thy mare*		סוּסוֹתֶיךָ	*thy mares*
2 f. sg.	סוּסָתֵךְ	*thy mare*		סוּסוֹתַיִךְ	*thy mares*
3 m. sg.	סוּסָתוֹ	*his mare*		סוּסוֹתָיו	*his mares*
3 f. sg.	סוּסָתָה	*her mare*		סוּסוֹתֶיהָ	*her mares*
1 c. pl.	סוּסָתֵנוּ	*our mare*		סוּסוֹתֵינוּ	*our mares*
2 m. pl.	סוּסַתְכֶם	*your mare*		סוּסוֹתֵיכֶם	*your mares*
2 f. pl.	סוּסַתְכֶן	*your mare*		סוּסוֹתֵיכֶן	*your mares*
3 m. pl.	סוּסָתָם	*their mare*		סוּסוֹתֵיהֶם	*their mares*
3 f. pl.	סוּסָתָן	*their mare*		סוּסוֹתֵיהֶן	*their mares*

NOTES

1. In the singular the old feminine form is used, and the endings are joined directly to it. There is no vowel change before the heavily accented syllables כֶם and כֶן, but before all the light suffixes the ־ַ is heightened to ־ָ. We have סוּסָתוֹ instead of סוּסַתוֹ (The vowel must be long in an open syllable unless accented.) סוּסַתְכֶם can stand because the ־ַ is in a half-open syllable.

2. In the plural there is a double plural ending. The feminine plural וֹת is retained and the regular plural suffixes are added, סוּסוֹתֵינוּ.

EXERCISES

1. Write the pronominal suffixes to the following:
יוֹם *day*, יוֹנָה *dove*, דּוֹרוֹת *generations*, טוֹבִים *good*.

2. Translate.

אוּרִי, אוֹרִים, אוֹר הַבֹּקֶר, אוֹר פָּנִים, קוֹלוֹ, קוֹלִי, אָבִי, קוֹלְךָ,
קוֹלְכֶם, קוֹלָהּ, גְּבוּרֵנוּ, דוֹרוֹתֵיהֶם, יוֹנָתָם, טוֹבוֹתֶיךָ, יוֹנָתָהּ,
יוֹמָהּ, דְּרוֹתַי, טוֹבִים, סוּסָתְךָ, סוּסוֹתֵינוּ, קוֹלוֹתֵיהֶם, תּוֹרָתְךָ,
תּוֹרוֹת, סוּסַיָ, צוּרִים, צוּרֵינוּ, גְּבוּרִים, גְּבוּרֶיךָ, גְּבוּרָם,
בְּרִיתִי, בְּרִיתוֹ, בְּרִיתְכֶם:

LESSON XV

OTHER SUBSTANTIVES WITH SUFFIXES

In our last lesson the student was introduced to the pronominal suffixes as attached to a word that had unchangeable
vowels in it. In other words, we were concerned with the terminations. We now turn to the consideration of a word that is
subject to internal vowel changes when suffixes are added. In
this study let the student remember that the vowel of an open
syllable must be long unless accented. The vowel of the ante-
penultimate syllable is usually volatilized, מְלָכִים, דְּבָרִים.

	Singular		Plural	
	דָּבָר	word	דְּבָרִים	words
	דְּבַר	word of (Const.)	דִּבְרֵי	words of (Const.)
1 c. sg.	דְּבָרִי	my word	דְּבָרַי	my words
2 m. sg.	דְּבָרְךָ	thy word	דְּבָרֶיךָ	thy words
2 f. sg.	דְּבָרֵךְ	thy word	דְּבָרַיִךְ	thy words
3 m. sg.	דְּבָרוֹ	his word	דְּבָרָיו	his words
3 f. sg.	דְּבָרָהּ	her word	דְּבָרֶיהָ	her words

1 c. pl.	דְּבָרֵנוּ *our word*	דְּבָרֵינוּ *our words*	
2 m. pl.	דְּבַרְכֶם *your word*	דִּבְרֵיכֶם *your words*	
2 f. pl.	דְּבַרְכֶן *your word*	דִּבְרֵיכֶן *your words*	
3 m. pl.	דְּבָרָם *their word*	דִּבְרֵיהֶם *their words*	
3 f. pl.	דְּבָרָן *their word*	דִּבְרֵיהֶן *their words*	

There are many classes of substantives. In each class the vowels show a different behavior. We present two of these examples and then append a list of some other nouns with the construct form of each.

Eternity		*King*	
עוֹלָם	עוֹלָמִים	מֶלֶךְ	מְלָכִים
עוֹלַם	עוֹלְמֵי	מֶלֶךְ	מַלְכֵי
עוֹלָמִי	עוֹלָמַי	מַלְכִּי	מְלָכַי
עוֹלָמְךָ	עוֹלָמֶיךָ	מַלְכְּךָ	מְלָכֶיךָ
עוֹלָמֵךְ	עוֹלָמַיִךְ	מַלְכֵּךְ	מְלָכַיִךְ
עוֹלָמוֹ	עוֹלָמָיו	מַלְכּוֹ	מְלָכָיו
עוֹלָמָהּ	עוֹלָמֶיהָ	מַלְכָּהּ	מְלָכֶיהָ
עוֹלָמֵנוּ	עוֹלָמֵינוּ	מַלְכֵּנוּ	מְלָכֵינוּ
עוֹלַמְכֶם	עוֹלְמֵיכֶם	מַלְכְּכֶם	מַלְכֵיכֶם
עוֹלַמְכֶן	עוֹלְמֵיכֶן	מַלְכְּכֶן	מַלְכֵיכֶן
עוֹלָמָם	עוֹלְמֵיהֶם	מַלְכָּם	מַלְכֵיהֶם
עוֹלָמָן	עוֹלְמֵיהֶן	מַלְכָּן	מַלְכֵיהֶן

	Absolute	Construct			Absolute	Construct
overseer	פָּקִיד	פְּקִיד	*death*	מָוֶת	מוֹת
wise	חָכָם	חֲכַם	*fruit*	פְּרִי	פְּרִי
old man	זָקֵן	זְקַן	*sea*	יָם	יַם (יְם)
book	סֵפֶר	סֵפֶר	*queen*	מַלְכָּה	מַלְכַּת
youth	נַעַר	נַעַר	*righteousness*	צְדָקָה	צִדְקַת
work	פֹּעַל	פֹּעַל			

SOME IRREGULAR NOUNS

	Singular		Plural	
	Absolute	Construct	Absolute	Construct
father	אָב	אֲבִי	אָבוֹת	אֲבוֹת
brother	אָח	אֲחִי	אַחִים	אֲחֵי
one	אֶחָד	אַחַד	אֲחָדִים	אַחֲדֵי
sister	אָחוֹת	אֲחוֹת	אֲחָיוֹת	אַחְיוֹתַי
man	אִישׁ	אִישׁ	אֲנָשִׁים	אַנְשֵׁי
house	בַּיִת	בֵּית	בָּתִּים	בָּתֵּי
wife	אִשָּׁה	אֵשֶׁת	נָשִׁים	נְשֵׁי
son	בֵּן	בֶּן (בִּן)	בָּנִים	בְּנֵי
name	שֵׁם	שֵׁם	שֵׁמוֹת	שְׁמוֹת
daughter	בַּת	בַּת	בָּנוֹת	בְּנוֹת
water	———	———	מַיִם	מֵי (מֵימֵי)
day	יוֹם	יוֹם	יָמִים	יְמֵי
city	עִיר	עִיר	עָרִים	עָרֵי

	Absolute	Construct	Absolute	Construct
mouth	פֶּה	פִּי	פִּיוֹת	פִּיוֹת
head	רֹאשׁ	רֹאשׁ	רָאשִׁים	רָאשֵׁי
heavens	——	——	שָׁמַיִם	שְׁמֵי
implement	כְּלִי	כְּלִי	כֵּלִים	כְּלֵי

EXERCISES

Translate.

זְקֵנִים, זִקְנֵי, חַכְמֵי, יַמִּים, מְלָכוֹת, זִקְנֵי, מוֹתִי, נְעָרִים,
סִפְרִי, פְּרִיהֶם, זִקְנֵיכֶם, מוֹתִי, נַעֲרָה, סְפָרִים, פְּעָלוֹ, פְּעָלִים,
פְּקִידִים, פְּקִידוֹ, צִדְקָתִי, צְדָקוֹת, צִדְקוֹת, דְּבָרַי, קוֹלָם,
יוֹמָן, קוֹלֵךְ, פִּיךָ, בְּרִיתָם, אֱלֹהֵינוּ׃

LESSON XVI

SOME PRINCIPLES OF SYNTAX

1. The verb usually stands first in the sentence. However
when either the negative or the interrogative pronoun occurs
in the sentence it precedes the verb.

מָכַר הָאִישׁ סוּס   *the man sold a horse.*

לֹא שָׁמַר אֶת הַתּוֹרָה   *he did not keep the law.*

מִי כָתַב אֶת־הַסֵּפֶר   *who wrote the book?*

2. When particular emphasis is wanted, any word may be
given first place.

לִי הַכֹּהֵן נָתַן סֵפֶר   *the priest gave me a book.*

3. The subject usually follows the verb.

אָמַר אֱלֹהִים *God said.*

4. The subject is followed by its modifiers. The adjective agrees with the substantive in gender, number, and definiteness.

הַסּוּס הַטּוֹב *the good horse.*

הַסּוּסִים הַטּוֹבִים *the good horses.*

הַסּוּסוֹת הַטּוֹבוֹת *the good mares.*

5. The demonstrative behaves like the adjective. When attributive, it follows the substantive and both take the article.

הַקּוֹל הַזֶּה *this voice.*

If another adjective is used, the demonstrative follows it, and each word is made definite by the article.

הַקּוֹל הַטּוֹב הַזֶּה *this good voice.*

6. The direct object of the verb is the next in order. If definite, it is preceded by the particle אֵת.

מָכַר הָאִישׁ אֶת הָעֵץ *the man sold the tree.*

7. By way of summary, we may note the regular word order.

Verb, subject (and its modifiers), direct object (and its modifiers), indirect object. When any other order is used, it is for special emphasis.

כָּתַב הַמֶּלֶךְ הַגָּדוֹל הַזֶּה אֶת הַדָּבָר הַטּוֹב לַשַּׂר *This great king wrote the good word to the prince.*

8. The comparative degree is expressed by means of the preposition מִן.

הָאִישׁ גָּדוֹל מִן־הַבֵּן *the man is larger than the son.*

9 The use of *He directive* to express the idea of the accusative

as the limit of motion is common. The suffix הָ‎ is attached
to the substantive.

אַרְצָה‎ *toward the land.*

10. The Cohortative ending הָ‎ is attached to the first person
of the imperfect or to the imperative to give added strength.
In the case of the imperative the request is made more hearty
and impressive.

אֶמְשְׁלָה‎ *let me rule* or *I will rule.*

נִכְרְתָה‎ *we will cut* (a covenant)

שְׁמָעוּ־נָא‎ *hear, I pray*

זָכְרָה‎ *think!*

11. A prohibition cannot be expressed by an imperative. The
usual means is to use אַל‎ with the jussive.

וְדָם נָקִי אַל־תִּשְׁפֹּכוּ‎ *and shed not innocent blood.*

VOCABULARY

בֵּין‎	between	דּוֹר‎	generation	עוֹד‎	again
בַּיִת‎	house	דָּם‎	blood	עֵת‎	time (f.)
גָּדוֹל‎	great	הַר‎	mountain	פֶּה‎	mouth

EXERCISES

Translate.

הַשָּׁנִים הָאֵלֶּה, הָאָרֶץ הַזֹּאת, נָתַן אֱלֹהִים אֶת־הַדָּבָר בַּיּוֹם
הַהוּא: שָׁמַר הָאָדָם אֶת־הַשַּׁבָּת: לָמַד הַיֶּלֶד מִן־הַסֵּפֶר: לֹא
מְשַׁלְתֶּם אֶת־הַיֶּלֶד: הָאִישׁ הַגָּדוֹל הָיָה בָהָר: זָכְרוּ אֶת הַצּוּרִים
בַּגַּן בֵּין הַבַּיִת וּבֵין הָעֵץ: כָּתְבָה הַבַּת אֶת הַסֵּפֶר לַיֶּלֶד:

LESSON XVII

The Stems of the Verb

In addition to the verb forms already studied we have six other stems, each representing a different aspect of the primary meaning of the verb. To find a suitable name for these sets of forms is difficult. They can hardly be called conjugations, or moods, or voices. Perhaps it will be best to speak of them as stems. These derived stems are formed from the simple (*Qal*) stem (or the root) by means of prefixes, vowel changes, and the doubling of certain letters.

The root idea or meaning of the verb is presented in three conditions or degrees: (1) the **simple,** *to love,* (2) the **intensive,** *to love passionately*, (3) the **causative,** extending the action over a second agent, *to make to love, to cause to love.* Each of these has an active and a passive form. The intensive has a reflexive form also. The names for these stems, except Qal which means "light," are derived from the Hebrew word פָּעַל. (Niph'al, Pi'el, Pu'al, Hithpa'el, Hiph'il, Hoph'al).

SIMPLE	INTENSIVE	CAUSATIVE
Active	Active	Active
(Qal) קַל	(Pi'el) פִּעֵל	(Hiph'il) הִפְעִיל
Passive	Passive	Passive
(Niph'al) נִפְעַל	(Pu'al) פֻּעַל	(Hoph'al) הָפְעַל
	Reflexive	
	(Hithpa'el) הִתְפַּעֵל	

Using קָטַל as the paradigm word the stems are as follows:

1. The Simple Active (Qal) — קָטַל — *he killed*

2. The Simple Passive (Niph'al) — נִקְטַל — *he was killed*

3. The Intensive Active (Pi'el) — קִטֵּל — *he killed (brutally)*

4. The Intensive Passive (Pu'al) — קֻטַּל — *he was killed (brutally)*

5. The Intensive Reflexive (Hithpa'el) — הִתְקַטֵּל — *he killed himself*

6. The Causative Active (Hiph'il) — הִקְטִיל — *he caused to kill*

7. The Causative Passive (Hoph'al) — הָקְטַל — *he was caused to kill*

Characteristics of these Stems

1. Qal קָטַל, the simple verb stem as found in the lexicon.

2. Niph'al (נִקְטַל) נִפְעַל, the passive of the Qal, has a prefixed נ (shortened from הִן). It may be reflexive in force.

3. Pi'el (פִּעֵל) קִטֵּל, always active, middle radical always doubled by means of daghesh-forte (in strong verbs). It may be iterative or emphatic.

4. Pu'al (פֻּעַל) קֻטַּל always passive, middle radical always doubled (in strong verbs).

5. Hithpa'el (הִתְפַּעֵל) הִתְקַטֵּל, reflexive (middle voice), middle radical doubled and a prefixed הִת always present.

6. Hiph'il (הִפְעִיל) הִקְטִיל active, always has a prefixed ה.

7. Hoph'al (הָפְעַל) הָקְטַל passive, always has a prefixed ה.

NOTES

1. We use קְטַל as a paradigm word because the old word פָּעַל contains a guttural, the presence of which causes some irregularities.

2. The complete paradigm of the seven stems is given, although only six verbs out of fourteen hundred make use of all these stems.

3. The names of the stems indicate the vowels to be used in the perfects. Learn to pronounce each word correctly, getting the proper vowel sound.

נִקְטַל	nĭk-ṭăl	נִמְשַׁל	nĭm-shăl	*Niph'al*
קִטֵּל	kĭt-ṭēl	מִשֵּׁל	mĭsh-shēl	*Pi'el*
קֻטַּל	kŭt-ṭăl	מֻשַּׁל	mŭsh-shăl	*Pu'al*
הִתְקַטֵּל	hĭth-kăṭ-ṭēl	הִתְמַשֵּׁל	hĭth-măsh-shēl	*Hithpa'el*
הִקְטִיל	hĭk-ṭîl	הִמְשִׁיל	hĭm-shîl	*Hiph'il*
הָקְטַל	hŏk-ṭăl	הָמְשַׁל	hŏm-shăl	*Hoph'al*

4. Remember the doubling of the second radical of the three intensive stems.

5. The causative stems are increased from without. Remember the prefixed ה, הָקְטַל, הִקְטִיל.

6. The first syllable of Niph'al, Hiph'il and Hoph'al stems is closed and the second radical of the verb takes daghesh-lene if it is ב, ג, ד, כ, פ, ת; נִשְׁבַּר, הִזְכִּיר, הָרְדַּף.

VOCABULARY

גָּבַר *be strong, prevail*   סָגַר *close, shut*

דָּרַשׁ *tread, seek*   שָׂרַף *burn*

כָּבֵס *wash*   שָׁכַב *lie down*

כפר *cover* (Pi.)   שׁכם *rise early* (Hi.)

EXERCISES

1. Write the 3rd masculine, singular of each of the stems treated above, using קָטַל ,מָשַׁל ,כָּשַׁל ,גָּנַב, מָלַךְ.

2. Translate and locate fully:*

גָּבַר, נִדְרַשׁ, כִּבֵּס, כִּפֶּר, נִסְגַּר, הִשְׁכִּיב, הִגְבִּיר, כָּבַס, הִתְכַּפֵּר, סָגַר, הִשְׁכִּים, שָׁכֵן, הִתְגַּבֵּר, כִּפֵּר, סִגֵּר, נִשְׁבַּר, הִשְׁבִּית, נִשְׁפַּט, הִסְגִּיר, נִשְׂרַף, הִשְׁכִּין, שִׁבֵּר, הָשְׁבַּר, שָׁלַם, הִשְׁבִּיר, נִשְׁבַּת, הִשְׁלִים, נִקְרַב, הִקְרִיב, הִשְׂכִּיל, נִקְבַּר, קָבַר, נִצְדַּק, הִצְדִּיק, נִמְכַּר, הִתְמַכֵּר, הִזְכִּיר, פָּקַד:

*To locate דִּבַּרְתָּ let the student use the following order: "Pi'el, perfect, 2nd, masculine, singular from דִּבֵּר *to speak. Thou didst speak.*"

LESSON XVIII
THE REMAINING PERFECTS

We turn now to a consideration of each of these stems.

The Niph'al (נִקְטַל).

The simple passive stem has a prefixed נ (from the ground form נִקְטַל). Note how closely the inflection resembles the simple active (Qal) stem.

Singular   Plural

נִקְטַל *he was killed (he killed himself)*

נִקְטְלָה *she was killed*   נִקְטְלוּ *they were killed*

נְקְטַלְתָּ *thou* (m.) *wast killed*   נְקְטַלְתֶּם *you* (m.) *were killed*

נְקְטַלְתְּ *thou* (f.) *wast killed*   נְקְטַלְתֶּן *you* (f.) *were killed*

נְקְטַלְתִּי *I was killed*   נְקְטַלְנוּ *we were killed*

The Pi'el (קְטֵל) (קַטֵּל ground form).

The intensive active stem doubles the middle radical.

Singular

קַטֵּל *he killed (brutally)*

קַטְּלָה *she killed (brutally)*

קַטַּלְתָּ *thou* (m.) *didst kill (brutally)*

קַטַּלְתְּ *thou* (f.) *didst kill (brutally)*

קַטַּלְתִּי *I killed (brutally)*

Plural

קַטְּלוּ *they killed (brutally)*

קַטַּלְתֶּם *you* (m.) *killed (brutally)*

קַטַּלְתֶּן *you* (f.) *killed (brutally)*

קַטַּלְנוּ *we killed (brutally)*

The Pu'al (קֻטַּל) (קֻטַּל or קֻטָּל)

The intensive passive stem doubles the middle radical.

Singular

קֻטַּל *he was killed (brutally)*

קֻטְּלָה *she was killed*

קֻטַּלְתָּ *thou* (m.) *wast killed*

קָטַלְתְּ *thou* (f.) *wast killed*

קָטַלְתִּי *I was killed*

Plural

קָטְלוּ *they were killed* (*brutally*)

קָטַלְתֶּם *you* (m.) *were killed*

קָטַלְתֶּן *you* (f.) *were killed*

קָטַלְנוּ *we were killed*

The Hithpaʻel (הִתְקַטֵּל) (הִתְקַטַּל)

The intensive reflexive stem doubles the middle radical and prefixes הִת.

Singular

הִתְקַטֵּל *he killed himself*

הִתְקַטְּלָה *she killed herself*

הִתְקַטַּלְתָּ *thou* (m.) *didst kill thyself*

הִתְקַטַּלְתְּ *thou* (f.) *didst kill thyself*

הִתְקַטַּלְתִּי *I killed myself*

Plural

הִתְקַטְּלוּ *they killed themselves*

הִתְקַטַּלְתֶּם *you* (m.) *killed yourselves*

הִתְקַטַּלְתֶּן *you* (f.) *killed yourselves*

הִתְקַטַּלְנוּ *we killed ourselves*

NOTE: When the prefix (הִת) precedes the sibilants ס, שׂ, שׁ, the ת of the prefix changes places with the sibilant, הִשְׁתַּמֵּר *he*

kept himself, הִסְתַּתֵּר *he concealed himself.* The תּ of the prefix
may be assimilated before ד, ת, ט. It may be changed to ט
and transposed before צ, הִטַּהֵר for הִתְטַהֵר *he purified himself,*
הִצְטַדֵּק for הִתְצַדֵּק *he sanctified himself.* (See Isa. 1:16 הִזַּכּוּ
for the assimilation of ת before ז).

The Hiph'il (הִקְטִיל) (הַקְטֵל)

The causative stem has a prefixed ה. The ground form is
הַקְטֵל which becomes הִקְטִיל in 3rd masculine singular. Before vowel additions (הָ__ and וּ) the יִ__ is retained and accented
(הִקְטִילוּ). Before consonant additions the original ◌ֵ is re-
stored (הִקְטַלְתָּ).

Singular

הִקְטִיל	*he caused to kill*
הִקְטִילָה	*she caused to kill*
הִקְטַלְתָּ	*thou* (m.) *didst cause to kill*
הִקְטַלְתְּ	*thou* (f.) *didst cause to kill*
הִקְטַלְתִּי	*I caused to kill*

Plural

הִקְטִילוּ	*they caused to kill*
הִקְטַלְתֶּם	*you* (m.) *caused to kill*
הִקְטַלְתֶּן	*you* (f.) *caused to kill*
הִקְטַלְנוּ	*we caused to kill*

The Hoph'al (הָקְטַל) (הֻקְטַל or הָקְטַל)

The causative passive has the prefixed ה with the vowel ◌ֻ (ŏ).
Sometimes the original ◌ָ takes its place.

Singular

הָקְטַל   *he was caused to kill*

הָקְטְלָה   *she was caused to kill*

הָקְטַלְתָּ   *thou (m.) wast caused to kill*

הָקְטַלְתְּ   *thou (f.) wast caused to kill*

הָקְטַלְתִּי   *I was caused to kill*

Plural

הָקְטְלוּ   *they were caused to kill*

הָקְטַלְתֶּם   *you (m.) were caused to kill*

הָקְטַלְתֶּן   *you (f.) were caused to kill*

הָקְטַלְנוּ   *we were caused to kill*

EXERCISES

Translate and locate fully.

הִמְשִׁילוּ, נָתְנָה, שְׁמַרְתָּ, גֻּדְלָה, דִּבַּרְנוּ, לָמַדְתִּי, לְמַדְתֶּם,
רֻדַּף, הָפְקַדְתִּי, כֻּתְּבוּ, קֻבַּרְתֶּן, נִשְׁבַּתְנוּ, מֻשַׁלְתֶּם, הִסְתַּתֵּר,
הִמְשִׁילָה, מָשַׁלְתִּי, הִתְקַדְּשָׁה, הִצְדַּקְנוּ, קֻדַּשְׁתֶּן, סֻפַּרְתָּ, כָּשֵׁל,
הֻכְשַׁלְתָּ, שֻׁבְּרוּ, הָזְכַּרְתִּי, נִזְכַּרְנוּ, זְכַרְתֶּם, נִשְׁמְרָה, הִמְלַכְתִּי,
לֻבַּדְנוּ, הָשְׁבַּרְתִּי:

LESSON XIX

THE REMAINING IMPERFECTS

The Niph'al (יִקָּטֵל)

The prefix in the imperfect is יִן (yĭn). Since the נ is always assimilated when followed by a syllable-divider we have יִקָּטֵל

instead of יִנְקֶטֶל *he will be killed.* (The original form was probably יִהְנְקַטֵל).

Singular

יִקָּטֵל	*he will be killed*
תִּקָּטֵל	*she will be killed*
תִּקָּטֵל	*thou* (m.) *wilt be killed*
תִּקָּטְלִי	*thou* (f.) *wilt be killed*
אֶקָּטֵל	*I shall be killed*

Plural

יִקָּטְלוּ	*they* (m.) *will be killed*
תִּקָּטַלְנָה	*they* (f.) *will be killed*
תִּקָּטְלוּ	*you* (m.) *will be killed*
תִּקָּטַלְנָה	*you* (f.) *will be killed*
נִקָּטֵל	*we shall be killed*

The Pi'el (יִקַטֵּל) (יְקַטֵּל)

The intensive active requires that the middle radical be doubled. The meaning is properly intensive; יִשְׁבֹּר (Qal) *he will break.* יְשַׁבֵּר (Pi'el) *he will break* (into bits). It may have a causative force, יִלְמַד *he will learn,* יְלַמֵּד *he will teach* (cause to learn). The preformative has ־ְ except under א. The vowel before נָה is usually ־ֵ, תְּקַטֵּלְנָה.

Singular

יְקַטֵּל	*he will kill* (brutally)
תְּקַטֵּל	*she will kill*

תְּקַטֵּל *thou* (m.) *wilt kill*

תְּקַטְּלִי *thou* (f.) *wilt kill*

אֲקַטֵּל *I shall kill*

Plural

יְקַטְּלוּ *they* (m.) *will kill* (*brutally*)

תְּקַטֵּלְנָה *they* (f.) *will kill*

תְּקַטְּלוּ *you* (m.) *will kill*

תְּקַטֵּלְנָה *you* (f.) *will kill*

נְקַטֵּל *we shall kill*

The Puʻal (יְקַטֵּל) (יְקֻטַּל)

The intensive passive requires the doubling of the middle radical. It has the dull vowel ◌ֻ under the first radical. The ◌ַ is under the preformative. Before נָה we usually find ◌ַ. It is the regular intensive passive, יְבֻקַּשׁ *he will be sought diligently.*

Singular

יְקֻטַּל *he will be killed* (*brutally*)

תְּקֻטַּל *she will be killed*

תְּקֻטַּל *thou* (m.) *wilt be killed*

תְּקֻטְּלִי *thou* (f.) *wilt be killed*

אֲקֻטַּל *I shall be killed*

Plural

יְקֻטְּלוּ *they* (m.) *will be killed* (*brutally*)

תְּקֻטַּלְנָה *they* (f.) *will be killed*

תִּקָּטְלוּ   *you* (m.) *will be killed*

תִּקָּטֵלְנָה   *you* (f.) *will be killed*

נִקָּטֵל   *we shall be killed*

The Hithpa'el (יִתְקַטֵּל) (יִתְקַטֵּל)

The intensive reflexive has the prefix יִת and is inflected regularly. The middle radical (of the stem) is doubled. The vowel before נָה is usually ֵ. (See page 51 for note on change before sibilants.)

Singular

יִתְקַטֵּל   *he will kill himself*

תִּתְקַטֵּל   *she will kill herself*

תִּתְקַטֵּל   *thou* (m.) *wilt kill thyself*

תִּתְקַטְּלִי   *thou* (f.) *wilt kill thyself*

אֶתְקַטֵּל   *I shall kill myself*

Plural

יִתְקַטְּלוּ   *they* (m.) *will kill themselves*

תִּתְקַטֵּלְנָה   *they* (f.) *will kill themselves*

תִּתְקַטְּלוּ   *you* (m.) *will kill yourselves*

תִּתְקַטֵּלְנָה   *you* (f.) *will kill yourselves*

נִתְקַטֵּל   *we shall kill ourselves*

The Hiph'il (יַקְטִיל) (יְהָקְטַל)

The causative active stem holds the original ◌ַ under the preformative (יַקְטִיל). The יִ◌ is retained and accented before vowel additions (יִ◌ and וּ). The vowel ◌ַ occurs before נָה.

Singular

יַקְטִיל	*he will cause to kill*
תַּקְטִיל	*she will cause to kill*
תַּקְטִיל	*thou* (m.) *wilt cause to kill*
תַּקְטִילִי	*thou* (f.) *wilt cause to kill*
אַקְטִיל	*I shall cause to kill*

Plural

יַקְטִילוּ	*they* (m.) *will cause to kill*
תַּקְטֵלְנָה	*they* (f.) *will cause to kill*
תַּקְטִילוּ	*you* (m.) *will cause to kill*
תַּקְטֵלְנָה	*you* (f.) *will cause to kill*
נַקְטִיל	*we shall cause to kill*

The Hoph'al (יָקְטַל) (יְהָקְטַל)

The causative passive is perfectly regular in its inflection. A secondary form of Hoph'al, with ◌ֻ under the preformative, occurs in a few strong verbs and certain classes of weak verbs.

Singular

יָקְטַל	*he will be caused to kill*
תָּקְטַל	*she will be caused to kill*

תָּקְטַל   *thou (m.) wilt be caused to kill*

תָּקְטְלִי   *thou (f.) wilt be caused to kill*

אָקְטַל   *I shall be caused to kill*

Plural

יָקְטְלוּ   *they (m.) will be caused to kill*

תָּקְטַלְנָה   *they (f.) will be caused to kill*

תָּקְטְלוּ   *you (m.) will be caused to kill*

תָּקְטַלְנָה   *you (f.) will be caused to kill*

נָקְטַל   *we shall be caused to kill*

EXERCISES

Translate and locate fully.

יִשָּׁבֵר, יְקַדְּשׁוּ, תְּדַבֵּר, תְּכֻפַּר, תְּקֻדְּשׁוּ, יְסֻגְּרוּ, תִּתְקַדְּשׁוּ,
יַזְכִּירוּ, יָפְקְדוּ, אַקְרִיב, תִּזָּכֵרְנָה, נְלַמֵּד, יְמָכֵר, יְלֻבַּשׁ, יְקֻדְּשׁוּ,
תִּקְרְבִי, תַּשְׁכִּילוּ, נַזְכִּיר, יְשֻׁבְּרוּ, תִּשָּׁמַרְנָה, יֻנְתַּן, נַגְדִּיל, נִכָּרֵת,
אֶשָּׁבֵר, אֶתְדַּבֵּר, יְסֻפְּרוּ, אֶכָּשֵׁל, אֶתְגַּדֵּל, תֻּזְכִּיר, נִלָּבֵשׁ,
יִמָּלֵט:

LESSON XX

THE IMPERATIVES, INFINITIVES AND PARTICIPLES

THE IMPERATIVES

The stem of the imperative is the same as the imperfect. The passive stems, Pu'al and Hoph'al, have no imperatives. The imperative is found only in the second person (singular and plural).

Niph'al

2 m. sg.	הִקָּטֵל	*be killed (kill thyself)*
2 f. sg.	הִקָּטְלִי	*be killed (kill thyself)*
2 m. pl.	הִקָּטְלוּ	*be killed (kill yourselves)*
2 f. pl.	הִקָּטַלְנָה	*be killed (kill yourselves)*

Pi'el

2 m. sg.	קַטֵּל	*kill (thou) (brutally)*
2 f. sg.	קַטְּלִי	*kill (thou) (brutally)*
2 m. pl.	קַטְּלוּ	*kill (ye) (brutally)*
2 f. pl.	קַטֵּלְנָה	*kill (ye) (brutally)*

Hithpa'el

2 m. sg.	הִתְקַטֵּל	*kill thyself*
2 f. sg.	הִתְקַטְּלִי	*kill thyself*
2 m. pl.	הִתְקַטְּלוּ	*kill yourselves*
2 f. pl.	הִתְקַטֵּלְנָה	*kill yourselves*

Hiph'il

2 m. sg.	הַקְטֵל	*cause (one) to kill*
2 f. sg.	הַקְטִילִי	*cause (one) to kill*
2 m. pl.	הַקְטִילוּ	*cause (one) to kill*
2 f. pl.	הַקְטֵלְנָה	*cause (one) to kill*

The Infinitives

There are two infinitives for each stem. The Hithpa'el infinitive absolute and the Pu'al infinitive construct are not found in the Bible. The Niph'al infinitive absolute has two forms. Either form may be used. Prepositions may precede and suffixes may be added to the construct infinitives but never to the absolute.

Absolute

Niph'al	הִקָּטֹל (נִקְטֹל)	*being killed*
Pi'el	קַטֹּל (קַטֵּל)	*killing (brutally)*
Pu'al	קֻטֹּל	*being (brutally) killed*
Hithpa'el	(הִתְקַטֹּל)	*killing one's self*
Hiph'il	הַקְטֵל	*causing to kill*
Hoph'al	הָקְטֵל	*being caused to kill*

Construct

Niph'al	הִקָּטֵל	*to be killed*
Pi'el	קַטֵּל	*to kill (brutally)*
Hithpa'el	הִתְקַטֵּל	*to kill one's self*
Hiph'il	הַקְטִיל	*to cause to kill*
Hoph'al	הָקְטַל	*to be caused to kill*

The Participles

Each stem has a participle. The Qal has both an active and a passive form. The Niph'al participle has the same form as

the perfect except for the long vowel in the ultima (נִקְטָל).
The other participles are formed by prefixing מ to the stem in
the place of the preformative of the imperfect (מְקַטֵּל, יְקַטֵּל).

Qal	(active)	קֹטֵל	*killing, one killing*
	(passive)	קָטוּל	*killed, one killed (dead)*
Niphʻal	passive or reflexive	נִקְטָל	*killed, one killed or killing one's self*
Piʻel	(active)	מְקַטֵּל	*killing (brutally), one killing (brutally)*
Puʻal	(passive)	מְקֻטָּל	*being (brutally) killed, one killed*
Hithpaʻel	(reflexive)	מִתְקַטֵּל	*killing one's self, one who kills himself*
Hiphʻil	(active)	מַקְטִיל	*causing to kill, one who causes to kill*
Hophʻal	(passive)	מָקְטָל	*caused to kill, one caused to kill*

Vocabulary

בָּגַד *deal treacherously*   בדל (Hi.) *divide, separate*

בקש *seek* (Pi.)   שלך *cast* (Hi.)

מלט *escape* (Ni., Hi., Hith.)   תָּפַשׂ *catch, seize*

Exercises

Translate and locate fully.

לִשְׁכֹּן, לָמוּד, לְדַבֵּר, מַשְׁכִּים, נִמְלָט, כָּתוּב, נִשְׁבָּר, מְדַבֵּר,
מְקֻדָּשׁ, מַזְכִּיר, דַּבֵּר, שָׁבוּר, נִפְקָד, מְבַקֵּשׁ, מַקְרִיב, מָפְקָד,
מִתְקַדֵּשׁ, הַנָּתֹן, הַשְׁכֵּם, בַּקְּשִׁי, הַכְרֵת, הַמָּלֵט, הִסְתַּתַּרְנָה,
הִשָּׁמֵר, לְהִתְקַדֵּשׁ, לִכְרֹת, מַלֵּט, זָכוֹר:

LESSON XXI

A Synopsis of the Strong Verb

	Simple		Intensive			Causative	
	Qal	Niph'al	Pi'el	Pu'al	Hithpa'el	Hiph'il	Hoph'al
Perf.	קָטַל	נִקְטַל	קִטֵּל	קֻטַּל	הִתְקַטֵּל	הִקְטִיל	הָקְטַל
Impf.	יִקְטֹל	יִקָּטֵל	יְקַטֵּל	יְקֻטַּל	יִתְקַטֵּל	יַקְטִיל	יָקְטַל
Imv.	קְטֹל	הִקָּטֵל	קַטֵּל	—	הִתְקַטֵּל	הַקְטֵל	—
Inf. A.	קָטוֹל	הִקָּטֹל נִקְטֹל	קַטֹּל	קֻטֹּל			הָקְטֵל
Inf. C.	קְטֹל	הִקָּטֵל	קַטֵּל	קֻטַּל	הִתְקַטֵּל	הַקְטִיל	הָקְטַל
Ptc. A.	קֹטֵל	—	מְקַטֵּל	—	מִתְקַטֵּל	מַקְטִיל	—
Ptc. P.	קָטוּל	נִקְטָל	—	מְקֻטָּר	—	—	מָקְטָל

Notes

1. Too much emphasis cannot be given to the importance of this synopsis. Nothing short of an absolute mastery of every form can be considered.

2. Learn to pronounce the names of the stems perfectly. If the word, "Niph'al," is pronounced correctly it should be easy to write the Hebrew form, using the short *i* and the short *a*. (נִקְטַל, נִמְשַׁל).

3. In writing the imperfects let the student make sure of the following order of the vowel of the preformative:

Qal Niph'al Pi'el Pu'al Hithpa'el Hiph'il Hoph'al

בְ בְ בִ בֻ יִתְ בַ בָ

Pronounce them over and over until they are mastered.

4. The imperfects have as the vowel of the first radical:

Qal Niph'al Pi'el Pu'al Hithpa'el Hiph'il Hoph'al

קְ קָּ קַ קַּ קַ קְ קְ

5. The second radical with its vowel is as follows:

Qal Niph'al Pi'el Pu'al Hithpa'el Hiph'il Hoph'al

ט טֵ טֵּ טַּ טֵּ טִי טַ

6. The Niph'al has נ in every form. It is assimilated except in the perfect and the participle.

7. The intensive stems have the second radical doubled *everywhere*. The active and passive stems are distinguished by the vowels and the reflexive by the prefixes מְ, נְת, תְּת, יְת, הְת.

8. The Hiph'il has ־ֵ under the preformative in all forms except in the perfect.

9. The Hoph'al has ־ָ (ŏ) under the preformative in all forms.

10. The passive stems have no imperatives (except Niphal).

11. The preformative letter for all participles (except in Qal and Niph'al) is מְ.

12. Before נָה in active stems the vowel is ־ֵ. In the passive stems the vowel is ־ֵ.

Vocabulary

גָּנַב	steal	סָפַד	mourn
מטר	rain	שָׁטַף	overflow
סָמַך	sustain	קָבַץ	collect

Exercises

Translate and locate fully.

תִּמָּטֵר, הִמְטִיר, אַמְטִיר, מַמְטִיר, יָמָלֵט, הַזְכִּיר, לַמְלֹךְ,

מְקַדֵּשׁ, גָּנְבוּ, גֹּנֵב, יִסְמֹךְ, גָּנוֹב יִגְנֹב, מְדַבֵּר, לָבוּשׁ, סָמַךְ,

סָפְדוּ, קָבַץ, יִגְנֹב, סָמְכָה, סְפָדִים, קֹבֵץ, הִתְקַבְּצוּ, שָׁטַף,

יִתְגַּנֵּב, סָמוּךְ, סִפְדוּ, תִּקְבַּץ, יִשְׁטֹף, יָכָרֵת, יִסָּפְדוּ, לִסְפֹּר,

הַקָּבַץ, שָׁטַף, יִסְגֹּר, יָנָתֵן, מְבַקֵּשׁ, הַשְׁכִּים, יְלַמֵּד, הִמְשִׁיל,

יִכָּתֵב:

LESSON XXII

Waw Consecutive (Conversive)

Hebrew makes a peculiar use of the conjunction. It is called waw consecutive. The simple conjunction may connect verbs or nouns. Waw consecutive is used to connect finite verbs only and indicates that the state of the verb to which it is joined is a consequence of a preceding verb. It must be joined to its verb. Any conjunction not attached directly to its verb is not waw consecutive.

In continued narration after a perfect the verbs that follow may be put in the imperfect with waw consecutive.

The man kept (שָׁמַר) *the law, and he rested* (וַיִּשְׁבֹּת) *on the Sabbath and he did not sell* (וְלֹא מָכַר) *anything.*

After a simple imperfect the verbs that follow may be in the perfect with waw consecutive.

The man will keep (יִשְׁמֹר) *the law and he will rest* (וְשָׁבַת) *on the Sabbath and he will not sell* (וְלֹא יִמְכֹּר) *anything.*

It seems from these illustrations that the waw has the power of converting the perfect into an imperfect and *vice versa.* In fact, older grammars named it "waw conversive." It is best to drop this name and use the term that more accurately describes the actual function. The verbs, connected by ן, form in the mind of the author one chain or series, in which the verbs with waw consecutive are judged from the point of view of the first verb and, from that point of view, are considered as expressing a completed or incomplete action.

מָשַׁל	*he ruled*	יִמְשֹׁל	*he will rule*
וּמָשַׁל	*and he will rule*	וַיִּמְשֹׁל	*and he ruled*

The Form of the Conjunction

1. With the perfect, it is the same as the waw conjunctive with its various pointings, וְחַי, וּמָשַׁל, וְקָרָא.

2. With the imperfect, it is ן followed by daghesh-forte, and pointed just as the article, וַיָּקָם, וָאֶקְטֹל, וַיִּקְרָא.

(NOTE: The daghesh-forte may be omitted when supported only by simple sheʷwa).

THE VERBAL FORM USED

1. The usual verbal form is used in the perfect. The accent is frequently shifted from the penult to the ultima, וְאָמַרְתָּ instead of וְאָמַרְתָּ.

2. The imperfect prefers a shortened form. The accent is usually shifted from the ultima to the penult when the penultimate syllable is open, וַיֵּשֶׁב, וַיֹּאמֶר, וַיִּרָא, וַיְהִי.

VOCABULARY

אָסַר   *bind, imprison*   גֵּרֵשׁ   *drive out*

בָּלַע   *swallow*   נבא   *prophesy*

בָּרַח   *flee*   נָטָה   *spread out*

EXERCISES

Translate and locate verb forms:

אָסְרָה, אָסוּר, אָסְרוּ, בֶּלְעוּ, מִבְלָע, בָּרְחוּ, הִבְרִיחוּ, גֵּרֵשׁ, נִגְרַשׁ, יְנַבֵּא, יִתְנַבֵּא, מִתְנַבֵּא, זָכַר אֱלֹהִים אֶת־בְּרִיתוֹ וַיִּפְקֹד אֶת־הָעָם: יִפְקֹד אֱלֹהִים אֶת־עַמּוֹ וְשָׁמַר אֹתָם: דִּבַּרְתִּי אֶת־הַדָּבָר וְלֹא כָשָׁלוּ: יַשְׁכִּים וְנִמְלַט וּבִקֵּשׁ אֶת הָעִיר: יִזְכֹּר אֹתָם וְהָלַךְ וְדִבֶּר לָהֶם: הִשְׁכִּים וַיְדַבֵּר וְלֹא בָרַח מִן־הַבָּיִת:

LESSON XXIII

PRONOMINAL SUFFIXES WITH VERBS

The direct object of the verb, when a pronoun, may be written as a suffix to אֵת (אֹתוֹ *him*) or as a suffix to the verb. These

fragmentary pronouns are joined to active verbs and point out
the person or thing acted upon.

הִקְטִילוֹ *he caused him to kill*, or *he caused (one) to kill him.*

The suffixes for perfect and imperfect, when the verbal form
ends in a vowel, are as follows:

Singular		Plural	
נִי	*me*	נוּ	*us*
ךָ	*thee* (m.)	כֶם	*you* (m.)
ךְ	*thee* (f.)	(כֶן)	*you* (f.)
הוּ	*him*	ם	*them* (m.)
הָ	*her*	ן	*them* (f.)

When the verbal form ends in a consonant, a connecting
vowel is required. In the perfects this vowel is ־ָ or ־ַ. In the
imperfects and imperatives it is ־ֵ.

After verbal forms ending in a consonant

Perfect		Impf. and Impv.	
־ַנִי	*me*	־ֵנִי	*me*
־ְךָ	*thee* (m.)	־ְךָ	*thee* (m.)
־ָךְ (־ֵךְ)	*thee* (f.)	־ֵךְ	*thee* (f.)
וֹ = (־ָהוּ)	*him*	־ֵהוּ	*him*
־ָהּ	*her*	־ֶהָ	*her*
־ָנוּ	*us*	־ֵנוּ	*us*
־ְכֶם	*you* (m.)	־ְכֶם	*you* (m.)

‏־כֶן‎	*you* (f.)	‏־כֶן‎	*you* (f.)
‏־ם‎	*them* (m.)	‏־ם‎	*them* (m.)
‏־ן‎	*them* (f.)	—	*them* (f.)

Notes

1. These suffixes resemble very closely the noun suffixes. Note carefully the differences. (See paradigm M, page 216, for suffixes added to ‏קָטַל‎).

2. The imperative takes the same suffixes and the same connecting vowel as the imperfect.

3. The infinitive construct takes noun suffixes.

4. The suffixes to the participle are practically always those of the noun.

5. Singular suffixes to the imperfect and imperative are sometimes strengthened by the addition of *Nun* which is usually assimilated to the following consonant.

6. It is our purpose in this lesson to learn to recognize and translate the suffix to the verb. We shall use the Hiph'il form of the verb because it presents no internal vowel changes. The student will find many mystifying changes in ordinary verb forms. Let him be content, for the time being, with the location of the form and the proper translation of the verb and the pronominal suffix.

Suffixes to the Hiph'il

Perfect

הִקְטִיל	*he caused to kill*
הִקְטִילַנִי	*he caused to kill me*
הִקְטִילְךָ	*he caused to kill thee* (m.)
הִקְטִילֵךְ	*he caused to kill thee* (f.)
הִקְטִילוֹ	*he caused to kill him*
הִקְטִילָהּ	*he caused to kill her*
הִקְטִילָנוּ	*he caused to kill us*
הִקְטִילְכֶם	*he caused to kill you* (m.)
הִקְטִילְכֶן	*he caused to kill you* (f.)
הִקְטִילָם	*he caused to kill them* (m.)
הִקְטִילָן	*he caused to kill them* (f.)

Imperfect

יַקְטִיל	*he will cause to kill*
יַקְטִילֵנִי	*he will cause to kill me*
יַקְטִילְךָ	*he will cause to kill thee* (m.)
יַקְטִילֵךְ	*he will cause to kill thee* (f.)
יַקְטִילֵהוּ	*he will cause to kill him*
יַקְטִילָהּ	*he will cause to kill her*
יַקְטִילֵנוּ	*he will cause to kill us*
יַקְטִילְכֶם	*he will cause to kill you* (m.)

יַקְטִילְךָ   he will cause to kill you (f.)

יַקְטִילֵם   he will cause to kill them (m.)

(יַקְטִילֵן)   he will cause to kill them (f.)

VOCABULARY

אָבַד *perish*   בָּרָא *create*
(Hi.) *destroy*

אָהַב *love*   בָּרַךְ *bless*

אָמַר *say*   עָמַד *stand*

EXERCISES

Translate and locate fully

הַלְבִּישַׁנִי, הִמְלִיכוּ, יַלְבִּישֵׁם, תְּלַמְּדֵם, לְהַבְדִּילְךָ,

הַזְכִּירַנִי, יַמְשִׁילְכֶם, הִמְטִיר, הִמְלִיכַנִי, הִמְשִׁילָהּ, אַלְבִּישֵׁם,

הַצְדַּ יֵּקַנִי, הִשְׂכִּילְךָ, יַזְכִּירֵךְ, נַשְׂכִּימֵם, יַשְׁבִּירֵנִי, נַמְשִׁילוֹ,

יַפְקִידֵנוּ, הִשְׁלִיכוּ, יַגְבִּירְכֶם, הִגְדִּילְךָ, יַגְדִּילְכֶם:

LESSON XXIV

A STORY CONCERNING THE COVENANT WITH ISRAEL

לִמֵּד יהוה אֶת־יִשְׂרָאֵל בַּמִּדְבָּר: וַיְדַבֵּר לוֹ כַּדְּבָרִים

הָאֵלֶּה כַּאֲשֶׁר דִּבַּרְתִּי לְאַבְרָהָם אָבִיךְ כֵּן אֲנִי מְדַבֵּר לָךְ:

אֲנִי כֹרֵת בְּרִית עִמְּךָ: זְכֹר אֶת־מִצְוֹת יהוה אֱלֹהֶיךָ לִשְׁמֹר

אֹתָן וְאָנֹכִי אֲגַדֵּל אֹתְךָ: הִתְקַדֵּשׁ וְכַבֵּד אֶת־אֱלֹהֶיךָ: תִּלְמַד

אֶת־הַדְּבָרִים הָאֵלֶּה וּקְשַׁרְתָּם לְאוֹת עַל יָדֶיךָ וּכְתַבְתָּם עַל־
מְזוּזוֹת בֵּיתֶיךָ וּבִשְׁעָרֶיךָ: גַּם לַמֹּד תְּלַמֵּד אֹתָם לְבָנֶיךָ: כָּכָה
הַשְׂכֵּל תַּשְׂכִּיל אֶת־בָּנֶיךָ: לָכֵן אָמְרוּ בְּנֵי יִשְׂרָאֵל טוֹב לָנוּ
לִלְמֹד עַל יְדֵי יהוה: מִשְׁפְּטֵי יהוה אֱמֶת גַּם עַבְדְּךָ נִזְהָר בָּהֶם
בְּשָׁמְרָם עֵקֶב רָב: יהוה יִמְלֹךְ לְעוֹלָם וָעֶד:

NOTES

1. For words not yet studied see vocabulary, page 158. A
translation of this reading lesson may be found on page 191.
It is to be used by the student in preparation.

2. לָמַד in the Pi'el (לִמֵּד) means "make to learn, teach."

3. לוֹ "to him." The antecedent noun being a collective noun
(יִשְׂרָאֵל), all the pronouns referring to it may be rendered as
plurals.

4. כַּאֲשֶׁר preposition כְּ and the indeclinable relative pronoun אֲשֶׁר. Literal rendering "according to the thing which;"
hence, "just as."

5. מְדַבֵּר a participle may be used as a finite verb. It denotes continuous action. The subject usually precedes (as in
this case) the participle. Cf. כָּרַת in sentence following.

6. עִמְּךָ a pausal form. Preposition עִם + 2nd m. sg. suffix.

7. אֹתָן sign of the accusative אֵת + 3rd f. plu. suffix. So אֹתְךָ
and אֹתָם later.

8. תִּלְמֹד impf. with the force of an imperative. וּקְשַׁרְתָּם perfect with וְ consecutive + 3rd m. pl. suffix. Again, the force of an imperative.

9. וּבִשְׁעָרֶיךָ mas. plu. of שַׁעַר "gate" + וְ conjunctive, the preposition בְּ + 2nd m. sg. suffix.

10. לַמֹּד when the infinitive absolute precedes the verb, it adds intensity to the action. Literal rendering: "teaching, thou shalt teach;" thus, "thou shalt *indeed* teach." Cf. הַשְׂכֵּל in next sentence.

11. לְבָנֶיךָ mas. plu. of בֵּן + the preposition לְ and 2nd m. sg. suffix. The mas. const. plu. of בֵּן is בְּנֵי.

12. Literal rendering of עַל יְדֵי יהוה : "upon the hands of Yahweh." Const. plu. of יָד.

13. עֶבֶד, עַבְדְּךָ + 2nd m. sg. suffix.

14. בְּשָׁמְרָם infinitive construct (שְׁמֹר) + preposition בְּ and 3rd m. pl. suffix.

15. Literal rendering of לְעוֹלָם וָעֶד : "To the ages (collective noun) and on."

LESSON XXV
IRREGULAR VERBS

Statives

Less than one fifth of the verbs in Hebrew are inflected like the strong verb קָטַל. There are certain verbs known as "statives," usually intransitive, which express a state or condition, *he is full, thirsty, in fear, in love, heavy, strong,* etc. They are regular except in the Qal. In the ultimate syllable of the Qal they may take ־ֵ, ־ַ, or ־ָ; שָׁכַב *to lie down,* כָּבֵד *to be heavy,* קָטֹן *to be small.* The ־ֵ is changed to ־ַ before all consonantal afformatives, יָשַׁבְתָּ but the ־ָ is retained before the conso-nantal afformatives (except תֶם and תֶן) קָטָנְתָּ, but קְטָנְתֶם.

Some of the more common statives are:

כָּבֵד	be heavy	גָּדַל	be great
זָקֵן	be old	שָׂכַל	be wise
יָכֹל	be able	שָׁכֹל	be bereaved
קָטֹן	be small	חָזַק	be strong
יָרֵא	be afraid	צָדַק	be righteous
שָׁכַב	lie down	קָדַשׁ	be holy
שָׁלֵם	be whole	קָרַב	be near
רָחַק	be far off	שָׂמַח	be glad

Guttural Verbs

It must be remembered that gutturals have certain pecu-liarities, that affect the vowels under and before them. The verb that has a guttural in it differs from קָטַל only in vocaliza-tion. The consonants do not change. א and ה are not classed as gutturals at the end of a word. נָחַם, לָקַח, שָׁבַע, גָּאַל, עָמַד.

Weak Verbs

In addition to the gutturals א, ה, ח, ע and the letter ר there are other consonants that give trouble. These letters נ, י, and ו may be assimilated and disappear with or without trace. Verbs whose second and third consonants are identical show certain peculiarities that we shall consider.

The Paradigm Word, פָּעַל

It is convenient to have a system for designating the radicals, and for this purpose the old Jewish paradigm word, פָּעַל, is adopted. The letters *Pe*, *Ayin*, and *Lamedh*, are used in speaking of the radicals. פ (*Pe*) stands for the first radical. ע (*Ayin*) for the second, and ל (*Lamedh*) for the third. Thus a *Pe Nun* verb is one which has a *Nun* as its first radical, נָפַל. A *Pe Yodh* verb is one that has a *Yodh* as its first radical, יָטַב. An *Ayin Waw* verb is one whose middle radical is a *Waw*, קוּם. A verb like סָבַב whose second and third radicals are the same is called a *Double Ayin* verb. A *Lamedh Aleph* verb has an *Aleph* for its third radical, קָרָא.

Using פָּעַל and watching for א, ה, ח, ע, ר, נ, י, and ו we get:

Pe Guttural	עָמַד, חָזַק, עָבַד
Ayin Guttural	בָּחַר, צָעַק, שָׁאַל
Lamedh Guttural	תָּקַע, שָׁמַע, שָׁלַח
Pe Nun	נָבַט, נָצַל, נָפַל
Lamedh Aleph	חָטָא, קָרָא, מָצָא

Lamedh He	בָּנָה, פָּדָה, גָּלָה
Double Ayin	מָדַד, גָּלַל, סָבַב
Ayin Waw	שׁוּב, רוּץ, קוּם
Ayin Yodh	שִׁיר, בִּין, שִׂים
Pe Yodh	יָתַר, יָלַד, יָשַׁב

In studying the guttural verbs it will be well to remember that the radicals remain the same throughout just as in the strong verb. For example the Pi'el which doubles the middle radical (קִטֵּל) will necessarily assume a special form when the middle radical is a guttural, as gutturals cannot be doubled. The form is determined by the laws governing gutturals. It is not some arbitrary thing to be committed to memory. We find בֵּרֵךְ instead of בִּרֵךְ however, because the middle radical refuses the doubling and the short vowel in the open pretone must be heightened. So it is with the other types of "irregular" verbs, which are thoroughly regular to one who clearly understands the fundamental principles of the language.

VOCABULARY

אָשֵׁם	transgress, offend	שָׁאַל	ask
רָכַב	ride	רָגַז	be excited
תָּקַע	strike	רָאָה	see
שָׁבַע	swear	עָרַךְ	arrange

4. Five verbs beginning with אָ have certain peculiarities in the Qal;

אָבַד *perish,* אָכַל *eat,* אָמַר *say,* אָבָה *be willing,* אָפָה *bake.*

In the Qal imperfect the preformative vowel is ô and the second vowel is ă. (In pause the short ă may become long ē, יֹאכֵל)

לֵאמֹר becomes לֶאֱמֹר, יֹאכַל, יֹאמַר.

5. The verb אָהֵב is irregular. The imperative is אֱהַב, plural אֱהָבוּ.

VOCABULARY

אָסַף	gather	חָפֵץ	desire, delight *in*	עָבַר	pass over
הָפַךְ	overturn	חָשַׁב	think, devise	עָזַב	abandon
הָרַג	kill	עָבַד	serve	עָזַר	assist

EXERCISES

Translate and locate fully:

עִזְבוּ, עֲמַדְתֶּם, יַעֲבֹר, תַּעֲבִיר, יֵעָזֵר, אֹהֵב, נֶאֶסְפָה,

יֵהָפְכוּ, עָבַר, נַעֲמֹד, מֵעֲמָד, יֹאכַל, עֲבַרְתֶּם, עָזוֹב, אֱמֹר,

וַיֹּאמְרוּ, נֹאמַר, לֵאמֹר, אָכוֹל תֹּאכֵל, תֹּאמְרוּ, הֶעֱמִידָה,

תַּעֲזְבִי, עָמֹד, הָפַכְתִּי, עֹמֵד, מַעֲמִיד, יַעֲמֹד:

LESSON XXVII

The Ayin Guttural Verb

(The Middle Radical a Guttural)

See Paradigm C (page 200)

Types: שָׁאַל *ask,* שָׁחַט *slay,* בָּעַר *consume.*

Verbs whose second radical is a guttural exhibit the following peculiarities:

1. The guttural *refuses the doubling* (Cf. Pi., Pu., Hithpa.).

   (1) Before א and ר (and sometimes ע) the preceding vowel is heightened ⸺ to ⸺, ⸺ to ⸺, ⸺ to ⸺.

   בֵּרֵךְ becomes בֵּרֵךְ

   יְבָרֵךְ becomes יְבָרֵךְ

   יְמָאֵן becomes יְמָאֵן.

   (2) Before ה, ח (and sometimes ע) the preceding vowel usually remains short (doubled by implication).

   יְנַחֵם, נִחַם, מִהַר, יְנַעֵם.

2. The guttural *prefers compound shᵉwa* **under** it. Wherever the strong verb has vocal shᵉwa, the four gutturals (א, ה, ח, ע) take ⸺ while ר usually takes simple shᵉwa.

   שָׁחֲטָה instead of שָׁחְטָה

   בָּחֲרוּ instead of בָּחְרוּ

   תִּשְׂחֲקוּ instead of תִּשְׂחְקוּ.

3. The guttural *prefers an "a" class vowel*. ⸺ usually replaces ⸺ in the Qal imperfect and imperative, יִשְׂחַט instead of יִשְׂחֹט.

In the Pi'el perfect the ⸺ sometimes gives way to ⸺, נָחַם instead of נָחֵם.

VOCABULARY

פָּרַד *separate*	מִהַר (Pi.) *hasten*	שָׁחַט *slaughter*
מָאֵן (Pi.) *refuse*	כָּעַס *provoke, be vexed*	בָּעַר *consume, burn*
שָׂחַק *laugh*	צָעַק *cry out*	גָּאַל *deliver, redeem*

Exercises

1. Write in full:

    a. The Pi'el of גְרשׁ.

    b. The Pu'al of בער.

    c. The Qal of שׁחט.

2. Translate and locate fully:

הִכְעִיס, אַכְעִיס, בֹּעֵר, לְבָעֵר, גָּאַל, נִמְהָר, מְשַׁחֵק, שָׁחוּט,
בֵּעֵר, הִבְעַרְתִּי, נִגְאַל, מִהַר, מַשְׁחִיקִים, יִשְׁחַט, בְּעַרְתָּ,
תַּבְעִיר, מֵאֵן, תִּגְּאֵל, יְמַהֵר, יְבַעֵר, מַהֵר, יִשְׁחַט, מַבְעִיר,
מֵאַנְתָּ, מְמַהֵר, שָׁחֲטוּ, לִשְׁחֹט, שָׁחֲקוּ, יִשְׁחַק, יְמָאֵן, גָּאַל, מָאֵן,
יִגְאַל, מְבַעֲרִים, יִבְעַר, בַּעֲרָה, הִכְעִיס, גְּאוּלִים:

LESSON XXVIII

The Lamedh Guttural Verb

(The Final Radical a Guttural)

See Paradigm D (page 202)

Types: שָׁמַע *hear,* בָּטַח *trust,* גָּבַהּ *be high.*

This class includes verbs ending in ח, ע, הּ. Verbs with ר as the final guttural behave as strong verbs. Final א and ה are not gutturals. They form distinct classes of weak verbs.

The peculiarities of the Lamedh Guttural are:

1. Every final guttural must have an "*a*" sound before it,

יַקְטַח, קָטַח, יִקְטַח, קָטַח:

2. Unchangeably long vowels naturally are retained, taking pathaḥ furtive between the vowel and the guttural.

שָׁלוּחַ becomes שָׁלוּחַ (shā-lû°ḥ)

יַשְׁלִיחַ becomes יַשְׁלִיחַ (yăsh-lî°ḥ).

3. When afformatives are added the form stands just as the strong verb, הִשְׁמַעְתֶּם, קָטְחוּ, שָׁלְחָה, יִשְׁלְחוּ.

4. In the perfects the 2nd feminine singular forms have a helping vowel (◌ֲ) under the guttural שָׁלַחַתְּ. (Note the daghesh-lene in the תּ and the syllable-divider under it. This ◌ֲ is very probably a pathaḥ furtive).

VOCABULARY

זֶבַח	sacrifice	בָּקַע	cleave, split	בָּטַח	trust
לָקַח	take	פָּשַׁע	transgress	גָּבַהּ	be high, (Hi.) exalt
מָשַׁח	anoint	שָׁמַע	hear	שָׁלַח	send

EXERCISES

1. Write the 3rd singular masculine perfect and imperfect of שלח in all stems.

2. Write the participles of שמע in all formations.

3. Write the Hiph'il perfect and the Qal imperfect of בטח.

4. Translate and locate fully:

יִבְטַח, מַבְטִיחַ, מַגְבִּיהַ, לִזְבֹּחַ, בֹּקֵעַ, הִתְבַּקְּעוּ, אֶלְקָחָה,

נִשְׁמַע, מְשֻׁלָּח, בְּטַח, גָּבַהְתָּ, זָבַחְתִּי, זֶבַח, יִבְקַע, לָקַח,

מַשְׁמִיעַ, בָּטוּחַ, גְּבֹהוּ, מַשְׁלִיחַ, זֶבַח, לְהִבָּקַע, לְקַחְתָּ, זָבְחוּ,
לָקַח, נִמְשַׁח, שָׁלַח, יִפְשַׁע, בָּטוּחַ, יִגְבַּהּ, וַיִּזְבַּח, לִזְבֹּחַ,
מִבְקָעִים, לֹקֵחַ, מָשׁוּחַ, הַמָּשׁחַ, שָׁלוּחַ, נִשְׁלַח, פָּשְׁעוּ, הַבְטַחְתָּ,
יַגְבִּיהַּ, אֶזְבַּח, מִזַּבֵּחַ, בָּקַעְתָּ, לְהַבְקִיעַ, נִלְקַח, יִשְׁמַע, שָׁמֵעַ,
שָׁלַח, נִפְשַׁע, שָׁלַח:

LESSON XXIX

A Story Concerning the Crossing of the Jordan

אָמַר יְהוֹשֻׁעַ אֶל־בְּנֵי יִשְׂרָאֵל הַיּוֹם הַזֶּה נַעֲבֹר אֶת־הַיַּרְדֵּן:
יַעַבְרוּ הַכֹּהֲנִים לִפְנֵי הָעָם וְעָמְדוּ בְתוֹךְ הַיַּרְדֵּן עַד־אֲשֶׁר
עָבְרוּ כֹל הָעָם: יהוה שָׁלַח אֹתָנוּ בַּדֶּרֶךְ הַזֹּאת וְשָׁמוֹעַ נִשְׁמַע
בְּקוֹלוֹ:   אֲנִי בָּטוּחַ כִּי כֻלָּנוּ בְּטֻחִים בּוֹ:   הוּא מַבְטִיחַ אֹתָנוּ:
נֹאמַר יהוה עִמָּנוּ וְלֹא נֹאבֵד:

וַיְדַבֵּר יְהוֹשֻׁעַ עוֹד לֵאמֹר הַעֲבִירוּ עִמָּכֶם שְׁתֵּים־עֶשְׂרֵה
אֲבָנִים וְהַעֲמִידוּ אֹתָם בְּמִלּוֹנְכֶם: יִשְׁאֲלוּ בְנֵיכֶם מָחָר לֵאמֹר
מָה לָכֶם הָאֲבָנִים הָאֵלֶּה וַאֲמַרְתֶּם לָהֶם נִכְרְתוּ מֵי הַיַּרְדֵּן
מִפְּנֵי אֲרוֹן בְּרִית יהוה: לֹא מֵאֲנוּ בְנֵי־יִשְׂרָאֵל לַעֲבֹר כִּדְבַר
יהוה וְלֹא נִמְאֲסוּ כַּאֲשֶׁר נִמְאֲסוּ אֲבוֹתֵיהֶם בַּמִּדְבָּר עַל־כֵּן
הָאֲבָנִים הָאֵלֶּה לְזִכָּרוֹן לִפְנֵי יִשְׂרָאֵל עַד עוֹלָם:

Notes

1. For new words consult the vocabulary on page 158.

2. בְּנֵי mas. const. plu. of בֵּן, cf. בְּנֵיכֶם.

3. הַיּוֹם emphatic by virtue of its position.

4. לִפְנֵי const. plu. of פָּנֶה + preposition לְ, "in the presence of."

5. עַד־אֲשֶׁר with finite verb, "until."

6. כֹּל הָעָם a collective subject; hence, a plural verb עֲבָדוּ.

7. שֹׁלֵחַ a ptc. used as a finite verb. The subject precedes when ptc. is employed.

8. וְשָׁמוֹעַ נִשְׁמַע בְּקוֹלוֹ literal rendering: "and hearkening we shall hearken to his voice." Note use of inf. absolute. שָׁמַע – – – בְּ means "to hearken to."

9. בָּטוּחַ literally: "am made trustful," ptc. used as finite verb.

10. כֻּלָּנוּ "all of us," כֹּל + the pronom. suffix.

11. הַעֲבִירוּ "cause ye to pass over." Hiph. imperative.

12. שְׁתֵּים־עֶשְׂרֵה "twelve."

13. וְהַעֲמִידוּ Hiph. imperative of עָמַד.

14. מָחָר "tomorrow."

15. מֵי construct of מַיִם.

16. עַל־כֵּן "upon so"="therefore."

17. עַד עוֹלָם collective noun "unto ages."

LESSON XXX

THE PE NUN VERB ·

(The First Radical a Nun)

See Paradigm E (page 204)

Types: נָפַל *fall*, נָגַשׁ *approach*.

When the letter נ is supported by a syllable-divider it is assimilated into the following letter, יַנְגִּיד becomes יַגִּיד, יִנְפֹּל becomes יִפֹּל, נָתַנְתָּ becomes נָתַתָּ.

1. This assimilation comes in Qal imperfect, Niph'al perfect and participle, and throughout the Hiph'il and Hoph'al. When the נ is dropped a daghesh-forte is always placed in the second radical. This assimilation does not take place in verbs that are also Ayin Guttural.

2. The Qal imperative is usually regular (נְפֹל) although in certain cases (the Qal in *a*) the נ is lost, leaving the form טַל, גַּשׁ.

3. The Qal infinitive construct is usually regular (נְטֹל) although in the verbs that have *a* in the imperfect the נ is dropped. As a sort of compensation ת is added, making a segholate form. (נָגַשׁ becomes גַּשׁ then גַּשְׁתּ then גֶּשֶׁת).

4. The preposition before such a segholate form is always written לְ (לָגֶשֶׁת).

5. The verb לָקַח follows the analogy of the Pe Nun verb in the Qal and Hoph'al. יִלְקַח becomes יִקַּח, נִלְקַח (Qal im-

perfect) becomes נִקַּח but נִלְקַח (Niph'al perfect) remains un-
assimilated.

NOTE: On account of the sharpened syllable in the Hoph'al,
the original preformative ־ָ appears, יֻגַּד; הֻגַּד.

<h2>VOCABULARY</h2>

נָגַע touch   נָטַע plant

נָגַשׁ approach   נגד announce, declare
(Hi.) bring near

נָפַל fall   נבט (Hi.) look, gaze, behold

נצל (Hi.) snatch, deliver   נָסַע depart
(Ni.) (passive)
(Pi.) plunder

<h2>EXERCISES</h2>

1. Write synopses of Qal, Niph'al, and Hiph'il stems, using
נָפַל, נָגַשׁ.

2. Translate and locate fully:

יִפֹּל, נֹסֵעַ, יִגַּע, לָגֶשֶׁת, נָטַעְתִּי, מַפִּיל, יַנְצֵל, תַּסִּיעַ, יַפִּיל,
הַבִּיט, גַּע, נִגַּשׁ, יִטַּע, מַפִּילִים, הִצִּיל, מַסִּיעַ, קַח, הִגִּיד, מַבִּיט,
נֹגֵעַ, יְנַגַּע, נַגִּישׁ, נֹטֵעַ, הִתְנַפֵּל, הַצֵּל, מַצִּיל, נָסְעוּ, הִגַּדְתָּ, יַגִּיד,
הִגִּיעַ, מַגִּישׁ, נָטוּעַ, מִתְנַפֵּל, יִתְנַצְּלוּ, גַּשׁ, מַגִּיד, הַגִּיעַ, מְנַגֵּשׁ,
אֶפֹּל, נִפֵּל, יִנָּצֵל, יִסַּע, יַקַּח, הֻגַּד, יֻגַּד, מַגִּיעַ, הִתְנַגְּשׁוּ, הִפִּיל,
נִצַּלְתֶּם:

LESSON XXXI
THE LAMEDH ALEPH VERB
(Last Radical an Aleph)
See Paradigm F (page 206)

Types: מָצָא *find*, מָלֵא *be full*, קָרָא *call*.

At the beginning of a syllable א is always a guttural; at the end of a syllable it is always quiescent (silent). When quiescent the preceding vowel is always long, מָצָא *he found*, יִמְצָא *he will find*, נִקְרָא *he was called*.

1. To write the **synopsis** of the Lamedh Aleph verb it is only necessary to write the synopsis of the strong verb, substitute an א for the ל of קָטַל and heighten the short vowels. (The Qal imperfect and imperative prefer the *a* instead of the *o* (יִקְטָא and קְטָא).

2. To write the various **inflections** note:

(a) Before the consonant afformatives the same rule applies מָצָאתָ, הִקְטֵאתִי, קְטֵאתָ.

(b) Before the vowel additions (הָ_, יְ_, וּ) the א is a consonant (guttural) and is treated like a strong consonant רָפְאוּ, מָצְאָה.

NOTES

1. In the inflection of the perfects the vowel before א is ◌ָ in the Qal, and ◌ֵ in all the other perfects, נִקְטֵאת, מָצָאתָ, קְטֵאתָ.

2. In the imperfects and imperatives before א with the termination נָה the vowel is ◌ֵ (é) (heightened from ◌ַ) קְטֶאנָה.

3. The infinitive construct may be formed by adding ת
(מְלֹאת) although the regular form is קְרֹא *to call*.

4. The quiescent א frequently falls out in the writing, מָצָתִי
for מָצָאתִי.

חָבָא	(Ni.) *hide, withdraw*	נָשָׂא	*lift up*	שָׂנֵא	*hate*
חָטָא	*sin*	קָרָא	*call, meet,*	מָלֵא	*be full*
מָצָא	*find*	רָפָא	*heal, care*	צָמֵא	*be thirsty*

EXERCISES

1. Write a complete synopsis using מָצָא.

2. Translate and locate fully:

חָטְאָה, חָטָא, מַחֲטִיא, תַּחֲבִיא, מָלֵא, מָצָאתְ, מַמְצִיא,

מְנַשְּׂאִים, תֵּרָפֵא, יִקְרָא, שָׂנֵא, יִתְחַטָּאוּ, יִתְחַבֵּא, מָלֵא, נִמְצָא,

נָשְׂאוּ, יְרֻפָּא, לְהִתְרַפֵּא, קֹרֵא, שָׂנוֹא, הֶחֱטִיא, חֹטֵא, נֶחְבָּא,

מִתְחַבֵּא, מְמַלֵּא, מֹצֵא, רֻפָּא, צָמְאוּ, יַקְרֵא, מְשֻׁנָּא, נִקְרָא,

יִצְמָא, לִרְפֹּא, יִנָּשֵׂא, נַמְצִיא, יִמָּלֵא, מָלְאוּ, תֵּחָבֵא, תַּחֲטִיא,

חֻבְּאוּ, מֻלְאוּ, נִמְצָא, נָשָׂא, נָשָׂא, רֻפֵּא, קָרָאת, יִשָּׂנֵא:

LESSON XXXII

THE LAMEDH HE (LAMEDH YODH) VERB

(Last Radical ה)

See Paradigm G (page 208)

Types: גָּלָה *reveal*, כָּסָה *conceal*.

These verbs originally ended in י (or ו). This final consonant has been lost. As a protection for the vowel and to preserve the appearance of the triliteral root the final הּ is now written as the third consonant. The הּ is not a genuine part of the root. It is a vowel sign with the ָ of the root. (When the הּ is truly consonantal, it takes mappiḳ. The verb then belongs to the Lamedh Guttural class, גָּבַהּ *to be high*, תָּמַהּ *to wonder*).

1. In the **synopsis** of this verb (in all forms without afformatives) the letter הּ appears as the final letter (except in infinitives construct and the Qal passive participle).

Note the endings for the various stems:

הָ֫ in all perfects הָקְטָה, נִקְטָה, קְטָה, קָטָה.

הֶ֫ in all imperfects יִקְטֶה, יָקְטֶה, יְקַטֶּה, יַקְטֶה.

הֵ֫ in all imperatives הַקְטֵה, הִקְטֵה, קַטֵּה, קְטֵה.

Regular vowel in all infinitives absolute הַקְטֵה, קָטֹה, קָטוֹ.

וֹת in all infinitives construct הַקְטוֹת, הִקְטוֹת, קְטוֹת.

הֶ֫ in all participles (except Qal passive) מְקַטֶּה, קֹטֶה, נִקְטֶה, מַקְטֶה, מַקְטֶה.

Write the synopsis of the strong verb, change the ל to an הּ, substitute the vowel given above and the new synopsis is complete.

2. In the **inflection,** when afformatives are added, the following rules apply:

    (a) Before consonant afformatives the י is preserved as the third radical. The י unites with the preceding vowel, forming a diphthong.

In active perfects it is יְ (The Pi'el and Hiph'il may have יֵ).

In passive perfects it is יֻ.

In imperfects and imperatives before נָה it is יֶ,
קְטֶינָה ,תִּקְטֶינָה ,הִקְטִיתָ ,קְטִיתָ ,קָטִיתָ.

(b) Before vowel afformatives (and before suffixes) the יְ with its vowel is lost.

קָטוּ instead of קָטְיוּ
קֻטוּ instead of קֻטְיוּ
יַקְטוּ instead of יַקְטְיוּ
יֵרְדוּ instead of יֵרְדְיוּ

Notes

1. The feminine singular of all perfects has the old feminine ending ת to which the regular ending הָ is added, (קָטְתָה and קֻטְתָה).

2. The jussive of all voices is formed by dropping the הָ of the imperfect. יַקְט instead of יַקְטָה. This process is called "apocopation" and the resultant forms "apocopated forms." The addition of ו consecutive also causes this apocopation, וַיִּגֶל for וַיִּגְלָה.

Vocabulary

בָּכָה weep	כָּלָה be complete (Pi.) complete	רָעָה feed
גָּלָה disclose (Pi.) reveal (Hi.) carry away	צוה (Pi.) command	פָּדָה ransom
	כָּסָה cover, conceal	קָנָה get, obtain
אָבָה be willing	בָּנָה build	פָּנָה turn

Exercises

1. Write a synopsis of the verb using נָלָה.

2. Translate and locate fully:

בָּכִיתִי, אָבוּ, יֵגְלֶה, תִּבְכֶּה, אֹבֶה, הָגְלוּ, יִגְלוּ, נִבְכֶּה,
נָגְלָה, בָּכוּ, גָּלָה, גָּלִית, בֹּכֶה, נַשׁ, נָּלוּי, הֻגְלָה, מְבַכֶּה, מְגֻלָּה,
הָגְלוּ, הִתְגַּלּוֹת, מְגֻלָּה, בָּנִיתָ, יִבְנֶה, בֹּנֶה, בָּנֹה, בָּנוֹת, נִבְנָה,
נִבְנֶה, לְהִבָּנוֹת, כֹּסָה, הַכָּסוֹת, כִּסָּה, כִּסִּיתִי, יְכַסֶּה, כַּסּוֹת,
מְכֻסֶּה, יִתְכַּסּוּ, מִתְכַּסֶּה, כָּלוּ, כְּלוֹת, כָּלָה, כֻּלּוּ, אֲכַלֶּה,
כַּלֵּה, יִפְדֶּה, פְּדֵה, פֻּדֶּה, יָפְדֶה, פָּנִיתָ, פָּנֶה, יִפְנֶה, לִפְנוֹת, פְּנֵה,
מַפְנֶה, מָפְנֶה, יִרְעֶה, רָעֹה, לִרְעוֹת, רֹעֶה, קֶנָתָה, קָנֹה, קָנֶה,
יִקְנוּ, צַנֵּה, יְצַוֶּה, וַיְצַו, מְצַוֶּה, צַוֵּיתָ:

LESSON XXXIII

A Story Concerning the Crossing of the Jordan (Continued)

אָמַר יהוה אֶל־יְהוֹשֻׁעַ הַיּוֹם הַזֶּה אָחֵל גַּדֶּלְךָ בְּעֵינֵי כָּל־
יִשְׂרָאֵל כִּי יֵדְעוּ כִּי כַּאֲשֶׁר הָיִיתִי עִם־מֹשֶׁה אֶהְיֶה עִמָּךְ: אֱמֹר
לָהֶם בְּזֹאת תֵּדְעוּ כִּי אֵל חַי בְּקִרְבְּכֶם וְהוֹרֵשׁ יוֹרִישׁ בַּעֲבוּרֵיכֶם
אֶת הַגּוֹיִים אֲשֶׁר יֹשְׁבִים בָּאָרֶץ: כְּנוֹחַ כַּפּוֹת רַגְלֵי הַכֹּהֲנִים
בְּמֵי הַיַּרְדֵּן יִכָּרְתוּ הַמַּיִם הַיֹּרְדִים מִלְמַעְלָה וְיַעַמְדוּ נֵד־אֶחָד
וְהַמַּיִם הַיֹּרְדִים עַל יָם־הַמֶּלַח יָתַמּוּ עַד אֲשֶׁר תַּמּוּ כָל־הָעָם
לַעֲבֹר: אֶת־זֹאת יַעֲשֶׂה יהוה לְמַעַן דַּעַת כָּל־עַמֵּי הָאָרֶץ אֶת־
יַד יהוה כִּי חֲזָקָה הִיא וּלְמַעַן שׂוֹם יִרְאַת יהוה בִּלְבַבְכֶם:

וּבַיּוֹם הַהוּא הָחֵל החל יהוה לְגַדֵּל אֶת־יְהוֹשֻׁעַ: הָיוּ הַכֹּהֲנִים
עֹמְדִים בְּתוֹךְ הַיַּרְדֵּן עַד תֹּם כָּל־הַדָּבָר אֲשֶׁר צִוָּה יהוה אֶת־
יְהוֹשֻׁעַ: וַיְהִי כַּאֲשֶׁר תַּמּוּ הַכֹּהֲנִים לַעֲבֹר הֶחֱלוּ הַמַּיִם לָשׁוּב
לִמְקוֹמָם: וַיֹּאמְרוּ בְנֵי יִשְׂרָאֵל בִּלְבָבָם חֶסֶד יְסוֹבֵב אֶת־כָּל־
הַבֹּטְחִים בְּיהוה כְּמוֹ מְסוֹבֵב הוּא אֶת־יְהוֹשֻׁעַ הַיּוֹם הַלְלוּ־יָהּ
הַלְלוּ אֶת־שֵׁם יהוה:

NOTES

1. גַּדְּלוֹ Pi'el inf. const. + pronom. suffix. ־ is changed to
־ֵ before heavy suffix ךָ.

2. בְּעֵינֵי construct plural of עַיִן + preposition.

3. בְּזֹאת is emphatic by position.

4. הַיֹּרְדִים When the article is used with the ptc., it is practically equivalent to a relative clause.

5. כְּנוֹחַ "At the resting of the souls of the feet." Inf. const.
from נוּחַ.

6. עַד אֲשֶׁר תַּמּוּ "until that all the people will have finished
with reference to passing over."

7. לֵב, בִּלְבַבְכֶם (reduplicated form) + prep. בְּ + 2nd plu.
suffix.

8. וַיְהִי apocopated (shortened) form of Qal impf. יְהֶיֶה.

9. יְסוֹבֵב Po'el impf. from סָבַב.

10. מְסוֹבֵב Po'el ptc. from סָבַב.

11. הַיּוֹם "the day"="this day," "today." (Recurrence of
original demonstrative force of the article.)

LESSON XXXIV

The Double Ayin Verb
(Second and Third Radical the Same)
See Paradigm H (page 210)

Types: סָבַב *surround*, קָלַל *be light.*

The weakness of these verbs lies in the fact that the second
and third radicals, being identical, are in many cases written as
one letter, סָבַב becomes סַב, קָלַל becomes קַל. Where this
occurs, the second radical must bear daghesh-forte before afformatives, קַלּוּ instead of קָלֲלוּ.

1. To find the **synopsis** we write קָטַט as in the strong verb.
The next step is to cancel the second radical and the vowel of
the first. קָטַט becomes קַט, יִקְטַט becomes יִקַּט. In the intensive stems and in the Qal infinitive absolute and participles
the form remains uncontracted קָטַט, קָטוֹט, קֹטֵט.

2. The stem vowel, which, after contraction, stands with the
first radical instead of the second, is the same as that of the corresponding form of the strong verb except in

Niph'al imperfect and imperative הִקַּט, יִקַּט,

Hiph'il perfect, imperfect, infinitive construct and participle
מֵקַט, הָקֵט יָקֵט, הָקֵט.

The ground form is retained in the Niph'al while the vowel
of the ground form is heightened in the Hiph'il.

3. The vowel of the preformative, now in an open syllable
before the tone, is heightened, ־ to ־ in Qal and Niph'al, ־

to ‑ in Hiph'il perfect and participle; נִקְטַט becomes נָקַט,
הֶקְטַט becomes הֶקַט.

4. The regular intensive stems are found frequently uncontracted, הִלֵּל *praise*. Certain special forms are also found,
קוֹטֵט (here called *Po'el*), קוֹטַט (*Po'al*), and הִתְקוֹטֵט (*Hith-po'el*). In rare instances a *Pilpel* form is found גִּלְגֵּל from גָּלַל
to roll.

5. Before consonantal afformatives a long helping vowel is
inserted to insure pronunciation of the full letter of the stem.
In all the perfects it is וֹ and in the imperfects and imperatives
(before נָה) it is יְ.

תִּצְלֶיְנָה, נְקַטוֹתָ, סַבּוֹת

These vowels are always accented except before תֶּם and תֶּן.

6. An Aramaic form of the Qal imperfect, made by doubling
the first radical, is quite common, יְקֹב *he will curse*, יִדֹּם *he will
be silent*.

VOCABULARY

גָּלַל	roll	פלל	(Pi.) *intervene, meditate* (Hith.) *pray*
מָדַד	measure	אָרַר	curse
סָבַב	surround, turn	הלל	(Pi.) *praise* (Hith.) *boast*
קָלַל	be insignificant (Ni.) be light (Hi.) make light	חָנַן	be gracious (Pi.) make gracious (Hith.) make entreaty

EXERCISES

1. Write a synopsis of Qal, Niph'al, and Hiph'il using גָּלַל.

2. Translate and locate fully:

קָלוּ, קִלֵּל, אָרוֹר, אָרוּר, גַּל, גֻּלַּל, יְקַלַּל, הָקֵל, קַלְקַל,
לְהִתְגֹּלֵל, מִתְגֹּלֵל, הָלֵל, אֲהַלֵּל, חַנּוֹתִי, מִתְחַנֵּן, יִתְמֹדֵד,
הֵסֵב, הַלְלוּ, יָחֹן, מַדּוֹתִי, סַבּוֹתִי, נָסֵב, מֵסֵב, הַלֵּל, חֹנֵן, יָמֹד,
סֹבִּי, סֹב, פִּלַּלְתָּ, מְהֻלָּל, חָנוֹן, נְהַלַּל, חָנוּן, יִמַּד, סֹבֵב, יְפַלֵּל,
מִתְהַלֲלִים, יְחֻנַּן, יְמַדֵּד, נָסַבּוּ, הִתְפַּלֵּל, מְדַד, סַבֵּב:

LESSON XXXV

THE MIDDLE VOWEL VERBS
(Ayin Waw and Ayin Yodh)
See Paradigm I (page 212)

Types: קוּם *rise*, בּוֹשׁ *be ashamed*, בִּין *discern*

In certain verbs the middle radical was originally ו or י, but this letter has either dropped out altogether, or remains only as a vowel letter. As a result, in many forms only two of the radicals appear. This is usually true of the Qal perfect: e. g., בָּן, בָּא, מֵת, קָם. Since there is in these forms no indication of the original middle radical, the *infinitive construct* form is usually cited as the root, for there the ו or י is preserved: e. g., קוּם, בִּין, בּוֹא, מוּת.

Not all verbs which have a ו or י as the middle radical exhibit this peculiarity. In some cases the letter is strong enough to be retained as a consonant: e. g., צָוָה *command*, גָּוַע *expire*, חָיָה *live*, הָיָה *be*. These verbs are not classed as Middle Vowel verbs, and the rules here given do not apply to them.

As in strong verbs there are three classes of Middle Vowel verbs: *a*, *e*, and *o*. (Cf. קָטֹל, כָּבֵד, קָטֹן.) קוּם has the Qal perfect in *a*: קָם; מוּת in *e:* מֵת; בּוֹשׁ in *o*. The *o* type verb often retains the middle vowel letter where other types reject it: בּוֹשׁ, בּוֹשָׁה, בּוֹשׁוּ. (Note, however, that בּוֹא, *go in*, takes Qal perfect בָּא. So also the Ayin Yodh verbs: בִּין, Qal perfect, בָּן).

The following general rules apply to Middle Vowel verbs:

1. Medial ו never appears as a consonant. It either falls out or unites with the form:

קַוַל becomes קַל

קְוֻל becomes קוּל

נָקְוַם becomes נָקוּם

2. The vowel of the preformative, which, after the contraction, stands in an open syllable before the tone, is heightened ־ָ to ־ֵ in Hiph'il perfect and participle, (וּ in Hoph'al) and ־ָ to ־ָ elsewhere:

נָקוֹם יָקוּם, הוּקַם יָקִים, הֵקִים

3. Before vowel afformatives the stem vowel, instead of being volatilized, as in the strong verb, is retained and accented:

יָמֹלוּ, נָפֹצוּ, יָבֹאוּ

4. Before consonantal afformatives a separating vowel (וֹ in perfect and ־ִי in imperfect and imperative) is found in Niph'al and Hiph'il perfects and Qal imperfect. The Qal perfect shortens ־ָ to ־ַ, קַמְתִּי instead of קָמֹותִי.

NOTES

1. In the Ayin Yodh verbs the Qal imperfect is identical in form with the Hiph‘il imperfect: יָשִׂים ,יָבִין ,יָשִׁיר ,יָשִׂית.

2. The verb בּוֹא (*come in*) keeps וֹ in the Qal imperfect where the other verbs have וּ (יָבוֹא).

3. Instead of the regular intensive stems we usually find Polel, Pilpel, Polal, or Hithpolel forms: קוֹמָם, כִּלְכֵּל, קוֹמֵם, הִתְקוֹמֵם.

4. When the separating vowel (וֹ) of the Niph‘al perfect is accented, the וֹ of the stem is changed to וּ (for the sake of euphony): נְקוּלוֹת.

5. When the preposition לְ is prefixed to the infinitive construct it is pointed לָ (לָשׁוּב).

VOCABULARY

גּוּר	sojourn	שׁוּב	turn, return
טוֹב	be good	בּוֹשׁ	be ashamed
קוּם	rise (Hi.) *raise up*	בִּין	discern (Hi.) *explain*
רוּץ	run	מוּת	die
שִׂים	put, place	שִׁיר	sing

EXERCISES

1. Write synopses using בּוֹשׁ, שִׂים, גּוּר.

2. Translate and locate fully:

יָבִין, בִּין, הֵבִין, אֶתְבּוֹנֵן, בּוֹשָׁה, מֵבִין, מֵבִישׁ, בּוֹשִׁים, גָּר,

יָגוּר, גַּרְתִּי, גּוּרִי, טוֹב, נָרִים, מִתְגּוֹרֵר, טוֹבוּ, הַטִּיבוֹתָ, אָמוּת,

מֵת, קַמְתָּ, מוֹת, נָקוֹם, מְמוֹתֵת, קוּם, הֵמִית, יָמִית, הֲקִים,

יָקִים, מֵמִית, יוּמַת, רָץ, מֵקִים, הָקֵם, יָרוּץ, תָּרִיץ, לָרוּץ,

שָׁמוּ, שַׂמְתִּי, שׁוּב, יָשִׂים, שָׁב, מֵשִׂים, שַׁבְתָּ, יוּשַׁם, הֲשִׁיבוֹתִי,

מֵשִׁיב, הוּשַׁב, שָׁר, יָשִׁיר, יוּשַׁר, לָשִׁיר:

LESSON XXXVI

The Pe Yodh and Pe Waw Verbs

(The First Radical Yodh or Waw)

See Paradigm K (page 214)

Types: יָטַב *be good,* יָדַע *know,* יָרַשׁ *inherit*

Since Yodh and Waw are weak letters they become quiescent after certain vowel sounds. They lose their consonantal character after most preformatives.

1. Six verbs are properly **Pe Yodh,** יָטַב *be good,* יָנַק *suck,* יָמַן *go to right,* יָשַׁר *be straight,* יָקַץ *awake,* יָלַל *howl.*

They retain the Yodh, יָטֵב, יְטֹב, יְטוֹב, יָטַב, יֵיטַב, יִטֹב, יְטוֹב.

In the Hiph'il the Yodh unites with the vowel of the preformative, giving מֵיטִיב, יֵיטִיב, הֵיטִיב, ־ֵ.

2. Others are properly **Pe Waw** verbs, and are divided into two classes:

(a) Some **reject** the Waw in the Qal impf., imper. and inf. construct, יָרַד *go down,* יָדַע *know,* יָצָא *go out,* יָקַע *be dislocated,* יָשַׁב *sit, dwell,* יָלַד *bear,* יָחַד *be united,* (הָלַךְ *walk*).

Qal pf.	impf.	imper.	inf. construct
יָשַׁב	יֵשֵׁב	שֵׁב	שֶׁבֶת
יָדַע	יֵדַע	דַּע	דַּעַת
יָצָא	יֵצֵא	צֵא	צֵאת
הָלַךְ	יֵלֵךְ	לֵךְ	לֶכֶת

(b) Others **retain** the Waw, allowing it to stand as a Yodh with the vowel of the preformative, יָרֵשׁ *possess*, יָרֵא *fear*, יָעַץ *advise*, יָעֵף *be weary*, יָשֵׁן *sleep*.

Qal pf.	impf.	imper.	inf. construct
יָרֵשׁ	יִירַשׁ	יְרשׁ (רַשׁ)	יְרשׁ (רֶשֶׁת)
יָבֵשׁ	יִיבַשׁ	יְבַשׁ	יְבשׁ (יְבֶשֶׁת)

3. In the Hiph‘il of verbs properly Pe Waw the original הוְשִׁיב (הַוְשַׁב) appears as הוֹשִׁיב. (Likewise, מוֹשִׁיב, יוֹשִׁיב).

4. In the Niph‘al perfect the original נַוְשַׁב becomes נוֹשַׁב. This is true both of Pe Yodh and of Pe Waw types. The Niph‘al imperfect, imperative and infinitives behave as the strong verb יִוָּלֵד, הִוָּתֵר, תִּוָּרֵשׁ.

5. In the Hoph‘al the original הוְשַׁב becomes הוּשַׁב. (Likewise, מוּשַׁב, יוּשַׁב).

NOTES

1. The verb, יָכֹל *be able*, is irregular. The only imperfect used is the form יוּכַל which is a true Hoph‘al. The infinitive construct is יְכֹלֶת.

2. The verb, הָלַךְ *walk*, is treated as a Pe Waw verb except in the Qal perfect, participle and infinite absolute, and throughout the Hithpaʻel. The infinitive construct is לֶכֶת.

3. When the preposition לְ is written with the infinitive construct it takes the form לָ (לָשֶׁבֶת).

4. The Qal imperative sometimes takes the cohortative ending רְדָה, שְׁבָה, לְכָה, ֶ,ָה.

VOCABULARY

יָבֵשׁ	be dry, dry up	יָטַב	be good (Hi.) do good
יָלַד	bring forth (Hi.) beget	יָרֵא	fear
יָעַץ	give counsel	יָשַׁר	be straight (Pi.) make straight
יָשַׁב	sit, dwell	הָלַךְ	go, walk
יָדַע	know		

EXERCISES

1. Write a full synopsis of this verb using יָלַד.

2. Translate and locate fully:

יָלַד, הוֹדַע, אוֹבִישׁ, נוֹדַע, יָבְשׁוּ, הוֹלִיד, יֵיטַב, יִוָּדַע,

יָדַעְתִּי, תִּיבַשׁ, יָבוֹשׁ, יֵדַע, נוֹדָע, הֵיטִיב, מוֹלִיד, תִּיבֵשׁ, דַּע,

יָדַעְתָּ, מֵיטִיב, יוֹעֵץ, הוֹבִישׁ, יֵדַע, יוֹדִיעַ, תֵּלֵךְ, יָעוּץ, הוֹבַשְׁתָּ,

יָדוּעַ, מוֹדִיעִים, יֵלֵד, נוֹעַץ, נוֹלַד, יְשַׁבְתֶּם, יִישַׁר, מִתְהַלֵּךְ,

אוֹלִיד מוֹלִיכִים, לֵךְ, הוֹלֵךְ, הֲלַכְתִּי, נְהַלֵּךְ, מְהַלֵּךְ, יְיַשֵּׁר,

יֵרָאֶה, יִירָא, יְרָא, תִּוָּרֵא, אֵשֵׁב, שֵׁב, שֶׁבֶת, שְׁבוּ, מוֹשִׁיב:

LESSON XXXVII

A Story Concerning the Crossing of the Jordan (Continued)

וַיְדַבֵּר יְהוֹשֻׁעַ אֶל־בְּנֵי יִשְׂרָאֵל עוֹד לֵאמֹר כַּאֲשֶׁר יָסַע
הָאָרוֹן מִמְּקוֹמוֹ וְאַתֶּם תִּסְעוּ מִמְּקוֹמְכֶם: אַךְ כַּעֲמֹד הַכֹּהֲנִים
עַל גְּדוֹת הַנָּהָר תַּעֲמְדוּ נַם אַתֶּם: אַגִּיד לָכֶם מָתַי לִנְסֹעַ עוֹד
לֵאמֹר זֹאת הָעֵת לָגֶשֶׁת קְחוּ אֶת־כָּל־אֲשֶׁר־לָכֶם וּשְׂאוּ אֶת־
מַשָּׂאֲכֶם: בָּעֵת הַהִיא נָתַן אָמֵץ אִישׁ לְרֵעֵהוּ: נִקְרָא אִישׁ
לְרֵעֵהוּ לֵאמֹר אַל נִפְחָד: כָּכָה נִפְלָא: יֹאמְרוּ לָנוּ יַלְדֵינוּ
מָחָר קְרָאתֶם לָנוּ וַנַּעֲבֹר בְּלִי פַחַד: יֹאמַר בֵּן לְאָבִיו קָרָאתָ
לִי בַיּוֹם הַהוּא בַּת לְאִמָּהּ קָרוֹא קָרָאת לִי: כָּכָה יַפְלִיא יהוה
אֶת־הַיּוֹם הַזֶּה:

וַיַּעֲשׂוּ בְנֵי יִשְׂרָאֵל כִּדְבַר יהוה: אָמַר יְהוֹשֻׁעַ הִתְקַדְּשׁוּ כִּי
יַעֲשֶׂה יהוה נִפְלָאוֹת בְּקִרְבְּכֶם וְכֵן עָשׂוּ: וַיְצַוּוּ אֹתָם הַשֹּׁטְרִים
לַעֲשׂוֹת כַּאֲשֶׁר צִוָּה יהוה בַכֹּל וְכֵן עָשׂוּ: וּבַעֲלוֹת הָעָם אֶל
הֶחָרָבָה אָמְרוּ יהוה עָשָׂה כִדְבָרוֹ טוֹב לָנוּ לַעֲשׂוֹת אֶת־כָּל־
אֲשֶׁר מְצַוֶּה הוּא:

Notes

1. וְאַתֶּם literal rendering: "and ye." אַתֶּם used for emphasis: "then *ye, on your part,* shall journey."

2. כַּעֲמֹד infinitive construct with preposition כְּ. Literal rendering: "at the standing of . . . . . ." כְּ with infinitive construct denotes "at the point when, just as, as soon as;" בְּ with infinitive denotes duration: "in, when." Cf. בַּעֲלוֹת.

3. אֶת־כָּל־אֲשֶׁר־לָכֶם literally: "all which to you." A Hebrew idiom for expressing possession. "All that you have" (free translation).

4. בָּעֵת הַהִיא emphatic by virtue of position.

5. Distributive use of אִישׁ: "each to his fellow (or friend)." More literal rendering: "a man to his fellow."

6. יְלָדֵינוּ construct plural of יֶלֶד with 1st c. pl. suffix.

7. בְּלִי "without."

8. לְאִמָּה the noun אֵם with preposition לְ and 3rd f. sg. suffix.

9. קָרוֹא intensive use of infinitive absolute.

10. וַיְצַוּוּ Pi'el imperfect with ו consecutive from צָוָה (used mainly in the Pi'el stem). The first ו is a doubled consonant; the second a vowel=wă-yᵉtsăw-wû.

11. כֹּל, בְּכֹל and preposition בְּ (בָּ before tone).

12. וּבַעֲלוֹת infinitive construct from עָלָה with preposition בְּ and ו conjunctive. Literal rendering: "In the going up of . . ."

13. מְצַוֶּה הוּא participle used as finite verb. Here the subject follows the participle, contrary to common usage. This places the emphasis on the participle.

LESSON XXXVIII

THE NUMERALS

1. The cardinal numbers, from *one* to *ten* inclusive, have each an appropriate form for the masculine and feminine genders as well as for the absolute and construct states.

2. The number *one* אֶחָד is an adjective. It usually stands after and agrees with its noun, אִישׁ אֶחָד *one man;* אִשָּׁה אַחַת *one woman.*

3. The numeral *two* שְׁנַיִם (f. שְׁתַּיִם) is a noun. It usually stands before and agrees with its noun, שְׁנֵי אֲנָשִׁים *two men;* (or שְׁנַיִם אֲנָשִׁים); שְׁתֵּי נָשִׁים *two women* (or שְׁתַּיִם נָשִׁים).

4. The numbers from *three* to *ten* are nouns and disagree in gender. They may stand before the noun in construct or, either before or after it, in absolute state, חֲמִשָּׁה בָנִים *five sons* or בָּנִים חֲמִשָּׁה or חֲמֵשֶׁת בָּנִים. (Note the use of the feminine forms with masculine nouns and the masculine form with feminine nouns, שֵׁשׁ יְלָדוֹת *six girls.*)

5. The numbers *eleven* to *nineteen* are formed by two separate words: the unit and the ten. The unit is the possessive. The noun is usually in the plural, חֲמִשָּׁה עָשָׂר בָּנִים *fifteen sons.*

6. The numbers *thirty, forty, fifty, sixty, seventy, eighty* and *ninety* are formed from the corresponding units with plural terminations. *Twenty* is plural of *ten,* עֶשֶׂר, עֶשְׂרִים, שְׁלֹשִׁים, etc. The noun is in the singular when the numeral precedes, in the plural when it follows the noun, שְׁלֹשִׁים שָׁנָה, שְׁלֹשִׁים שָׁנִים.

CARDINAL NUMBERS

	WITH MASCULINE NOUNS			WITH FEMININE NOUNS	
	Absolute	Construct		Absolute	Construct
1.	אֶחָד	אַחַד	א	אַחַת	אַחַת
2.	שְׁנַיִם	שְׁנֵי	ב	שְׁתַּיִם	שְׁתֵּי
3.	שְׁלֹשָׁה	שְׁלֹשֶׁת	ג	שָׁלֹשׁ	שְׁלֹשׁ
4.	אַרְבָּעָה	אַרְבַּעַת	ד	אַרְבַּע	אַרְבַּע
5.	חֲמִשָּׁה	חֲמֵשֶׁת	ה	חָמֵשׁ	חֲמֵשׁ
6.	שִׁשָּׁה	שֵׁשֶׁת	ו	שֵׁשׁ	שֵׁשׁ
7.	שִׁבְעָה	שִׁבְעַת	ז	שֶׁבַע	(שְׁבַע)
8.	שְׁמֹנָה	שְׁמֹנַת	ח	שְׁמֹנֶה	שְׁמֹנֶה
9.	תִּשְׁעָה	תִּשְׁעַת	ט	תֵּשַׁע	(תְּשַׁע)
10.	עֲשָׂרָה	עֲשֶׂרֶת	י	עֶשֶׂר	עֶשֶׂר
11.	{ אַחַד עָשָׂר / עַשְׁתֵּי עָשָׂר }		יא	{ אַחַת עֶשְׂרֵה / עַשְׁתֵּי עֶשְׂרֵה }	
12.	{ שְׁנֵים עָשָׂר / שְׁנֵי עָשָׂר }		יב	{ שְׁתֵּים עֶשְׂרֵה / שְׁתֵּי עֶשְׂרֵה }	
13.	שְׁלֹשָׁה עָשָׂר		יג	שְׁלֹשׁ עֶשְׂרֵה	
14.	אַרְבָּעָה עָשָׂר		יד	אַרְבַּע עֶשְׂרֵה	
15.	חֲמִשָּׁה עָשָׂר		טו	חֲמֵשׁ עֶשְׂרֵה	
16.	שִׁשָּׁה עָשָׂר		טז	שֵׁשׁ עֶשְׂרֵה	

WITH MASCULINE NOUNS		WITH FEMININE NOUNS
17.	שִׁבְעָה עָשָׂר יז	שְׁבַע עֶשְׂרֵה
18.	שְׁמֹנָה עָשָׂר יח	שְׁמֹנֶה עֶשְׂרֵה
19.	תִּשְׁעָה עָשָׂר יט	תְּשַׁע עֶשְׂרֵה

	WITH MASCULINE NOUNS		WITH FEMININE NOUNS
20.	עֶשְׂרִים	600.	שֵׁשׁ מֵאוֹת
21.	אֶחָד וְעֶשְׂרִים	700.	שְׁבַע מֵאוֹת
30.	שְׁלֹשִׁים	800.	שְׁמֹנֶה מֵאוֹת
40.	אַרְבָּעִים	900.	תְּשַׁע מֵאוֹת
50.	חֲמִשִּׁים	1,000.	אֶלֶף אֶחָד
60.	שִׁשִּׁים	2,000.	שְׁנֵי אֲלָפִּים
70.	שִׁבְעִים	3,000.	שְׁלֹשֶׁת אֲלָפִּים
80.	שְׁמֹנִים	4,000.	אַרְבַּעַת אֲלָפִּים
90.	תִּשְׁעִים	5,000.	חֲמֵשֶׁת אֲלָפִּים
100.	מֵאָה אַחַת	6,000.	שֵׁשֶׁת אֲלָפִּים
200.	שְׁתֵּי מֵאוֹת	7,000.	שִׁבְעַת אֲלָפִּים
300.	שְׁלֹשׁ מֵאוֹת	8,000.	שְׁמֹנַת אֲלָפִּים
400.	אַרְבַּע מֵאוֹת	9,000.	תְּשַׁעַת אֲלָפִּים
500.	חֲמֵשׁ מֵאוֹת	10,000.	עֲשֶׂרֶת אֲלָפִּים / רְבָבָה

The Ordinals from *one* to *ten* are adjectives formed from the corresponding cardinal numerals by the addition of the termination יִ_. Another יִ_ is inserted (when possible) between the second and third radical. After *ten* the cardinals are used for ordinals.

First	רִאשׁוֹן	*Sixth*	שִׁשִּׁי
Second	שֵׁנִי	*Seventh*	שְׁבִיעִי
Third	שְׁלִישִׁי	*Eighth*	שְׁמִינִי
Fourth	רְבִיעִי	*Ninth*	תְּשִׁיעִי
Fifth	חֲמִישִׁי	*Tenth*	עֲשִׂירִי

EXERCISES

שִׁשָּׁה בָנִים, בָּנוֹת שֵׁשׁ, שֵׁשׁ שָׁנִים, שֵׁשֶׁת יָמִים. עֲשָׂרָה אֲנָשִׁים,
פָּרִים עֲשָׂרָה, עֶשֶׂר שָׁנִים, עֲשֶׂרֶת יָמִים, עֲשֶׂרֶת הַדְּבָרִים.
אַרְבָּעָה עָשָׂר כְּבָשִׂים, שְׁלֹשָׁה עָשָׂר פָּרִים, שְׁנֵים עָשָׂר שִׁבְטֵי
יִשְׂרָאֵל; שְׁתֵּים עֶשְׂרֵה אֲבָנִים, שְׁלֹשׁ עֶשְׂרֵה עָרִים; עָרִים תֵּשַׁע
עֶשְׂרֵה. חֲמִשָּׁה עָשָׂר שֶׁקֶל, שְׁמֹנָה עָשָׂר אֶלֶף, אַרְבָּעָה עָשָׂר
יוֹם, שְׁנֵים עָשָׂר אִישׁ, שְׁנֵי עָשָׂר בָּקָר; שְׁמֹנֶה עֶשְׂרֵה אַמָּה, שֵׁשׁ
עֶשְׂרֵה נֶפֶשׁ, תֵּשַׁע עֶשְׂרֵה שָׁנָה.

חָמֵשׁ שָׁנִים וְשִׁשִּׁים שָׁנָה, אַרְבָּעִים וְחָמֵשׁ שָׁנָה, שִׁבְעִים שָׁנָה
וְחָמֵשׁ שָׁנִים.

מֵאָה אִישׁ, מָאתַיִם שָׁנָה, תְּשַׁע מֵאוֹת שָׁנָה, שְׁלֹשׁ מֵאוֹת.
אֶלֶף אִישׁ, אֶלֶף פְּעָמִים, שִׁבְעַת אֲלָפִים פָּרָשִׁים, עֲשֶׂרֶת
אֲלָפִים אִישׁ:

LESSON XXXIX

READING ASSIGNMENT

וַיֹּאמֶר שְׁמוּאֵל אֶל־כָּל־יִשְׂרָאֵל הִנֵּה שָׁמַעְתִּי בְקוֹלְכֶם לְכֹל
אֲשֶׁר־אֲמַרְתֶּם לִי וָאַמְלִיךְ עֲלֵיכֶם מֶלֶךְ: וְעַתָּה הִנֵּה הַמֶּלֶךְ
מִתְהַלֵּךְ לִפְנֵיכֶם וַאֲנִי זָקַנְתִּי וָשַׂבְתִּי וּבָנַי הִנָּם אִתְּכֶם וַאֲנִי
הִתְהַלַּכְתִּי לִפְנֵיכֶם מִנְּעֻרַי עַד־הַיּוֹם הַזֶּה: הִנְנִי עֲנוּ בִי נֶגֶד יהוה
וְנֶגֶד מְשִׁיחוֹ אֶת־שׁוֹר מִי לָקַחְתִּי וַחֲמוֹר מִי לָקַחְתִּי וְאֶת־מִי
עָשַׁקְתִּי אֶת־מִי רַצּוֹתִי וּמִיַּד־מִי לָקַחְתִּי כֹפֶר וְאָשִׁיב לָכֶם:
וַיֹּאמְרוּ לֹא עֲשַׁקְתָּנוּ וְלֹא רַצּוֹתָנוּ וְלֹא־לָקַחְתָּ מִיַּד־אִישׁ מְאוּמָה:
וַיֹּאמֶר אֲלֵיהֶם עֵד יהוה בָּכֶם וְעֵד מְשִׁיחוֹ הַיּוֹם הַזֶּה כִּי לֹא
מְצָאתֶם בְּיָדִי מְאוּמָה וַיֹּאמְרוּ עֵד: וַיֹּאמֶר שְׁמוּאֵל אֶל־הָעָם
יהוה אֲשֶׁר עָשָׂה אֶת־מֹשֶׁה וְאֶת־אַהֲרֹן וַאֲשֶׁר הֶעֱלָה אֶת־
אֲבוֹתֵיכֶם מֵאֶרֶץ מִצְרָיִם: וְעַתָּה הִתְיַצְּבוּ וְאִשָּׁפְטָה אִתְּכֶם
לִפְנֵי יהוה אֵת כָּל־צִדְקוֹת יהוה אֲשֶׁר־עָשָׂה אִתְּכֶם וְאֶת
אֲבוֹתֵיכֶם:

NOTES

1. שָׁמַע + בְּ means *to hearken*.

2. עֲלֵיכֶם the preposition עַל + the 2nd m. plu. suffix.

3. מִתְהַלֵּךְ note the force of the participle – continuous action (at present).

4. לִפְנֵיכֶם the preposition לְ + the substantive פָּנִים in the construct + the 2nd m. plu. pronominal suffix.

5. וַאֲנִי note the force of the pronoun (emphasis).

6. וְשַׂבְתִּי from שִׂיב *to be hoary with age.*

7. הֵנָּם the particle הִנֵּה (*behold*) + the 3rd m. plu. suffix.

8. אֶתְכֶם the preposition אֵת (*with*) + the 2nd plu. suffix.

9. מִנְּעָרַי the preposition מִן + the substantive נַעַר (*youth*) + 1st c. sg. suffix.

10. הִנְנִי see הֵנָּם (above).

11. עֲנוּ Qal imperative from עָנָה *to answer, respond.*

12. מְשִׁיחוֹ noun + 3rd m. sg. suffix from מָשַׁח *to anoint.*

13. אֶת־שׁוֹר־מִי a question. Note the accusative.

14. רַצּוֹתִי from רָצַץ *to crush.*

15. אֲלֵיהֶם preposition אֶל (*unto*) + 3rd m. plu. suffix.

16. אֲבוֹתֵיכֶם plural of אָב + 2nd m. plu. suffix.

17. מִצְרַיִם *Egypt, the Egyptians.*

18. הִתְיַצְּבוּ note the force of the Hithpa'el imperative, *get yourselves set.*

19. וְאִשָּׁפְטָה in the Niph'al this verb means *to enter into controversy.*

LESSON XL

READING ASSIGNMENT

וַיֹּאמֶר יהוה אֶל־שְׁמוּאֵל עַד־מָתַי אַתָּה מִתְאַבֵּל אֶל־שָׁאוּל
וַאֲנִי מְאַסְתִּיו מִמְּלֹךְ עַל־יִשְׂרָאֵל מַלֵּא קַרְנְךָ שֶׁמֶן וְלֵךְ אֶשְׁלָחֲךָ
אֶל־יִשַׁי בֵּית־הַלַּחְמִי כִּי־רָאִיתִי בְּבָנָיו לִי מֶלֶךְ: וַיֹּאמֶר שְׁמוּאֵל
אֵיךְ אֵלֵךְ וְשָׁמַע שָׁאוּל וַהֲרָגָנִי: וַיֹּאמֶר יהוה עֶגְלַת בָּקָר תִּקַּח
בְּיָדֶךָ וְאָמַרְתָּ לִזְבֹּחַ לַיהוה בָּאתִי: וְקָרָאתָ לְיִשַׁי בַּזָּבַח וְאָנֹכִי

אוֹדִיעֲךָ אֵת אֲשֶׁר־תַּעֲשֶׂה וּמָשַׁחְתָּ לִי אֵת אֲשֶׁר־אֹמַר אֵלֶיךָ:

וַיַּעַשׂ שְׁמוּאֵל אֵת אֲשֶׁר דִּבֶּר יהוה וַיָּבֹא בֵּית לָחֶם וַיֶּחֶרְדוּ

זִקְנֵי הָעִיר לִקְרָאתוֹ וַיֹּאמֶר שָׁלוֹם לִזְבֹּחַ לַיהוה בָּאתִי

הִתְקַדְּשׁוּ וּבָאתֶם אִתִּי בַּזָּבַח וַיְקַדֵּשׁ אֶת־יִשַׁי וְאֶת־בָּנָיו וַיִּקְרָא

לָהֶם לַזָּבַח: וַיַּעֲבֵר יִשַׁי שִׁבְעַת בָּנָיו לִפְנֵי שְׁמוּאֵל וַיֹּאמֶר

שְׁמוּאֵל אֶל־יִשַׁי לֹא־בָחַר יהוה בָּאֵלֶּה:

וַיִּשְׁלַח וַיְבִיאֵהוּ: וַיֹּאמֶר יהוה קוּם מְשָׁחֵהוּ כִּי־זֶה הוּא:

וַיִּקַּח שְׁמוּאֵל אֶת־קֶרֶן הַשֶּׁמֶן וַיִּמְשַׁח אֹתוֹ בְּקֶרֶב אֶחָיו וַתִּצְלַח

רוּחַ־יהוה אֶל־דָּוִד מֵהַיּוֹם הַהוּא:

Notes

1. עַד־מָתַי the preposition עַד *up to* + interrogative adverb מָתַי *when*.

2. וַאֲנִי Note the emphatic use of this pronoun.

3. מְאַסְתִּיו Qal perfect + the 3rd m. sg. suffix, written defectively.

4. מִמְּלֹךְ the preposition מִן + the infinitive construct.

5. וְלֵךְ Qal imperative from הָלַךְ *to walk* + waw conj.

6. בֵּית־הַלַּחְמִי *the Beth-lehemite.*

7. בְּבָנָיו the prep. בְּ + the noun בָּנִים + the 3rd m. sg. suffix.

8. אֵלֵךְ from הָלַךְ *to walk.*

9. תִּקַּח from לָקַח *to take.*

10. בָּאתִי from בּוֹא *to go in* or *come in* + 2 m. sg. suffix.

11. אוֹדִיעֲךָ Hiph'il from יָדַע *to know.*

12. אֹמַר from אָמַר *to say.* Note the defective writing.

13. אֵלֶיךָ the preposition אֶל *unto* + the 2nd m. sg. suffix.

14. וַיַּעַשׂ a shortened form for וַיַּעֲשֶׂה.

15. וּבָאתֶם note the use of waw consecutive and the imperfect used as an imperative.

16. אִתִּי the preposition אֵת *with* + the 1st c. sg. suffix.

17. וַיְבִיאֵהוּ Hiph'il impf. of בּוֹא + waw cons. + 3rd m. sg. suffix.

LESSON XLI

READING ASSIGNMENT

בְּרֵאשִׁית בָּרָא אֱלֹהִים אֵת הַשָּׁמַיִם וְאֵת הָאָרֶץ: וְהָאָרֶץ
הָיְתָה תֹהוּ וָבֹהוּ וְחֹשֶׁךְ עַל־פְּנֵי תְהוֹם וְרוּחַ אֱלֹהִים מְרַחֶפֶת
עַל־פְּנֵי הַמָּיִם: וַיֹּאמֶר אֱלֹהִים יְהִי אוֹר וַיְהִי־אוֹר: וַיַּרְא אֱלֹהִים
אֶת־הָאוֹר כִּי־טוֹב וַיַּבְדֵּל אֱלֹהִים בֵּין הָאוֹר וּבֵין הַחֹשֶׁךְ:
וַיִּקְרָא אֱלֹהִים לָאוֹר יוֹם וְלַחֹשֶׁךְ קָרָא לָיְלָה וַיְהִי־עֶרֶב וַיְהִי־
בֹקֶר יוֹם אֶחָד: נָתַן אֱלֹהִים מְאֹרוֹת לְהַבְדִּיל בֵּין הַיּוֹם וּבֵין
הַלָּיְלָה: וַיֹּאמֶר אֱלֹהִים נַעֲשֶׂה אָדָם בְּצַלְמֵנוּ כִּדְמוּתֵנוּ וְיִרְדּוּ:
וַיִּבְרָא אֱלֹהִים אֶת־הָאָדָם בְּצַלְמוֹ בְּצֶלֶם אֱלֹהִים בָּרָא אֹתוֹ
זָכָר וּנְקֵבָה בָּרָא אֹתָם: וַיַּרְא אֱלֹהִים אֶת־כָּל־אֲשֶׁר עָשָׂה
וְהִנֵּה־טוֹב מְאֹד וַיְהִי־עֶרֶב וַיְהִי בֹקֶר יוֹם הַשִּׁשִׁי:

NOTES

1. מְרַחֶפֶת a feminine participle from רָחַף, to agree with רוּחַ.

2. הַמָּיִם pausal form for הַמַּיִם.

3. יְהִי a jussive form from הָיָה, translated *let be.*

4. וַיַּרְא a shortened form instead of וַיִּרְאֶה.

5. נַעֲשֶׂה *let us make* (cohortative).

6. וְיִרְדּוּ a Qal imperfect of רָדָה *to have dominion.*

LESSON XLII

Reading Assignment

בְּרֵאשִׁית הָיָה הַדָּבָר וְהַדָּבָר הָיָה אֶת הָאֱלֹהִים וֵאלֹהִים
הָיָה הַדָּבָר: הוּא הָיָה בְּרֵאשִׁית אֶת הָאֱלֹהִים: הַכֹּל נִהְיָה
עַל־יָדוֹ וּמִבַּלְעָדָיו לֹא נִהְיָה כָּל־אֲשֶׁר נִהְיָה: בּוֹ הָיוּ חַיִּים
וְהַחַיִּים הָיוּ אוֹר לִפְנֵי הָאָדָם: וְהָאוֹר הֵאִיר בַּחֹשֶׁךְ לֹא הִשִּׂיגוֹ:
וַיְהִי אִישׁ שָׁלוּחַ מֵאֵת הָאֱלֹהִים וּשְׁמוֹ יוֹחָנָן: הוּא בָא לְעֵדוּת
לְהָעִיד עַד־הָאוֹר לְמַעַן יַאֲמִינוּ כֻלָּם עַל־יָדוֹ: הוּא לֹא־הָיָה
הָאוֹר כִּי אִם־לְהָעִיד עַל־הָאוֹר: בָּעוֹלָם הָיָה וְעַל־יָדוֹ נִהְיָה
הָעוֹלָם וְהָעוֹלָם לֹא יְדָעוֹ: הוּא בָא בְשֶׁלּוֹ וַאֲשֶׁר־הֵמָּה לוֹ לֹא
קִבְּלֻהוּ: וְהַמְקַבְּלִים אֹתוֹ הַמַּאֲמִינִים בִּשְׁמוֹ נָתַן עֹז לָמוֹ לִהְיוֹת
בָּנִים לֵאלֹהִים:

Notes

1. This translation into Hebrew was made by Professor
Delitzsch.

2. נִהְיָה Niph'al perfect from הָיָה.

3. וּמִבַּלְעָדָיו the conj. וְ + the prep. מִן + the form בִּלְעֲדֵי
without, apart from.

4. הֵאִיר the causative idea from אוֹר *to be light.*

5. הִשִּׂיגוּ from נָשַׂג (Hi.) *to reach, overtake.*

6. עוֹלָם *world, age, antiquity, eternity.*

7. בְּשֶׁלּוֹ *through that which belongs to him* (וֹ + שֶׁל + בְּ).

8. קִבְּלֻהוּ defective writing for קִבְּלוּהוּ.

9. הַמְּקַבְּלִים ⎫
   הַמַּאֲמִינִים ⎭ participles (plural) + the article.

10. לָמוֹ poetic for לוֹ.

LESSON XLIII
READING ASSIGNMENT (PSALM XXIII)

מִזְמוֹר לְדָוִד (1)יְהֹוָה רֹעִי לֹא אֶחְסָר: (2)בִּנְאוֹת דֶּשֶׁא
יַרְבִּיצֵנִי עַל־מֵי מְנֻחוֹת יְנַהֲלֵנִי: (3)נַפְשִׁי יְשׁוֹבֵב יַנְחֵנִי בְמַעְגְּלֵי־
צֶדֶק לְמַעַן שְׁמוֹ: (4)גַּם כִּי־אֵלֵךְ בְּגֵיא צַלְמָוֶת לֹא־אִירָא רָע
כִּי־אַתָּה עִמָּדִי שִׁבְטְךָ וּמִשְׁעַנְתֶּךָ הֵמָּה יְנַחֲמֻנִי: (5)תַּעֲרֹךְ לְפָנַי
שֻׁלְחָן נֶגֶד צֹרְרָי דִּשַּׁנְתָּ בַשֶּׁמֶן רֹאשִׁי כּוֹסִי רְוָיָה: (6)אַךְ טוֹב
וָחֶסֶד יִרְדְּפוּנִי כָּל־יְמֵי חַיָּי וְשַׁבְתִּי בְּבֵית־יְהֹוָה לְאֹרֶךְ יָמִים:

NOTES

1. מִזְמוֹר לְדָוִד — These two words form a title to the psalm, but in the Hebrew text are written as though a part of the poem. The prep. לְ here probably expresses genitive relationship. It is necessary to use this construction to express the idea of possession of an indefinite substantive. The construct relationship, מִזְמוֹר דָּוִד, would mean, "*the* psalm of David." Many of the psalms have this heading. It sometimes occurs in the form לְדָוִד מִזְמוֹר, and sometimes simply לְדָוִד.

יְהֹוָה — This is not to be read *Yᵉhowah*. The personal name of God (probably Yahweh) was considered too sacred to be pronounced. Accordingly, the Hebrew always substituted another word, usually אֲדֹנָי, *my lord*, sometimes אֱלֹהִים, *God*. To indicate this reading, the Massoretes inserted the vowels of the substitute, though no change could be made in the inviolable consonants of the sacred text. The reader was expected to supply the proper consonants.

רֹעִי — properly Qal act. part. of verb רָעָה, used as a substantive. When suffix is added, final ה is dropped.

אֶחְסָר — final vowel lengthened from ◌ַ because of the poetical accent *silluḳ;* the syllable is said to be "in pause."

2. מֵי — construct of מַיִם, which occurs only in plural.

מְנוּחֹת — plural of מְנוּחָה, *a quiet place.*

3. נַפְשִׁי — נֶפֶשׁ + 1st c. sg. suffix.

יְשׁוֹבֵב — Polel impf. of שׁוּב.

יַנְחֵנִי — Hiph. impf. of נָחָה, + 1st c. sg. suffix.

בְּמַעְגְּלֵי — construct plural of מַעְגָּל, *track, way, wagon trail.*

4. כִּי — This relative conjunction is used with various shades of meaning: indirect discourse ("that"); causal ("because"); result ("so that"); adversative ("but"); time ("when"); condition ("although", "even if"); etc. Here it expresses the conditional idea, reinforced by גַּם.

אֵלֵךְ — from הָלַךְ (וְיָלַךְ).

צַלְמָוֶת — a poetical word, compounded of צֵל, *shadow, darkness*, and מָוֶת, *death;* lit., "thickest darkness;" fig., "great calamity or distress."

אִירָא — from יָרֵא.

עִמָּדִי — The prep. עִם sometimes takes this form when 1st c. sg. suffix is added (also עִמִּי). It probably goes back to an old form of the prep., עִמָּד.

יְנַחֲמֻנִי — from נָחַם. יְנַחֲמוּ + 1st c. sg. suffix, with consequent shortening of וּ to ֻ.

5. תַּעֲרֹךְ — from עָרַךְ.

צֹרְרָי — Qal act. part. of צָרַר, to press, be hostile; as a substantive, an enemy, adversary; here m. pl. with 1 c. sg. suffix.

דִּשַּׁנְתָּ — The verb דָּשֵׁן in Qal means to be fat; in Pi'el, to make fat, or cover with fat, oil; hence, anoint. The more common word for anoint is מָשַׁח.

רְוָיָה — a rare noun meaning an abundant drink, satisfying abundance, derived from רָוָה, to drink to the full. Here used with כּוֹסִי as a nominal sentence: my cup (is, or contains) an overflowing abundance.

6. יִרְדְּפוּנִי — verb רָדַף, with 1st c. sg. suffix.

וְשַׁבְתִּי — This form as it stands is Qal perf., 1 c. sg. with waw consec. from שׁוּב, return: and I shall return. The general critical opinion, however, is that we should read וְשִׁבְתִּי, which is Qal inf. const. of יָשַׁב, dwell, + 1 c. sg. suffix: "my dwelling." The Massoretes give no indication that the vowel should be changed, but וְשַׁבְתִּי is difficult to construe, so we may assume the emendation: and my dwelling (shall be) in the house of Yahweh.

LESSON XLIV

READING ASSIGNMENT (ISAIAH 5:1–7)

⁽¹⁾אָשִׁירָה נָּא לִידִידִי שִׁירַת דּוֹדִי לְכַרְמוֹ כֶּרֶם הָיָה לִידִידִי
בְּקֶרֶן בֶּן־שָׁמֶן: ⁽²⁾וַיְעַזְּקֵהוּ וַיְסַקְּלֵהוּ וַיִּטָּעֵהוּ שֹׂרֵק וַיִּבֶן מִגְדָּל
בְּתוֹכוֹ וְגַם־יֶקֶב חָצֵב בּוֹ וַיְקַו לַעֲשׂוֹת עֲנָבִים וַיַּעַשׂ בְּאֻשִׁים:
⁽³⁾וְעַתָּה יוֹשֵׁב יְרוּשָׁלַיִם וְאִישׁ יְהוּדָה שִׁפְטרּנָא בֵּינִי וּבֵין כַּרְמִי:
⁽⁴⁾מַה־לַּעֲשׂוֹת עוֹד לְכַרְמִי וְלֹא עָשִׂיתִי בּוֹ מַדּוּעַ קִוֵּיתִי לַעֲשׂוֹת
עֲנָבִים וַיַּעַשׂ בְּאֻשִׁים: ⁽⁵⁾וְעַתָּה אוֹדִיעָה־נָּא אֶתְכֶם אֵת אֲשֶׁר־
אֲנִי עֹשֶׂה לְכַרְמִי הָסֵר מְשׂוּכָּתוֹ וְהָיָה לְבָעֵר פָּרֹץ גְּדֵרוֹ וְהָיָה
לְמִרְמָס: ⁽⁶⁾וַאֲשִׁיתֵהוּ בָתָה לֹא יִזָּמֵר וְלֹא יֵעָדֵר וְעָלָה שָׁמִיר
וָשָׁיִת וְעַל הֶעָבִים אֲצַוֶּה מֵהַמְטִיר עָלָיו מָטָר: ⁽⁷⁾כִּי כֶרֶם
יהוה צְבָאוֹת בֵּית יִשְׂרָאֵל וְאִישׁ יְהוּדָה נְטַע שַׁעֲשׁוּעָיו וַיְקַו
לְמִשְׁפָּט וְהִנֵּה מִשְׂפָּח לִצְדָקָה וְהִנֵּה צְעָקָה:

NOTES

1. אָשִׁירָה Qal impf. with cohortative ending. Cohortative
of entreaty or strong self-will. נָא is an enclitic particle: *I (we)*
pray, now. Hence, *let me sing, I pray,* or *I will sing now.*

לִידִידִי=לְיָדִיד, יָדִיד adj. (poet.) *beloved,* const.

שִׁירַת const. of שִׁירָה n. f. *song, ode.* Cognate accusative.

דּוֹד *beloved, friend, love;* from root דּוּד *rock, swing, fondle, love.*

שָׁמֶן pausal form for שֶׁמֶן (due to presence of silluḳ). Literal
rendering of the phrase: *on a horn, a son of fatness.* A Hebrew
idiom. A common construction for expressing a characteristic

or quality. Freely: *on a fatly nourished mountain horn* (i. e.,
Canaan).

2. יְעַזְּקֵהוּ Pi. impf. of עָזַק *dig: he digged it up thoroughly.*

סָקַל *stone, put to death by stoning;* Pi., *free from stones.*

יִטָּעֵהוּ Qal impf. of נָטַע. Verbs of planting, sowing, etc.,
take a double accusative.

שֹׂרֵק finest kind of eastern vine.

יִבֶן apocopated (shortened) form of imperfect. Full form:
יִבְנֶה.

מִגְדָּל for adornment and protection.

וְגַם gives emphasis to what follows: *and also.* A wine-vat
was hewn out of rock. This was a hard task. The performance
of it indicated confident expectation.

וַיְקַו apocopated form: יְקַוֶּה (with ו consec.). From קָוָה
wait for (orig. root prob. *twist, stretch;* idea of tension carried
over to *wait for, endure*); intensive: *he waited diligently, expectantly.*

וַיַּעַשׂ apocopated form: יַעֲשֶׂה (with ו consec.). From עָשָׂה
do, make, produce, yield (of grain, grapes, etc.).

בְּאֻשִׁים n. m. plu. *stinking, wild,* or *worthless grapes.* From
בָּאַשׁ *have a bad smell, stink.*

The meaning of the song, which ends with verse 2, becomes
evident: the vineyard, located in Canaan (the fatly nourished
mountain horn), belonged to God; He digged it up, "stoned" it,

i. e., prepared it carefully, removing all obstructions; He then planted in it His choice group, the Hebrew people; He built a tower, hewed out a wine-vat, and waited expectantly for His people to bring forth fruit worthy of Him. Some have suggested that the tower represents Jerusalem, and the wine-vat, the Temple.

3. The prophet is here speaking. So closely is he identified with God that he speaks for God.

וְעַתָּה *and now.* Emphatic.

יוֹשֵׁב and אִישׁ are used in a collective sense.

4. *What more could I have done to my vineyard that I ......?*

לַעֲשׂוֹת the inf. const. with the prep. לְ is sometimes used to express possibility and is best translated by *can* or *could.*

מַדּוּעַ seeks for actual cause: *why, wherefore?*

5. The Lord of the vineyard speaks. *And now!* A tense moment.

אוֹדִיעָה Hi. cohortative of יָדַע.

עֹשֶׂה use of participle for vividness. Subject precedes.

הָסֵר probably Hi. inf. abs. from סוּר. הָסֵר and פָּרֹץ carry the bare ideas of the verbs. They are to be translated as imperfects or imperatives. (Harper's Syntax, p. 88.)

גָּדֵר a low, stone wall. *For trampling,* i. e., an open way for man and beast.

6. אֲשִׁיתֵהוּ Qal or Hi. impf. of שִׁית, *put, set, make.*

בָּתָה or בַּתָּה n. f. *Something cut off, ruin, desolation.*

מֵהַמְטִיר Hi. inf. const. with prep. מִן, from מטר.

7. The husk of the parable falls off. The heart of it is laid bare.

the planting of His delight—Judah was the seat of the Davidic dynasty.

Observe the play of words: צְדָקָה and צְעָקָה; מִשְׁפָּט and מִשְׂפָּח. מִשְׂפָּח derived (according to B.D.B.) from סָפַח, *pour out;* hence *bloodshed* (opposite of מִשְׁפָט).

THE SYNTAX OF THE VERB

(These lessons on Syntax may be used as the teacher chooses.
The author has found it best to give them during
the second year of study).

SYNTAX OF HEBREW VERBS

Syntax (Lat. *syntaxis*, Grk. σύνταξις, from συντάσσειν, *to put together in order*) is "connected system or order." In reference to language, it means the due arrangement of words in sentences and their agreement.

The syntax of Hebrew verbs appears to depend upon three things: 1. the state of the verb; 2. the time indicated by the context; 3. the mood indicated by the verb and the context.

Clear interpretation of these points of syntax is essential to clear, distinctive translation. First of all, therefore, the broad fundamental facts concerning these points will be treated with a view to showing the way to distinctive translations. Afterwards the more varied developments will be treated.

I. STATE

State, as used in this discussion of distinctive translations, means condition of action, mind, body, or event. Let this use of the word "state" be carefully observed. Later it will be necessary to distinguish certain actions and states, setting them in contrast with each other, as in the comparison of stative and active verbs. Here the word "state" is much broader. It applies to the kind of condition indicated by any verb, active or stative, and describes it as complete, incomplete, continuous or imperative. In this connection, complete means finished or established; incomplete means not finished and so in beginning,

121

or not established and so subject to interruptions and repetitions; continuous means without interruption; imperative means commanded.

Obviously the state of a verb may be learned from its grammatical form. Perfects indicate completed states; imperfects, incompleted states; imperatives, imperative states; and participles, continuous states.

It needs to be remembered that those participial forms referred to here are the ones which serve as verbs. Many participial forms become nouns. They are to be treated as nouns.

Infinitives are not mentioned because they are never really verbs. They develop as verb forms and partake of certain verbal characteristics, but their true nature is nominal or adverbial. They will be treated later as nouns and adverbs.

II. TIME

Time, as used here, is that which distinguishes the state of the verb as before, now, or after.

The time of a Hebrew verb must be judged in the light of its context. There are no obvious markers in grammatical formation or syntactical arrangement. The reader must view the context as a whole, no matter whether it be a sentence, a paragraph, a passage, a book, or a sphere of knowledge, and discern the time that fits.

A time which is not related to another time, i. e. not indicated as coming before or after another time, will be designated by a single or simple name as a past, a present, or a future.

In beginning God created (a past) *the heavens and the earth,* Gen. 1:1.

The voice of thy brother's blood is crying (a present) *unto me,* Gen. 4:10.

And from thy face I shall be hid (a future) . . ., Gen. 4:14.

A time which is related to another time will be designated by a compound name, as previous-present or subsequent-past. Note that both parts of these names indicate time. Names like present perfect and future perfect are not used in the designation of time, because they mix the idea of state with that of time. It is desired that each point of syntax be judged separately.

A *previous past* is a time which was previous to another past time.

And he rested (a past) *on the seventh day from all his work which he had made* (a previous-past), Gen. 2:2.

A *previous present* is a present time which is previous to another present time.

Ah, sinful nation . . . children that deal corruptly! (a present) *They have forsaken* (a previous-present) *Yahweh,* Isa. 1:4.

A *previous future* is a future time which is thought of as previous to another future time.

Go (a future), *for Yahweh will have sent* (a previous-future) *thee,* I Samuel 20:22.

A *subsequent past* is a past time which was subsequent to another past time.

Then a breach was made (a past time) *in the city, and all the men of war proceeded to flee* (a subsequent-past) . . ., Jer. 52:7.

A *subsequent present* is a present time which is subsequent to another present time.

Lo, you see (a present) *the man is mad; wherefore then do you proceed to bring* (a subsequent present) *him to me,* I Sam. 21:15.

A *subsequent future* is a future time which will be subsequent to another future time.

And what will ye do (a future) *for the day of visitation* . . . . *Without me they shall bow down* (a future) *under the prisoners, and under the slain they shall proceed to fall* (a subsequent-future), Isa. 10:3,4.

III. MOOD

Mood originally meant mind, feeling, or heart. It is used now to describe one's spirit, attitude, or temper. In grammar it describes the subject's manner of feeling or thinking concerning the state of the verb.

The mood is indicative when the state is thought of as a fact, subjunctive when it is considered conditional or dependent, cohortative or jussive when one desires to urge the doing or the acceptance of it, imperative when one intends to command the doing or acceptance of it.

The **indicative** mood is indicated merely by the fact that the context calls for an affirmation. There is no special form of the verb to indicate it. However, it is helpful to note that the absence of those circumstances which mark the other moods is evidence that a verb is in the indicative.

The **subjunctive** mood is called for by the presence of a conditional idea. Subjunctive means sub-joined, dependent, conditional. When the context does not deal with a matter as an established fact but merely as possible, or desirable, or obligatory, we have a subjunctive mood.

The condition upon which the possibility, desirability or responsibility depends may be stated or merely understood. One may say, "I should go, because I am expected;" or, merely, "I should go," taking for granted that the reason for this responsibility is understood in view of the situation. The reader is expected to observe the occasion for a subjunctive idea in the context, no matter whether the condition be stated or not. It is not indicated by the verb form but by the context. It is helpful to note that almost all subjunctives are imperfects and apply to future time.

The **cohortative** and the **jussive** belong to the same mood. Both express desire, urgency, a sort of optative mood. Both appear with forms of the imperfect, the cohortative regularly with forms in the first person, and the jussive regularly with forms in the second or third person.

The cohortative is indicated by the addition of הָ‑ to the verb form.

Let me go, I pray thee, and return אֵלְכָה־נָּא וְאָשׁוּבָה, Ex. 4:18.

The jussive is indicated sometimes by the use of the negative particle אַל, sometimes by a vowel change, and sometimes by the context alone.

When the jussive idea is negative, אַל is used instead of the emphatic לֹא. Thus אַל with an imperfect practically always indicates a jussive.

. . . *Do not draw near* אַל־תִּקְרְבוּ *unto it* . . ., Josh. 3:4.

The vowel changes which occur in the jussive appear to be due to an added stress in pronunciation which the urgency of the mood produces. Such changes help to call attention to a jussive. However, the context must be considered. Similar changes occur under other conditions, and the context must also be considered in order to determine whether or not a plea is expressed.

And all the people said, Let live יְחִי *King Solomon*, I Kings 1:39. יְחִי appears here in place of יִחְיֶה.

And whatsoever of thine is with thy brother let thy hand release תַּשְׁמֵט (*it*), Deut. 15:3. תַּשְׁמֵט appears here in place of תַּשְׁמִיט.

Whenever a jussive occurs with the context only to indicate that it is a jussive, the context shows with reasonable clearness that a plea is called for rather than a statement or a command.

And now, O God of Israel, let be confirmed יֵאָמֶן *I pray, thy words* . . . I Kings 8:26.

יֵאָמֶן in certain contexts should be translated "Will be confirmed." Here it is part of a prayer. The attitude of prayer calls for the jussive force.

The imperative is sometimes indicated by its own special form, sometimes by the use of an imperfect in the second person with לֹא, and sometimes by the context alone.

The special form of the imperative is used to express positive commands only.

Honor כַּבֵּד *thy father and thy mother*, Ex. 20: 12.

The imperfect in the second person with לֹא is used to express prohibitions.

Thou shalt not do לֹא־תַעֲשֶׂה *any work*, Ex. 20:10.

The imperfect in the second person may also be used to express a positive command. In such a case the context alone is relied upon to indicate the imperative idea.

Six days shalt thou labor תַעֲבֹד, Ex. 20:9.

This word comes in the midst of the commandments, and a reader senses the fact immediately that God is commanding His people as to what to do in order to get ready for the Sabbath, not merely urging them to do it or making a statement as to what they will do.

IV. TYPES OF TRANSLATION

When the three foregoing points of syntax have been determined, their combination furnishes a guide to the translation. In existing translations there is a lack of uniformity in the handling of these points that causes a serious loss of clarity and vividness. Many have concluded that uniformity in the determination and translation of these points is impossible. Nevertheless, the present suggestions concerning them grow out of a belief that the Hebrew authors did work upon uniform principles in their use of them and that an attempt to regain the force of the original is worth the best of our efforts.

The table that follows suggests a distinctive translation for each. Only active verbs are used. However, the parallels for stative verbs may be worked out easily. These distinctive translations seek to express the essential idea in each combination in such a way that it may be clearly distinguished from all others. The manner of the distinctive translations cannot be rigidly emulated in every translation, but the essential idea can be maintained.

The examples given in the detailed treatments that follow are intended to demonstrate the possibility of maintaining the essential idea amid all the variations of translation. The wording of existing translations, preferably the American Revised, is used wherever it appears to be true to the essential idea, but a new wording is offered where existing translations seem to fail in making that idea clear. With each group of illustrations the combination of syntactical points is indicated so that comparison with the table of distinctive translations may be made.

A Table of Distinctive Translations for Hebrew Verbs

	State	Time	Mood	Translation
1.	Complete	Past	Indic.	*Killed.*
2.	Complete	Present	Indic.	*Kills.*
3.	Complete	Future	Indic.	*Shall kill.*
4.	Complete	Previous Past	Indic.	*Had killed.*
5.	Complete	Previous Pres.	Indic.	*Has killed.*
6.	Complete	Previous Fut.	Indic.	*Will have killed.* *Shall have killed.*
7.	Incomplete	Past	Indic.	*Repeatedly killed.*
8.	Incomplete	Present	Indic.	*Repeatedly kills.*
9.	Incomplete	Future	Indic.	*Will repeatedly kill.*
10.	Incomplete	Subseq't Past	Indic.	*Began to kill.* *Proceeded to kill.*
11.	Incomplete	Subseq't Pres.	Indic.	*Begins to kill.* *Proceeds to kill.*
12.	Incomplete	Subseq't Fut.	Indic.	*Will begin to kill.* *Will proceed to kill.*
13.	Continuous	Past	Indic.	*Was killing.*
14.	Continuous	Present	Indic.	*Is killing.*
15.	Continuous	Future	Indic.	*Will be killing.*
16.	Incomplete	Future	Subj.	*Could kill.* *Would kill.* *Should kill.*
17.	Complete	Previous Fut.	Subj.	*Could have killed.* *Would have killed.* *Should have killed.*
18.	Incomplete	Future	Cohor.	*Will kill.* *Let kill.*
19.	Incomplete	Future	Juss.	*Let kill.* *Do kill.*
20.	Incomplete	Future	Imper.	*Shalt kill.*
21.	Imperative	Future	Imper.	*Kill.*

THE INDICATIVE PERFECTS

A perfect designates an action or state as **completed** either in reality or in the thought of the speaker. It may represent its condition in the past, present or future. In any case the condition must be conceived of as **finished** or **completed**. The perfect always looks back upon a condition as belonging to the past just as the imperfect looks forward to it.

I.   A **Simple Action** (.) (Greek Aorist). The perfect of narration denotes an action or state completed at a specific moment or period as indicated by the context.

There is no reference to any other event.

1. Past time (narration) (combination 1).

God created בָּרָא *the heavens.* Gen. 1:1.

To the woman he said אָמַר. Gen. 3:16.

God proved נִסָּה *Abram.* Gen. 22:1.

He sent שָׁלַח *letters.* Isa. 39:1

2. Present time (perfect of the immediate past) (English present) (combination 2).

And him I appoint צִוִּיתִי *to be a prince.* I Kgs. 1:35.

And now I send שָׁלַחְתִּי *a wise man.* II Chr. 2:12.

I lift up הֲרִמֹתִי *my hand to Yahweh.* Gen. 14:22.

(Deut. 26:3; Isa. 8:11; "*Thus says Yahweh.*")

3. Future time (considered completed because already determined or prophesied) (combination 3).

Note, therefore, that the auxiliary verb used in each translation, the *will* or the *shall*, is the reverse of the one ordinarily used. Inasmuch as *will*, with the second and third persons, expresses mere futurity, the use of *shall* indicates the determination or prophecy. As *shall* with the first person indicates mere futurity, the use of *will* indicates the determination or prophecy.

a. **Perfect of Certainty** — The speaker is certain of the outcome or he has fully determined to make certain actions occur. This use is common in promises, decrees, threats, where the fulfilment is so certain that it is conceived as a completed act.

To thy seed I will give נָתַ֫תִּי *this land.* Gen. 15:18.
I know that Yahweh will save הוֹשִׁ֫יעַ. Ps. 20:7.
The field I will give to thee נָתַ֫תִּי. Gen. 23:11.
(Ruth 4:3; Gen. 30:13; Num. 17:27; I Kgs. 3:13.)

b. The **prophetic perfect** portrays vividly and boldly a confidence that the speaker has in the certain fulfilment of a prediction. This use is found in the highest type of prophetic diction. It often is thrown into the midst of imperfects to indicate absolute confidence.

A child shall be born יֻלַּד *to us.* Isa. 9:5.
A star shall proceed דָּרַךְ *from Jacob.* Num. 24:17.
The people . . . shall see רָאוּ *a great light.* Isa. 9:1.
It shall overflow שָׁטַף. Isa. 8:8.
(Isa. 5:13; 10:28; 11:8, 9; 28:2; Hos. 4:6; Amos 5:2.)

II. **A Simple Act completed** at a time previous to another act or state, thus resulting in a state of completion (cf. Greek Perfect) (•——).

1. Past time (**Pluperfect**)—The action is conceived of as finished prior to a point of time referred to in the past. (combination 4).

And he put there the man whom he had formed יָצַר. Gen. 2:8.

For he had not eaten אָכַל *bread.* I Sam. 28:20.

And he rested . . . from all the work he had done. עָשָׂה. Gen. 2:2.

(Gen. 2:5; 2:22; 18:8; 28:11; Isa. 6:6; I Kgs. 5:15.)

2. Present time (**Greek Perfect**)—The action is pictured as completed at some specific moment in the past but continues in its effects into the present (combination 5).

They have forsaken עָזְבוּ *Yahweh.* Isa. 1:4.

Who have set themselves שָׁתוּ *against me.* Ps. 3:7.

He has hidden הִסְתִּיר *his face.* Ps. 10:11.

(Gen. 32:11; Ps. 48:4; I Sam. 12:3; 14:29.)

3. Future time (**Future Perfect**)—Here we find finished action viewed in relation to another action still in the future (combination 6).

Yahweh will have gone forth יָצָא. II Sam. 5:24.

Yahweh will have given them נְתָנָם *into our hand.* I Sam. 14:10.

Yahweh will have sent thee away שִׁלֵּחֲךָ. I Sam. 20:22.

(Gen. 48:6; Mic. 5:2; Ruth 2:21; Isa. 4:4; 6:11.)

III. An action extended into a **state** (•-•-•-•-•).

1. State of **Specific Activity** (combination 1).

He reigned מָלַךְ *three years.* I Kgs. 15:2.

They were fruitful פָּרוּ *and multiplied.* Ex. 1:7.

Twelve years they served עָבְדוּ. Gen. 14:4.

(Gen. 13:12; Ps. 45:10.)

2. **Perfect of experience** (**Gnomic Aorist**). The statement is considered true because things of the same kind have already happened. The author is certain that such propositions of a general character will hold good generally (combination 2).

The cloud dissolves and goes כָּלָה וַיֵּלַךְ. Job 7:9.

An ox knows יָדַע *his master.* Isa. 1:3.

Grass withers יָבֵשׁ *flower fades* נָבֵל. Isa. 40:7.

(Jer. 8:7; Ps. 7:16.)

IV. A **State** (——) (no real action).

1. A mental or **emotional state.** Stative verbs express a physical or mental state or condition; see verbs to *know, trust, rejoice, refuse, hate, love,* etc. (combination 2).

We remember זָכַרְנוּ *the fish.* Num. 11:5.

I love אָהַבְתִּי. Gen. 27:4.

I know יָדַעְתִּי *not the day of my death.* Gen. 27:2.

(Gen. 32:11; Jud. 14:16; Ex. 10:3.)

2. A pure **state of being;** see verbs meaning to *be righteous, high, beautiful, old, weary, full, great, honorable,* etc.

I am old זָקַנְתִּי. Gen. 27:2.

I am little קָטֹנְתִּי. Gen. 32:11.

(Gen. 18:13; Isa. 1:11; 52:7; 55:9; Ps. 6:7.)

THE INDICATIVE IMPERFECTS

Action represented by the imperfect is unfinished whether in the past, present or future. The action is presented in movement rather than "in a condition of rest." It may be (1) repeated (**frequentative**), (2) just beginning (**incipient**), or (3) in a state of continuation (**progressive** or **adjectival**). It does not imply mere continuance. The participle is used to picture the uninterrupted action while the imperfect points to an action as beginning or recurring repeatedly.

> *A river was proceeding* יֹצֵא *out of the garden.* Gen. 2:10.
> (Participle)
> *A mist used to go up* יַעֲלֶה, Gen 2:6. (Imperfect)

I.   An action repeated (● ● ● ●). The **frequentative** imperfect is used to describe reiterated actions, habits, customs or universal truths.

1. Past time (combination 7).
   And a mist used to go up יַעֲלֶה. Gen. 2:6.
   Thus did Job continually יַעֲשֶׂה. Job 1:5.
   And so he did יַעֲשֶׂה *year by year.* I Sam. 1:7.
   (Jud. 14:10; 21:25; II Sam. 1:22.)

2. Present time (combination 8).
   a. Facts that are accustomed to occur often in certain limits. (**Definite frequentative**)
      Those who fear Yahweh he honors יְכַבֵּד. Ps. 15:4.
   b. Truths universally admitted and facts that may occur at any time. (**Indefinite frequentative**)

Man looks upon . . . but Yahweh looks יִרְאֶה *on the heart.* I Sam. 16:7.

3. Future time (combination 9).

He will be יִהְיֶה *to thee for a mouth.* Ex. 4:16.

I shall draw water אֶשְׁאָב *for thy camel.* Gen. 24:19.

The children that will be born יִוָּלֵדוּ. Ps. 78:6.

II. An action begun at a time subsequent to that of another act or state, the **incipient** imperfect.

1. Past time (**Historical present**). The action is pictured as beginning or in movement. Used for vividness and color in poetry and prose (combination 10).

Then Moses proceeded to sing יָשִׁיר. Ex. 15:1.

Perish the day on which I was born אִוָּלֵד. Job 3:3.

I proceeded to bring you up אַעֲלֶה *out of Egypt.* Jud. 2:1.

2. Present time. For force and vividness the action is pictured as taking place while words are spoken (combination 11).

Kings of the earth begin to set themselves יִתְיַצְּבוּ. Ps. 2:2.

The day has turned (pf.) *and the shadows of evening begin to lengthen* יִנָּטוּ. Jer. 6:4.

(Jud. 17:9; Num. 24:17; Hab. 3:9.)

3. Future time (combination 12).

I know (pf.) *that thou wilt surely proceed to be king* תִּמְלֹךְ. I Sam. 24:20.

Ye will henceforth be swept away תִּסָּפוּ. I Sam. 12:25.

Because the Egyptians will proceed to see יִרְאוּ *thee.*
Gen. 12:12.

(Gen. 16:12; 49:1; Ex. 6:1; 9:5.)

III. An action extended into a **state** (•–•–•–•–•), the **progressive** imperfect.

1. Past time (combination 7).
   And just as they continued to afflict them so they continued to multiply יִרְבֶּה. Ex. 1:12.

2. Present time (combination 8).
   As a lamp that burneth יִבְעַר. Isa. 62:1 (יִבְעַר).
   Afraid of a man that dies יָמוּת. Isa. 51:12.

3. Future time (combination 9).
   I will maintain אוֹכִיחַ *my ways.* Job 13:15.

IV. A **state** (——), the **adjectival** imperfect expressing a physical or mental state or a pure state of being. (No real action). See verbs to *know, trust, rejoice, refuse, hate, love, be high, be righteous, be full, be small, be old, be beautiful,* etc. (combinations 7, 8, 9).

   Benjamin is a wolf which ravens יִטְרָף. Gen. 49:27 (יִטְרָף).

NOTE THE FOLLOWING: When the reference to time is single, only one action or state being involved, all perfects represent simple conditions, all imperfects repeated ones; when the reference to time is double, two actions or states being involved, all perfects represent previous conditions, all imperfects subsequent ones.

THE PARTICIPLES

Where stress is to be laid on the continuance of the action described the participle is always used. Its descriptive power is great. As a noun it does not involve any idea of time. As a verb its time is to be discerned from the context as that of any other verb. נֹפֵל may mean *falling* (Num. 24:4), *fallen* (Jud. 4:22) or *about to fall* (Jer. 37:14). The subject is presented in the continuous exercise of the action denoted by the verb. In the case of the passive participle the subject is presented as having the action continuously exercised upon him. The imperfect represented by a series of dots (. . . . . .), multiplies an action, while the participle, represented by a line, (——), prolongs the action. One is **continual,** the other **continuous.**

> *Seraphim were standing* עֹמְדִים . . . *with two he covered* יְכַסֶּה *his face.* Isa. 6:2.

I.   The **verbal** participles are all indicatives.

   1. In its verbal use it may serve (a) to describe actions or (b) to emphasize the duration of a given state in the past. In reality it takes us back to the event and seeks to help us see the figures moving in the background. (combination 13).

   > *We were binding sheaves* אֲנַחְנוּ מְאַלְּמִים. Gen. 37:7.
   > *They were going up* הֵם עֹלִים.
   > *The sea was going* הוֹלֵךְ *and storming* וְסֹעֵר. Jon. 1:11.

   2. It may pull aside a screen and let us see what is going on at the present moment.   (combination 14).

Thy brother's blood is crying out צֹעֲקִים *unto me.* Gen. 4:10

From Sarai . . . I am fleeing בֹּרַחַת. Gen. 16:8.
Strangers are devouring אֹכְלִים *your land.* Isa. 1:7.
I am teaching you מְלַמֵּד. Deut. 4:1.

3. It may picture for us that which is about to happen. The action is represented as already under way. (combination 15).

Sarah will be bearing יֹלֶדֶת *a son.* Gen. 17:19.
We are about to destroy מַשְׁחִתִים *this place.* Gen. 19:13.
Behold I am bringing הִנְנִי מֵבִיא. Gen. 6:17.

NOTES

1. The subject usually precedes the participle.

2. When the subject is a pronoun it must be expressed.
Tomorrow thou shalt be slain אַתָּה מוּמָת. I Sam. 19:11.

3. The Niph'al participle has the sense of the Latin gerundive. נוֹרָא *to be feared,* נֶחְמָד *desirable,* נִכְבָּד *honorable.*

4. Some forms of the verb הָיָה are used with the active participle to form progressive tenses. The idea of duration is thus brought into fuller prominence.
Moses was keeping הָיָה רֹעֶה *the flock.* Ex. 3:1.
And let it be (permanently) *dividing* מַבְדִּיל. Gen. 1:6.

5. The negative used with the participle is usually אֵין. (It may be לֹא when attributive).

6. It may express the jussive sense.

Cursed be thou אָרוּר אַתָּה. Gen. 3:14.

II. The participle is construed as *a* **noun** in many cases and
may be either the subject, predicate or object of the sentence.

Saviour מוֹשִׁיעַ, *friend (one loving)* אֹהֵב, *enemy* אֹיֵב, *seer
(one seeing)* חֹזֶה, *shepherd (one feeding)* רֹעֶה.

In apposition with a noun it may be used as an adjective.

A devouring fire אֵשׁ אֹכֶלֶת. Ex. 24:17 (Cf. Isa. 29:6).

When the participle has the article it takes on a new emphasis and must be rendered as a relative clause.

Yahweh who had appeared (or, *the one appearing*) הַנִּרְאָה
unto him. Gen. 12:7.

His hand, the one stretched out הַנְּטוּיָה. Isa. 14:27.

THE SUBJUNCTIVE IMPERFECTS

The conditional ideas of the subjunctive mood are naturally
expressed by imperfects. Except in rare instances, and then
only in conditional sentences, imperfects are always used. More-
over, all subjunctives are in future time. The variations of
translations, therefore, are indicated entirely by the nature of
the contingency revealed in the context, i. e., whether it is a
possibility, a desirability or a responsibility. (Combination 16).

1. **Possibility** is frequently expressed by the auxiliary
could. *Can, may* and *might* are also used often.

If a man could be able יוּכַל *to number the dust of the*

earth, also thy seed could be numbered יִמָּנֶה. Gen. 13:16.

That it may be well יִיטַב *with thee.* Gen. 12:13.

Though your sins be as scarlet they may be white יַלְבִּינוּ
as snow. Isa. 1:18.

Who may ascend יַעֲלֶה *into thy holy hill.* Ps. 24:3.

2. **Desirability** is frequently expressed by *would*. Each of
these suggested auxiliaries, however, is subject to variations.

If thou wouldst give me תִּתֶּן *half thy house, I would not
go in* אָבֹא *with thee.* I Kgs. 13:8.

3. **Responsibility** is frequently expressed by *should*. This
idea, however, has such variations as obligation and
necessity; so *ought, must* and similar expressions are
used.

Who am I that I should go אֵלֵךְ *unto Pharaoh.* Ex. 3:11.

But thou shouldst rule תִּמְשָׁל *over him.* Gen. 4:7.

To know what Israel ought to do יַעֲשֶׂה. I Ch. 12:32.

THE SUBJUNCTIVE PERFECTS

In conditional sentences, the protasis sometimes states a condition which creates a responsibility, obligation or necessity so
fixed that it is looked upon as inescapable. Then the apodosis
uses a perfect to express the inescapable nature of that responsibility, obligation or necessity, though its mood be subjunctive
and its time future. (Combination 17).

If you had kept them alive I should not kill הֲרַגְתִּי *you.* Jud. 8:19.
Except Jehovah of hosts had left us a very small remnant, as Sod-
om we should become הָיִינוּ. Isa. 1:9.

THE COHORTATIVE, JUSSIVE, AND IMPERATIVE

In Hebrew just as in Arabic, there are two modified forms of
the imperfect to give expression to desire on the part of the
speaker. (Cf. Arabic, *Energic* and *Jussive*). The cohortative
used in the **first** person, expresses the intention, will or desire of
the author when he is the subject of the action, while the jussive,
used in the **second** and **third** persons, expresses the desire, will
or command of the author when some other person is the subject
of the action.

I.   The **cohortative** expresses the will of the speaker in ref-
      erence to his own actions. (Cf. Isa. 15:19; Deut. 33:16 and
      Ps. 20:4 for instances of its use in third person). When the
      speaker is free it expresses his **desire** or **determination**.
      When he is dependent upon others it expresses a **wish** or
      request. The form may be made more emphatic by the
      addition of the particle נָא.

The cohortative may express: (combination 18).

1. A strong **determination**—"*I will.*"
   I will eat אֹכְלָה *flesh.* Deut. 12:20.
   I will set אָשִׂימָה *a king over me.* Deut. 17:14.

2. An **exhortation** (in plural).
   Let vs return נָשׁוּבָה *to Egypt.* Num. 14:4.

3. A **self-excitement**.

Let us break asunder נְנַתְּקָה. Ps. 2:3.

4. A **request** or **entreaty**.

Let me go up, I pray אֶעֱלֶה־נָּא. Gen. 50:5.

Let me pass through אֶעְבְּרָה *thy land.* Num. 21:22.

5. A simple **consent** (yielding to constraint).

Now let me die אָמוּתָה. Gen 46:30.

6. A **conditional** or final sentence.

Ask of me and I will give וְאֶתְּנָה. Ps 2:8. (cf. use of co-hortative in imperative.)

II.　The **jussive** is used in the second and third persons to express: (combination 19).

1. A **command** or **injunction** or **prohibition**.

Let there be יְהִי *light.* Gen. 1:3.

Let multiply יֶרֶב (יִרְבֶּה). Gen. 1:22.

Do not listen אַל־תִּשְׁמַע.

2. A **wish**.

Let Yahweh establish יָקֶם *his word.* I Sam. 1:23.

3. **Permission**.

Let him go up יַעַל *and build* וְיִבֶן. Ezra 1:3.

4. **Advice** or **suggestion**.

Let Pharoah look out יֵרֶא *a man.* Gen. 41:33.

5. A **petition** or **entreaty** or **prayer**.

Let thy servant remain, I pray יֵשֶׁב־נָא. Gen. 44:33.

Let Yahweh watch יִצֶף *between me and thee.* Gen. 31:49.

6. **Conditional clauses** in the apodosis and the protasis. (cf. Arabic usage.)

III. The **imperfect** may also be used as an **imperative,** either in positive commands or prohibitions. (combination 20).

Six days thou shalt serve תַּעֲבֹד. Ex. 20:9.

Thou shalt not murder לֹא תִּרְצָח. ¡Ex. 20:13.

Upon thy belly thou shalt go תֵּלֵךְ. Gen. 3:14.

The following distinctions between prohibitions expressed by the imperfect and prohibitions expressed by the jussive are very helpful. "In prohibition, (1) in the second person, the ordinary imperfect takes לֹא and means *thou shalt not*, the jussive takes אַל and means *do not;* (2) in the third person, the ordinary imperfect takes לֹא and means *he shall not*, the jussive takes אַל and means *let him not.*"

IV. **Positive commands** are also expressed by the special imperative form but it never takes a negative. The force of this imperative appears to be practically the same as that of the imperative imperfect. The imperative imperfect may be more polite in certain situations, but the two are often interchanged for no apparent reason other than variety. This one is always used with the second person, and may express: (combination 21).

1. A **command.**

   Speak דַּבֵּר *unto the children of Israel.* Lev. 1:2.

   Fill מַלֵּא *the men's sacks.* Gen. 44:1.

   Arise קוּם *go* לֵךְ *unto Nineveh.* Jonah 1:2.

2. An **exhortation.**

Break up נִירוּ your fallow ground for it is time to seek Yahweh. Hos. 10:12.

3. An **entreaty.**

Deliver me הַצִּילֵנִי. Ps. 31:3.

Arise קוּמָה and save us. Ps. 44:27.

4. **Permission.**

Where it is good in thine eyes, dwell שֵׁב. Gen. 20:15.

And he said unto him, run רוּץ. II Sam. 18:23.

5. **Strong assurances** (either promises or threats).

Thou shalt see רְאֵה the prosperity of Jerusalem. Ps. 128:5.

Cry aloud צַהֲלִי with thy voice. Isa. 10:30.

Occasionally a cohortative ה is added to an imperative. Re-store הָשִׁיבָה unto me the joy of thy salvation. Ps. 51:14. The addition of the cohortative idea emphasizes the earnestness of the command, indicating that the author not merely calls for the fulfilment but also earnestly desires it. We might translate here after this fashion: Restore — please! — unto me the joy of thy salvation.

THE INFINITIVES

I.   The **Infinitive absolute,** an abstract verbal noun, is used to express the bare idea of the verbal action, or along with the inflected form to give emphasis to the expression of the action, or it may stand alone, almost with the force of an exclamation.

1. It may stand **instead of the finite verb** to express vividly and emphatically the essential idea of the verb.

Behold! slaying הָרֹג *oxen! and killing* וְשָׁחֹט *sheep! eating* אָכֹל *flesh! and drinking* וְשָׁתוֹת *wine!* Isa. 22:13.

Remembering זָכוֹר *the Sabbath day, six days thou shalt work.* Ex. 20:8, 9.

Disguising הִתְחַפֵּשׂ *and coming* וָבֹא *into battle (will it be for me).* I Kgs. 22:30.

Thus said Yahweh, eating אָכוֹל *and leaving over* וְהוֹתֵר (shall it be). II Kgs. 4:43.

He did so walking הָלֹךְ *naked and barefoot.* Isa. 20:2.

2. It may stand **with the finite verb** to add emphasis or to describe the action of the preceding verb. Standing before the verb it adds an expression of intensity.

He urgently besought me נִשְׁאֹל נִשְׁאַל. I Sam. 20:6.
Thou shalt surely die מוֹת תָּמוּת. Gen. 2:17.
The ox will certainly be stoned סָקוֹל יִסָּקֵל. Ex. 21:28.
Wilt thou indeed rule over us? הֲמָלֹךְ תִּמְלֹךְ. Gen. 37:8.

3. **Constant progress** or complete existence of the action may be expressed by the use of the infinitive absolute following the main verb.

He is gone (quite gone) (וַיֵּלֶךְ) הָלַךְ הָלוֹךְ. II Sam. 3:24.
He went repeatedly out and in וַיֵּצֵא יָצוֹא וָשׁוֹב. Gen. 8:7.
He went on, weeping וַיֵּלֶךְ הָלוֹךְ וּבָכֹה. II Sam. 3:16.
And he gradually became greater and greater וַיֵּלֶךְ הָלוֹךְ וְגָדוֹל. I Chr. 11:9.

4. Some absolute infinitives (chiefly Hiph'il) have come to be construed as **adverbs**.

To walk humbly הַצְנֵעַ לֶכֶת. Mic. 6:8.

More הוֹתֵר. *Quickly* מַהֵר.

Diligently הַשְׁכֵּם (*to rise early*).

Much הַרְבֵּה. *Far* הַרְחֵק.

II.   The **infinitive construct** as a verbal substantive is used like a gerund, taking suffixes and prepositions, and also has the government of its verb. It does not take the article.

1. **Standing alone** it may be:

   (1) The **subject** of a nominal sentence.

   Man's being alone is not good הֱיוֹת. Gen. 2:18.

   Is wearying men too little for you? הַלְאוֹת. Isa. 7:13.

   (2) In the **genitive**.

   In the day of Yahweh's making עֲשׂוֹת. Gen. 2:4.

   (3) In the **accusative** as object of the verb.

   I know not to go out or come in צֵאת וָבֹא. I Kgs. 3:7.

2. **With the preposition** לְ the infinitive may express.

   (1) **Design** or **purpose**.

   He went up to worship לְהִשְׁתַּחֲוֹת *and to sacrifice* וְלִזְבֹּחַ. I Sam. 1:3.

   (2) The **result**.

   Thou shalt keep the charge of Yahweh so as to walk לָלֶכֶת *in his ways, to keep* לִשְׁמֹר *his statutes.* I Kgs. 2:3f.

(3) The **time of an action.**

At Joab's sending לִשְׁלֹחַ (when Joab sent). II Sam. 18:29.

(4) A **periphrastic future.**

The sun was about to set לָבוֹא. Gen. 15:12.

Yahweh is (ready) to save me לְהוֹשִׁיעֵנִי. Isa. 38:20.

(5) A **gerundive** (must, ought, is to be).

What is to be done לַעֲשׂוֹת for thee? II Kgs. 4:13.

The **negative infinitive** is formed by the use of the particle בִּלְתִּי with לְ.

I command thee not to eat לְבִלְתִּי אֲכָל־ from it. Gen. 3:11.

With the periphrastic or gerundive we usually find לֹא לְ or אֵין לְ.

The name of Yahweh must not be mentioned לֹא לְהַזְכִּיר. Amos 6:10.

WAW CONSECUTIVE WITH THE IMPERFECT

The primary forms, perfect and imperfect, are supplemented in Hebrew by two secondary forms made by prefixing the conjunction *waw* to the verb. When prefixed to a perfect it is to be translated as an imperfect. Joined to an imperfect it is to be translated as a perfect. A sentence begins with an ordinary perfect and is followed by one or more verbs in the imperfect with *waw* consecutive. This is the historical or narrative tense.

He found מָצָא the place and lay down וַיִּשְׁכַּב.

A sentence begins with the imperfect and is followed by one or more perfects with *waw* consecutive.

He will find יִמְצָא *the place and will lie down* וְשָׁכָב.

These verbs with *waw* consecutive are used in narration or prediction to carry forward the same idea as the first verb indicates.

The imperfect with *waw* continues the narrative in a connective way.

The serpent deceived me הִשִּׁיאַנִי *and I ate* וָאֹכֵל. Gen. 3:13.

He had not respect לֹא שָׁעָה *and Cain was angry* וַיִּחַר. Gen. 4:5.

Thou hast hearkened שָׁמַעְתָּ *to the voice and hast eaten* וַתֹּאכַל. Gen. 3:17.

He heard that he had been sick חָלָה *and was better* וַיֶּחֱזָק. Isa. 39:1.

It may continue a perfect of experience, a prophetic perfect, a participle, an infinitive or another imperfect with *waw*.

He blows נָשַׁף *upon them and they wither* וַיִּבָשׁוּ. Isa. 40:24.

A son shall be given נִתַּן *to us and shall be* וַתְּהִי . . . *and he shall call* וַיִּקְרָא. Isa. 9:5. (Prophetic perfect followed by imperfects with same meaning).

When I lifted up כַּהֲרִימִי *my voice and cried* וָאֶקְרָא. Gen. 39:18.

And Balaam arose וַיָּקָם *and saddled* וַיַּחֲבֹשׁ *and went* וַיֵּלֶךְ *and the anger of God was kindled* וַיִּחַר. Num. 22:21f.

NOTES

1. The *waw* is prefixed with ־ַ and daghesh-forte. Before א it takes ־ָ without the daghesh-forte.

וָאֶקְרָא, וַיִּקְרָא (cf. pointing of the article).

2. The tone is usually retracted from the last syllable to the penult, when the syllable is open.

וַתֵּלֶךְ ,וַיֹּאמֶר.

3. Whenever possible the form is shortened.

וַיַּךְ ,וַיֵּרָא ,וַיָּבֶן ,וַיִּקְטֵל.

4. *Waw* consecutive practically disappears from later Hebrew. Aramaic and post-biblical Hebrew authors do not use it at all.

5. When the verb is separated from its *waw* it lapses into the perfect.

And he called וַיִּקְרָא *to the light day, and to the darkness he called* קָרָא *night.* Gen. 1:5.

WAW CONSECUTIVE WITH THE PERFECT

In the statement of successive events or acts in the future *waw* with the perfect is used after the main verb in the imperfect or imperative. That verb fixes the starting point as the speaker passes successively forward in thought viewing each as completed in its turn.

If Israel shall err יִשְׁגּוּ *and it be hid* וְנֶעְלַם *and they do* וְעָשׂוּ *and shall be guilty* וְאָשֵׁמוּ *and it shall become known* וְנוֹדְעָה *then they shall offer* וְהִקְרִיבוּ *and shall bring* וְהֵבִיאוּ *and shall lay* וְסָמְכוּ. Lev. 4:13ff.

These verbs have the same variety of usages as the imperfects for which they are substituted. The waw continues the imperfect in the sense of a future.

God will be יְהְיֶה *with me and keep me* וּשְׁמָרָנִי.

It is used in a conditional or a subjunctive sense, to express command, or volition and following telic particles.

Every man should come יָבֹא *to me and I would do him justice* וְהִצְדַּקְתִּיו. II Sam. 15:4.

Lest he come יָבוֹא *and smite me* וְהִכַּנִי. Gen. 32:12.

That they may go יֵלְכוּ *and stumble* וְכָשְׁלוּ *and be broken* וְנִשְׁבָּרוּ. Isa. 28:13.

Thou mayest give it תִּתְּנֶנָּה *and he may eat it* וַאֲכָלָהּ. Deut. 14:21.

It is used with the imperfect to express what is general or customary in the present or the past.

On which one leans יִסָּמֵךְ *and it goes* וּבָא *into his hand.* Isa. 36:6.

A man flees יָנוּס *from a lion and a bear meets him* וּפְגָעוֹ. Amos 5:19.

A mist used to go up יַעֲלֶה *and water* וְהִשְׁקָה. Gen. 2:6. (See Gen. 29:2f; Ex. 33:7–11; Jud. 2:18f; 6:2–6; I Sam. 1:4–7 and I Kgs. 5:6–8 for examples of the use of *waw* consecutive with perfects to express graphic descriptions of past events more or less customary).

VOCABULARIES

According to כְּ

Against עַל (אֶל), בְּ

All כֹּל (כָּל־)

Among בְּתוֹךְ, בְּ

And וְ (וָ, וּ)

Anoint מָשַׁח

Be able יָכֹל

Bring forth יָלַד

Before נֶגֶד, טֶרֶם

Begin חָלַל

Be great גָּדַל

Be heavy כָּבֵד

Be righteous צָדֵק

Between בֵּין

Bless בֵּרךְ (Pi.)

Blood דָּם

Book סֵפֶר

Bread לֶחֶם

Brother אָח

Bury קָבַר

By בְּ, אֶל

Call קָרָא

Capture לָכַד

Child יֶלֶד

Choose בָּחַר

City עִיר (f.)

Cleave, cling דָּבַק

Clothe לָבַשׁ

Command צִוָּה (Pi.)

Come near קָרַב

Conceal כִּסָּה, סתר (Ni.)

Consecrate קִדַּשׁ (Pi.)

Consume אָכַל, בָּעַר

Covenant בְּרִית (f.)

Cover כָּפַר

Create בָּרָא

Cry out צָעַק

Curse קָלַל, אָרַר

Cut כָּרַת

Darkness חֹשֶׁךְ

153

Daughter בַּת (f.)

Day יוֹם

Deliver נצל (Hi.)

Destroy שָׁמַד

Divide בדל (Hi.)

Do עָשָׂה

Door דֶּלֶת (f.), פֶּתַח

Dove יוֹנָה (f.)

Draw near קָרַב

Dwell שָׁכַן, יָשַׁב

Earth אֶרֶץ

Eat אָכַל

Egypt מִצְרַיִם

Escape מלט (Ni.)

Evil רָעָה

Faces פָּנִים

Father אָב

Fight לָחַם (Ni.)

Fill מָלֵא

Find מָצָא

Fire אֵשׁ (f.)

Flesh בָּשָׂר

Foot רֶגֶל (f.)

For לְ (Prep.), כִּי (Conj.)

Friend רֵעַ, אֹהֵב

From מִן

Garden גַּן

Give נָתַן

Glory כָּבוֹד

Go הָלַךְ

God אֵל, אֱלֹהִים

Go down יָרַד

Gold זָהָב

Good טוֹב

Go out יָצָא

Great גָּדוֹל

Ground אֲדָמָה

Hand יָד (f.)

Hate שָׂנֵא

Have mercy רָחַם

He הוּא

Head רֹאשׁ

Heal רָפָא

Hear שָׁמַע

Heart לֵב, לֵבָב	Light אוֹר
Heavens שָׁמַיִם	Lord אָדוֹן
Heavy כָּבֵד	Love אָהַב
Hero גִּבּוֹר	Luminary מָאוֹר
Hide סָתַר, חָבָא	Man אִישׁ, אָדָם
Holy קָדוֹשׁ	Make king מָלַךְ (Hi.)
Honor כבד (Pi.)	Make known יָדַע (Hi.)
Horse סוּס	נָגַד (Hi.)
House בַּיִת	Minister שָׁרֵת (Pi.)
I אֲנִי, אָנֹכִי	Morning בֹּקֶר
I pray thee נָא	Moses מֹשֶׁה
In בְּ	Mother אֵם (f.)
Jehovah יהוה (יְהֹוָה)	Mountain הַר
Judge שָׁפַט	Name שֵׁם
Keep שָׁמַר	Night לַיְלָה, לַיִל
King, be מָלַךְ	Not לֹא, אַל
King מֶלֶךְ	Number סָפַר
Lad נַעַר	On עַל, בְּ
Land אֶרֶץ, אֲדָמָה (f.)	Over עַל
Large גָּדוֹל	Peace שָׁלוֹם
Law תּוֹרָה (f.)	People עַם
Learn לָמַד	Perfect תָּמִים

Perish אָבַד

Place מָקוֹם

Plant זָרַע, נָטַע

Pray פלל (Hith.)

Prince שַׂר

Princess שָׂרָה (f.)

Prophet נָבִיא

Pursue רָדַף

Refuse מָאַס

Reign מָלַךְ

Remember זָכַר

Rest שָׁבַת

Reveal גָּלָה

Righteousness צֶדֶק

Rise early שכם (Hi.)

River נָהָר

Roll גָּלַל

Rule מָשַׁל

Sabbath שַׁבָּת

Samuel שְׁמוּאֵל

Sanctify קדש (Pi.)

Say אָמַר

Sea יָם

See רָאָה

Seek בקש (Pi.)

Sell מָכַר

Send שָׁלַח

Separate בדל (Hi.)

Serve שָׁרַת, עָבַד

She הִיא

Sin (noun) חַטָּאת, חַטָּאָה (f.)

Sin (verb) חָטָא

Sit יָשַׁב

Slaughter הָרַג, שָׁחַט

Son בֵּן

Song שִׁיר

Speak דָּבַר (Pi.)

Star כּוֹכָב

Stone אֶבֶן

Stumble כָּשַׁל

Surround סָבַב

Swear שָׁבַע

Sword חֶרֶב (f.)

Take לָקַח

Teach לִמֵּד (Pi.)

Tell אָמַר

That (dem.) הוּא, הִיא (f.)

That (rel.) אֲשֶׁר

The (הַ, הָ, הֶ·)

There שָׁם

They הֵם (m.), הֵן (f.)

These אֵלֶּה

This זֶה (m.), זֹאת (f.)

Those הֵם (m.), הֵן (f.)

Thou אַתָּה (m.), אַתְּ (f.)

Time עֵת (f.) פַּעַם (f.)

To אֶל, לְ

Tongue לָשׁוֹן

Toward אֶל, לְ

Tree עֵץ

Trust בָּטַח

Unto אֶל, לְ

Upon עַל, לְ

Vessel כְּלִי

Visit פָּקַד

Voice קוֹל

Walk הָלַךְ

Was (to be) הָיָה

Wash כָּבֵס

Water מַיִם

Way דֶּרֶךְ

We אֲנַחְנוּ, נַחְנוּ

What (int.) מָה

What (rel.) אֲשֶׁר

When כִּי, אִם

Which (rel.) אֲשֶׁר

Who (int.) מִי

Who (rel.) אֲשֶׁר

Why מַדּוּעַ, לָמָה

Wicked (adj.) רַע

With אֵת, עִם

Witness עֵד

Woman אִשָּׁה (f.)

Word דָּבָר

Write כָּתַב

You אַתֶּם (m.), אַתֵּנָה (f.)

Year שָׁנָה (f.)

Youth עֶלֶם, נַעַר

א

אָב father

אָבַד to perish, (Hi.) to destroy

אָבָה to be willing

אֶבְיוֹן needy, wretched

אָבַל mourn

אֶבֶן (f.) stone

אַבְרָם Abram

אָדוֹן lord, commander, master

אָדָם man

אֲדָמָה (f.) ground, earth

אֲדֹנָי Lord

אָהַב to love

אֹהֶל tent, hut, habitation

אָוֶן iniquity, vainness, emptiness

אוֹצָר treasury

אוֹר to be light, shine

אוֹר light

אוֹת sign

אָז then

אֹזֶן (f.) ear

אָזַן (Hi.) to listen, hear

אָח brother

אֶחָד (m.) one, (f.) אַחַת

אָחוֹת (f.) sister

אָחַז to seize, (Pi.) to enclose

אֲחֻזָּה (f.) possession

אַחַר after, behind

אַחֵר another, other

אַחֲרוֹן last

אַחֲרִית (f.) latter end

אַי where?

אֹיֵב enemy

אֵיךְ how? how!

אַיִל ram, stag

אַיִן nothing, there is not

אִישׁ man, husband

אַךְ yea, surely, only

158

אָכַל eat, devour, (Pu.) to be consumed, (Hi.) to feed

אֹכֶל food, (f.)

אַל־ no, not, let not

אֵל God

אֶל unto

אֵלֶּה these

אֱלֹהִים God

אֱלִיל worthless; (pl.) idols

אַלְמָנָה (f.) widow

אֶלֶף ox, thousand

אֵם (f.) mother

אִם if, whether

אָמָה (f.) handmaid

אֱמוּנָה (f.) faithfulness, fidelity

אָמַן to be firm, (Ni.) to be faithful, (Hi.) to believe, trust

אָמֵץ to be alert, to be strong, (Pi.) to make firm

אָמַר to say, (Hi.) to avow

אֹמֶר saying, song

אֱמֶת (f.) truth, firmness

אֱנוֹשׁ man, mankind

אֲנַחְנוּ we

אָנֹכִי I, אֲנִי

אָסַף to gather, (Ni.) to assemble

אָסַר to bind, imprison

אַף nose, anger

אֵפוֹד ephod

אַרְבָּעָה four, אַרְבַּע

אַרְבָּעִים forty

אָרוֹן ark, chest

אֶרֶז cedar

אֹרַח way, path

אֲרִי lion

אֹרֶךְ length

אֶרֶץ (f.) earth

אָרַר to curse

אֵשׁ (f.) fire

אִשָּׁה (f.) woman, wife, female

אִשֶּׁה fire-offering

אָשֵׁם to be guilty, (Hi.) to punish

אָשַׁר to be straight, walk straight

אֲשֶׁר who, which (rel.)

אֶת (sign used before the definite accusative.)

אֶת with

אַתְּ (f.) thou

אַתָּה (m.) thou

אַתֶּם (m.) you

אַתֵּן (f.) you, אַתֵּנָה (f.)

ב

בְּ in, on, among

בְּאֵר (f.) well

בְּאֻשִׁים odious grapes

בָּגַד to deal treacherously

בֶּגֶד garment

בדל (Hi.) to separate, select

בֹּהוּ emptiness

בָּהַל to be afraid, (Pi.) to terrify

בְּהֵמָה (f.) beast, dumb brute

בּוֹא to go in

בּוֹר pit, grave

בּוֹשׁ to be ashamed

בָּזַז to plunder, spoil

בָּחַר to choose, prove

בָּטַח to trust

בֶּטֶן (f.) womb

בֵּין between, among

בִּין to perceive, (Hi.) to explain

בַּיִת house, tent

בָּכָה to weep

בְּכוֹר first-born, eldest

בְּלִי nothingness, not

בָּלַל to mingle, confuse

בָּלַע to swallow, (Pi.) to consume

בִּלְתִּי lest, that not

בָּמָה (f.) high place

בֵּן son

בָּנָה to build

בַּעַד behind, after

בַּעַל master, Baal

בָּעַר to consume, (Hi.) to kindle

בָּקַע to cleave, split

בָּקָר herd, cattle

בֹּקֶר morning

בקשׁ (Pi.) to seek, ask

בָּרָא to create, form

בַּרְזֶל iron

בָּרַח to flee, (Hi.) to drive away

בְּרִית (f.) covenant

בָּרַךְ to kneel down, bless

בֶּרֶךְ (f.) knee

בְּרָכָה (f.) blessing

בָּשָׂר flesh

בָּשַׁל to boil, ripen

בַּת (f.) daughter, girl, grand-
daughter

בָּתָה (f.) desolation

בְּתוֹךְ in the midst of

ג

גָּאוֹן pride, swelling

גָּאַל to redeem, deliver

גָּבַה to be high, to be proud

גִּבּוֹר hero

גְּבוּרָה (f.) might, strength

גָּבַר to be strong, (Hi.) to con-
firm, (Hith.) to behave
proudly

גֶּבֶר mighty one, man

גָּדָה (f.) bank

גָּדוֹל great, elder

גְּדִי kid, young goat

גָּדַל to be great, (Pi.) to cause
to grow, magnify

גּוֹי nation

גּוּר to sojourn, tarry

גּוֹרָל lot, voting-stone

גָּזַל to tear away, plunder

גַּיְא valley

גִּיל joy, exultation

גָּלָה to uncover, reveal, (Ni.)
to uncover oneself

גָּלַל to roll

גַּם also

גָּמַל to deal with, to do (good
or evil)

גָּמָל camel

גַּן garden

גָּנַב to steal

גֶּפֶן (f.) vine

גֵּר sojourner, stranger

גָּרַשׁ to drive out

ד

דֹּב bear

דָּבַק to cleave, cling

דָּבַר to speak (usually Pi.)

דָּבָר word, thing

דֶּבֶר plague, pestilence

דְּבַשׁ honey

דָּג fish, דָּגָה (f.)

דָּוִד David

דּוֹר generation, age

דִּין to rule, judge, (Ni.) to contend at law

דָּכָה (Pi.) to crush, trample

דֶּלֶת (f.) gate, door

דָּם blood

דָּמָה to be like, (Pi.) to compare

דְּמוּת (f.) likeness, image

דַּעַת (f.) knowledge

דַּרְדַּר thorny plant, thistles (col.)

דֶּרֶךְ way, journey

דָּרַשׁ to resort to, seek

דֶּשֶׁא grass

ה

הַ the

הֲ־ (particle of interrogation)

הֶבֶל vapor, breath, Abel

הוּא (m.) he

הוּא (m.) that (dem.)

הוֹד glory, splendor

הִיא (f.) she

הִיא (f.) that (dem.)

הָיָה to be, to become

הֵיכָל temple

הָלַךְ to go, walk

הָלַל to be boastful, (Pi.) to praise

הֵם (m.) they, הֵמָּה

הָמוֹן multitude, tumult

הֵן (f.) they, הֵנָּה

הֵן behold!, הִנֵּה

הָפַךְ to turn, overthrow, (Ni.) to be changed

הַר mountain

הָרַג to kill

הָרָה to conceive

ו

וְ and

ז

זֹאת (f.) this (dem.)

זָבַח to sacrifice

זֶבַח sacrifice

זֶה (m.) this (dem.)

זָהָב gold

זָהַר (Ni.) to be enlightened, (Hi.) to teach, warn

זוּר to be a stranger, (Ni.) to be estranged

זָכַר to remember

זָכָר male

זָמַר to prune, (Pi.) to sing

זָנָה to commit fornication

זָעַק to cry out

זָקֵן to be old

זָקֵן old man, elder

זְרֹעַ arm, strength

זָרַע to sow, (Hi.) to produce seed

זֶרַע seed

ח

חָבָא to hide, (Ni.) to hide oneself

חֶבֶל line, cord

חַג feast, festival

חָגַג to keep a feast

חָדַל to cease

חָדַשׁ (Pi.) to renew

חָדָשׁ fresh, new

חֹדֶשׁ new moon, month

חוּל to be in pain, writhe, bring forth

חוֹמָה (f.) wall

חוּץ outside, abroad

חָזָה to see, to gaze

חֹזֶה seer, prophet

חָזַק to be strong, (Hi.) to seize

חָטָא to miss, sin

חַטָּאת (f.) sin

חַי (adj.) living, fresh; (subst.) life חַיִּים (m. pl.)

חָיָה to live, (Pi.) to preserve alive

חַיָּה (f.) living creature, beast

חָכָם wise, skilful

חָכְמָה (f.) wisdom

חֵל bulwark, wall, rampart

חֵלֶב fat, marrow

חָלָה to be sick

חֲלוֹם dream

חָלַל to pollute, to pierce, (Hi.) to begin

חָלַם to dream

חָלַק to divide, plunder

חֵלֶק portion, share

חָמַד to take delight in, desire

חַמָּה (f.) heat, sun

חֲמוֹר (he)-ass

חָמָס violence, wickedness

חֲמִשָּׁה five, חָמֵשׁ

חֲמִשִּׁים fifty

חֵן favor, grace

חָנָה to encamp, bend down

חָנַן to be gracious, (Hith.) to entreat

חֶסֶד mercy, kindness

חָפֵץ to delight in

חֵץ arrow, handle

חָצֵב to cut, hew out

חֲצִי half

חֹק statute, (f.)

חָרֵב to dry up, to be waste

חֶרֶב (f.) sword

חֹרֵב Horeb

חָרְבָּה (f.) dry land

חָרַד to tremble, (Hi.) to terrify

חָרָה to be angry, burn

חֶרְפָּה (f.) reproach, shame

חָרַשׁ to plow, engrave, (Hi.) to be silent

חָשַׁב to think, impute

חֹשֶׁךְ darkness

חָתַת to be dismayed, (Hi.) to terrify

ט

טָהוֹר clean, pure

טָהֵר to be clean, (Pi.) to purify

טוֹב to be good

טוֹב good, kind

טַל dew

טָמֵא to be unclean, (Pi.) to defile

טֶרֶם before, not yet

י

יְאוֹר river, Nile

יָבֵשׁ to be dry

יַבָּשָׁה (f.) dry land

יָד (f.) hand

יָדָה to throw, cast, (Hi.) to praise, confess

יָדִיד one beloved

יָדַע to know, understand

יְהוּדָה Judah

יְהוָה Yahweh, יהוה

יְהוֹשֻׁעַ Joshua

יוֹחָנָן John

יוֹם day

יוֹמָם daily, by day.

יוֹנָה (f.) dove

יַחַד (subst.) oneness, unity; (adv.) all alike, together

יָטַב to be good, (Hi.) to do well

יַיִן wine

יכח (Hi.) to decide, prove

יָכֹל to be able

יָלַד to bring forth, (Ni.) to be born, (Hi.) to beget

יֶלֶד child, youth

ילל (Hi.) to wail, lament

יָם sea

יָמִין (f.) right hand

ימן (Hi.) to turn to the right

יָנַק to suck

יָסַף to add, repeat

יָסַר to chastise, admonish

יָעַץ to advise, counsel, (Hith.) to conspire

יַעַר forest

יָצָא to go out, (Hi.) to bring out

יִצְחָק. Isaac

יָצַק to pour out

יָצַר to form

יֵצֶר form, imagination

יֶקֶב wine-press

יָקַץ to awake

יָרֵא to fear, (Ni.) to be awe-inspiring

יָרַד to descend

יַרְדֵּן Jordan

יָרָה to throw, (Hi.) to teach

יְרוּשָׁלַיִם Jerusalem

יָרֵחַ moon

יָרַשׁ to possess, inherit

יִשְׂרָאֵל Israel

יֵשׁ there is

יָשַׁב to sit, dwell

יֹשֵׁב inhabitant

יְשׁוּעָה (f.) deliverance

יִשַׁי Jesse

ישׁע (Hi.) to deliver

יָשַׁר to be straight, upright, (Pi.) to make straight

יָשָׁר straight, upright

יתר (Ni.) to be left, (Hi.) to leave

יֶתֶר remnant

כ

כְּ as, like, according to

כָּבֵד to be heavy, to be hon-
ored

כָּבוֹד honor, glory

כָּבַס to wash, trample

כֶּבֶשׂ lamb

כֹּה thus, here

כֹּהֵן priest, minister

כּוֹכָב star

כּוּן (Hi.) to prepare, establish

כּוֹס (f.) cup

כֹּחַ strength

כִּי that, for, because

כָּכָה so, thus

כֹּל all

כֶּלֶב dog

כָּלָה to be complete, (Pi.) to
finish

כְּלִי vessel, implement

כְּמוֹ as, like, as soon as

כֵּן thus, so

כָּנָף (f.) wing

כִּסֵּא throne, seat

כָּסָה to cover, conceal

כְּסִיל fool, dullard

כֶּסֶף silver, money

כָּעַס to be vexed, (Hi.) to
provoke

כַּף (f.) palm of hand, sole

כפר (Pi.) to cover, (Pu.) to
be atoned for

כֹּפֶר bribe, ransom

כְּרוּב cherub

כֶּרֶם vineyard

כָּרַת to cut off

כָּשַׁל to stumble

כָּתַב to write

כָּתֵף (f.) shoulder

ל

לְ to, for, at

לֹא not, no

לֵב heart, לֵבָב

לְבַד alone

לָבַשׁ to be clothed, put on

לוּן to lodge, pass the night

לחם to fight, do battle

לֶחֶם bread

לַיְל, לַיְלָה night,

לָכַד to capture

לָכֵן therefore

לָמַד to learn, (Pi.) to teach

לָמָה why?

לְמַעַן in order that, to

לָקַח to take

לָשׁוֹן tongue

מ

מְאֹד very, exceedingly

מֵאָה (f.) hundred

מְאוּמָה anything

מָאוֹר luminary

מָאַן (Pi.) to refuse

מָאַס to reject

מִגְדָּל tower

מָגֵן shield

מִגְרָשׁ pasture

מִדְבָּר wilderness, desert, pasture

מָדַד to measure

מִדָּה (f.) measure

מַדּוּעַ why? wherefore?

מְדִינָה (f.) province

מָה what? how?

מִהַר (Pi.) to hasten

מוֹעֵד season, place

מוּת to die

מָוֶת death

מִזְבֵּחַ altar

מְזוּזָה (f.) doorpost

מִזְמוֹר psalm

מִזְרָח east, sunrise

מַחֲנֶה camp, army

מָחָר tomorrow

מַטֶּה rod, tribe

מִטַר (Hi.) to give rain, to rain

מָטָר rain

מִי who?

מַיִם (pl.) water, waters

מָכַר to sell

מָלֵא to be full

מַלְאָךְ angel, messenger

מְלָאכָה (f.) work, business

מָלוֹן lodging-place

מֶלַח salt

מִלְחָמָה (f.) war, fight, battle

מלט (Ni., Hith.) to escape,
(Hi., Pi.) to deliver

מָלַךְ to be king, (Hi.) to make king

מֶלֶךְ king

מַלְכָּה (f.) queen

מַלְכוּת (f.) kingdom

מַמְלָכָה (f.) kingdom

מִן out of, from, away from

מִנְחָה (f.) offering, present

מִסְפָּר number

מְעַט little, a few

מַעַל above

מַעֲשֶׂה work, doing, deed

מָצָא to find

מִצְוָה (f.) commandment

מִצְרַיִם Egypt, Egyptian

מִקְדָּשׁ sanctuary

מָקוֹם dwelling, place, abode

מִקְנֶה property, cattle

מַרְאֶה appearance, sight

מָרוֹם high place, height

מַשָּׂא burden, tribute

מְשׂוּכָה (f.) hedge

מִשְׁפָּח bloodshed

מֹשֶׁה Moses

מָשַׁח to anoint

מָשִׁיחַ anointed one

מִשְׁכָּן tabernacle, dwelling

מָשַׁל to rule

מָשָׁל proverb

מִשְׁעָן staff

מִשְׁפָּט judgment, sentence

מִשְׁקָל weight

מָתַי when

נ

נָא (enclitic particle of entreaty) "I pray"

נָוֶה (f.) pasture, habitation (pl. נָאוֹת)

נְאֻם oracle, utterance

נבא (Ni.) to prophesy

נבט (Hi.) to look

נָבִיא prophet

נֶגֶב south country

נגד (Hi.) to declare, tell

נֶגֶד before, in the presence of

נָגַע to touch, smite

נָגַשׁ to approach

נָד fugitive (ptc.)

נֵד heap, wall

נָדַח to banish, expel

נָדַר to vow

נֶדֶר vow

נהל (Pi.) to guide, lead

נָהָר river

נוּחַ to rest

נֹחַ Noah

נָחָה to guide, (Hi.) to lead

נָחַל to inherit, take

נַחַל valley, brook

נַחֲלָה (f.) possession, inheritance

נחם (Ni.) to repent, pity, (Pi.) to comfort

נַחְנוּ we

נָחָשׁ serpent

נְחֹשֶׁת (f.) bronze, copper

נָטָה to spread out, (Hi.) to incline, turn

נָטַע to plant

נֶטַע plant, plantation

נכה (Hi.) to smite

נכר (Hi.) to regard, know, (Ni.) to be unrecognized

נֶסֶךְ libation

נָסַע to remove, set out

נַעַר lad, servant

נַעֲרָה (f.) maiden, maid servant

נָפַל to fall

נֶפֶשׁ soul

נצב (Ni.) to stand, (Hi.) to set, place

נצח (Ni.) to endure, (Pi.) to excel, direct

נצל (Pi.) to plunder, (Hi.) to deliver

נצר to watch, guard

נְקֵבָה (f.) female

נָקָה (Pi.) to acquit, (Ni.) to be innocent

נָקִי innocent

נָקַם to avenge

נָשָׂא to lift, carry

נשׂג (Hi.) to reach, attain

נָשִׂיא chief, prince

נָשַׁק to kiss

נָתַן to give, establish

ס

סָבַב to turn, surround

סָבִיב circuit, around

סָגַר to shut, (Hi.) to deliver over

סוּס horse

סוּר to turn aside, (Hi.) to put away

סֶלַע rock, crag

סֹלֶת (f.) fine flour

סָמַךְ to lean, support

סָפַד to lament, mourn

סָפַר to count, (Pi.) to re- hearse

סֵפֶר book

סָקַל to stone, (Pi.) to free from stones

סתר (Ni.) to conceal

ע

עָב dark, cloud

עָבַד to serve

עֶבֶד servant, laborer

עֲבוֹדָה (f.) slavery, servitude

עָבַר to pass over

עֵבֶר over, beyond

עֶגְלָה (f.) heifer

עַד (prep.) until; (subst.) eternity

עֵד witness

עֵדָה (f.) congregation, as- sembly

עֵדוּת (f.) testimony

עֵדֶן Eden

עָדַר to hoe

עוּד to bear witness, testify

עוֹד again

עוֹלָה (f.) burnt offering

עוֹלָם age, eternity, world

עָוֹן iniquity, guilt, punish- ment

עוֹף bird, fowl

עוּף to fly

עוּר to awake

עוֹר skin, leather

עֵז (f.) goat

עֹז strength

עָזַב to abandon, forsake

עזק (Pi.) to dig

עָזַר to help

HEBREW–ENGLISH VOCABULARY 171

עַיִן (f.) eye, fountain

עִיר (f.) city

עַל upon, over

עֵלִי Eli

עָלָה to go up

עֶלְיוֹן high, most high

עָלַם to hide, conceal

עַם people, nation

עִם along with, with

עָמַד to stand, (Hi.) to appoint

עִמָּד with

עָמָל labor, misery

עֵמֶק valley

עֵנָב grape

עָנָה to answer

עָנָה to suffer, (Pi.) to oppress

עֳנִי affliction

עָנָן cloud

עָפָר dust

עֵץ tree

עֵצָה (f.) counsel

עֶצֶם (f.) bone

עֵקֶב end, result; (prep. and conj.) because of

עֶרֶב evening

עֲרָבָה (f.) desert, plain

עֶרְוָה (f.) nakedness

עָרַךְ to arrange

עָשָׂה to do, make

עשק (Hith.) to strive, quarrel

עֶשֶׂר ten, (f.) עֲשָׂרָה

עֶשְׂרִים twenty

עָשָׁן smoke

עֵת (f.) time

עַתָּה now

פ

פֵּאָה (f.) side, corner

פָּדָה to ransom

פֶּה mouth

פֹּה here

פּוּץ to be scattered

פָּחַד to be afraid, tremble

פלא (Ni.) to be wonderful, to be extraordinary

פלל (Pi.) to intervene, pray

פְּלִשְׁתִּים Philistines

פֶּן lest (with imp.)

פָּנָה to turn

פָּנִים face (faces)

פָּעַל to do, make

פָּקַד to visit

פַּר bullock

פָּרַד to divide, separate

פְּרִי fruit

פָּרַץ to break through

פרר (Hi.) to break, frustrate

פָּרַשׂ to spread out

פָּשַׁע to rebel against

פֶּשַׁע rebellion, transgression

פָּתָה to be open, to be simple, (Pi.) to deceive, entice

פָּתַח to open

פֶּתַח door

צ

צֹאן (f.) flock

צָדַק to be right, (Pi., Hi.) to justify

צֶדֶק righteousness

צְדָקָה (f.) righteousness

צוה (Pi.) to command

צוּר rock

צָחַק to laugh

צֶלֶם image

צָמֵא to be thirsty

צֶמַח sprout, growth

צָעַק to cry out

צְעָקָה (f.) cry, outcry

צָפָה to keep watch

צַר adversary

צָרָה (f.) adversity

צָרַר to show hostility towards, vex

ק

קבל (Pi.) to receive, take

קָבַץ to collect, gather

קָבַר to bury

קָדוֹשׁ holy

קֶדֶם before, east

קָדַשׁ to be set apart, (Pi.) to consecrate, sanctify

קֹדֶשׁ holiness, sanctity, consecrated thing

קוֹל voice

קוּם to arise, stand

קָטַל to kill

קָטֹן small, younger

קָטֹן to be little

קְטֹרֶת (f.) incense

קַיִן Cain

קִיר wall

קָלַל to be light, swift, (Pu.) to be cursed

קָנָה to acquire

קָנָה stalk, reed

קֵץ end

קָצֶה end, extremity

קָצִיר harvest

קָרָא to call, to meet, to happen

קָרַב to come near

קָרְבָּן offering

קָרוֹב near

קֶרֶן (f.) horn

קָרַע to tear

קָשַׁר to bind, to conspire

קֶשֶׁת (f.) bow

ר

רָאָה to see

רֹאשׁ head

רִאשׁוֹן first, former

רֵאשִׁית (f.) beginning

רַב great, much, many

רֹב abundance

רָבַב to be many

רָבָה to be great, (Hi.) to multiply

רְבִיעִי fourth

רָבַץ to lie down

רָגַז to tremble, to be agitated

רֶגֶל (f.) foot

רָדָה to rule, have dominion

רָדַף to pursue

רוּחַ (f.) spirit, breath

רִיחַ (Hi.) to inhale, smell

רוּם to be exalted, to rise

רוּץ to run

רֹחַב breadth

רָחַם to love, (Pi.) to have compassion

רָחַף (Pi.) to hover, brood

רָחַץ to wash, bathe

רָחַק to be distant, (Hi.) to remove

רָחֹק distant

רִיב to strive, contend

רִיב strife

רֵיחַ savor, odor

רָכַב to ride

רֶכֶב chariot

רָם high (ptc.)

רָמַס to tread, trample

רָמַשׂ to creep

רָנַן to shout, give ringing cry

רַע evil

רֵעַ friend, neighbor

רָעָב famine

רָעָה to pasture, to tend

רֹעֶה shepherd

רָעַע to break, to be evil

רָפָא to heal

רָצָה to delight in, to be gracious to

רָצוֹן delight, favor

רָצַח to slay, murder

רָצַץ to break, crush, (Polel)
to oppress

רַק only, thin

רָקִיעַ expanse

רָשָׁע evil, wicked

שׂ

שָׂבַע to be satisfied, sated

שָׂדֶה field, plain

שָׂחַק to laugh

שִׂיב to be gray, aged

שִׂים to put, place

שׂכל (Hi.) to be prudent, wise

שָׂמַח to rejoice, to be glad

שִׂמְחָה (f.) rejoicing, joy, fes-
tivity

שָׂנֵא to hate

שָׂעִיר hairy, goat

שָׂפָה (f.) lip, edge

שַׂר prince, head, chief

שָׂרָה (f.) Sarah

שָׂרַף to burn

שׂרֵק choicest vine

שׁ

שֶׁ (rel.) who, which, what

שָׁאוּל Saul

שְׁאוֹל (f.) Sheol, underworld

שָׁאַל to ask

שׁאר (Ni.) to be left, (Hi.) to
leave

שְׁאֵרִית remnant

שֵׁבֶט rod, tribe, staff

שְׁבִיעִי seventh

שָׁבַע (Ni.) to swear, (Hi.) to bind with an oath

שִׁבְעָה seven, שֶׁבַע

שִׁבְעִים seventy

שָׁבַר to break in pieces

שָׁבַת to cease, rest, (Hi.) to abolish

שַׁבָּת rest, Sabbath

שָׁדַד to ruin, devastate

שָׁוְא emptiness, iniquity

שׁוּב to turn back, return

שׁוֹפָר trumpet

שׁוֹר ox, bull

שָׁחָה to bow down

שָׁחַט to slaughter

שִׁחַת (Ni.) to be corrupted, spoiled, (Hi.) to corrupt, spoil

שָׁטַף to flow, to overwhelm

שִׁיר to sing

שִׁיר song

שִׁית to put, set

שַׁיִת thorns, briers

שָׁכַב to lie down

שָׁכַח to forget

שָׁכֹל to be bereaved, (Pi.) to make childless

שׁכם (Hi.) to rise early

שָׁכַן to dwell, (Hi.) to lay

שָׁכַר to be drunk, (Pi.) to make drunk

שָׁלוֹם peace

שָׁלַח to send, (Pi.) to set free

שֻׁלְחָן table

שְׁלִישִׁי third

שׁלך (Hi.) to throw, cast

שָׁלֵם to be whole, to be complete, (Hi.) to make peace

שֶׁלֶם peace offering

שְׁלֹשָׁה three, שָׁלֹשׁ

שָׁם there

שֵׁם name

שׁמד (Ni. to be destroyed, (Hi.) to destroy

שָׁמָּה thither

שְׁמוּאֵל Samuel

שָׁמַיִם heavens, sky

שָׁמִיר thorn, thorns

שָׁמֵם to be desolate

שְׁמָמָה (f.) desolation, waste

שֶׁמֶן oil, fatness, ointment

שְׁמֹנָה eight, שְׁמֹנֶה

שָׁמַע to hear

שָׁמַר to keep, watch

שֶׁמֶשׁ sun

שֵׁן (f.) tooth

שָׁנָה (f.) year

שֵׁנִי second

שְׁנַיִם (m.) two, שְׁתַּיִם (f.)

שַׁעַר (f.) gate, entrance

שַׁעֲשׁוּעִים (pl.) delight, pleasure

שִׁפְחָה (f.) maid-servant

שָׁפַט to judge

שׁקה (Hi.) to give to drink

שֶׁקֶל shekel

שֶׁקֶר falsehood, deception

שָׁרַץ to swarm

שֶׁרֶץ creeping things (coll.)

שרת (Pi.) to serve, minister

שֵׁשׁ six, שִׁשָּׁה

שִׁשִּׁי sixth

שִׁשִּׁים sixty

שָׁתָה to drink

ת

תֵּבָה (f.) ark

תֹּהוּ waste, formlessness

תְּהוֹם (f.) deep, abyss

תּוֹלְדוֹת (f.) generations, history

תּוֹעֵבָה (f.) abomination

תּוֹרָה (f.) law, instruction

תַּחַת under, beneath, instead of

תָּם whole, complete

תָּמִיד continuity

תָּמִים perfect

תָּמַם to finish, be complete

תִּפְאָרָה (f.) glory, splendor

תְּפִלָּה (f.) prayer

תָּפַשׂ to seize, catch

תָּקַע to thrust, strike

תְּרוּמָה (f.) heave-offering

תֵּשַׁע nine, תִּשְׁעָה

WORD LISTS

Some of the more common words are given in this table for review lessons. The teacher may assign them as early as he likes. The Hebrew word is given on page 179 and the English translation on page 183. The numbers correspond.

WORD LIST

(See page 20)

SOME OF THE MORE COMMON VERBS

1	אָהַב	18	גָּנַב	35	חָטָא	52	לָחַם
2	אָכַל	19	גָּבַר	36	חָנַן	53	לָכַד
3	אָמַר	20	גָּדַל	37	חָשַׁב	54	לָמַד
4	אָסַף	21	גָּלָה	38	יָדָה	55	לָקַח
5	אָרַר	22	גָּלַל	39	יָדַע	56	מָאַס
6	בָּגַד	23	גָּרַשׁ	40	יָצָא	57	מָדַד
7	בָּחַר	24	דָּבַק	41	יָרֵא	58	מָהַר
8	בָּטַח	25	דָּבַר	42	יָרַד	59	מָטַר
9	בָּכָה	26	דָּרַשׁ	43	יָשַׁב	60	מָכַר
10	בָּנָה	27	הָלַל	44	כָּבַס	61	מָלֵא
11	בָּעַר	28	הָלַךְ	45	כָּלָה	62	מָלַט
12	בָּקַע	29	הָפַךְ	46	כָּסָה	63	מָלַךְ
13	בָּקַשׁ	30	הָרַג	47	כָּפַר	64	מָצָא
14	בָּרָא	31	זָבַח	48	כָּרַת	65	מָשַׁח
15	בָּרַךְ	32	זָכַר	49	כָּשַׁל	66	מָשַׁל
16	בָּשַׁל	33	זָקֵן	50	כָּתַב	67	נָבַט
17	גָּאַל	34	חָדַל	51	לָבַשׁ	68	נָגַד

69	נָגַע	85	עָבַד	101	קָטֹן	117	שָׁבַר
70	נָגַשׁ	86	עָבַר	102	קָלַל	118	שָׁבַת
71	נָחַל	87	עָזַב	103	קָרָא	119	שָׁחַט
72	נָטָה	88	עָזַר	104	קָרַב	120	שָׁטַף
73	נָטַע	89	עָמַד	105	רָאָה	121	שִׁיר
74	נָסַע	90	עָרַךְ	106	רָנַן	122	שָׁכַב
75	נָפַל	91	פָּדָה	107	רָדַף	123	שָׁכַן
76	נָצַל	92	פָּלַל	108	רָחַם	124	שָׁכַם
77	נָשָׂא	93	פָּקַד	109	רָנַן	125	שָׁלַח
78	נָתַן	94	פָּרַד	110	רָעָה	126	שָׁלַךְ
79	סָבַב	95	פָּשַׁע	111	רָפָא	127	שָׁמַע
80	סָגַר	96	צָדַק	112	שָׂכַל	128	שָׁמַר
81	סָמַךְ	97	צָוָה	113	שָׂנֵא	129	שָׁפַט
82	סָפַד	98	צָמֵא	114	שָׂרַף	130	תָּפַשׂ
83	סָפַר	99	קָבַר	115	שָׁאַל	131	תָּמַם
84	סָתַר	100	קָדַשׁ	116	שָׁבַע	132	תָּקַע

WORD LIST

(See page 34)

Some of the More Common Substantives

1	אָב	18	אַתָּה	35	דְּבַשׁ	52	חֵץ
2	אֶבֶן	19	בְּהֵמָה	36	דּוֹר	53	חֹק
3	אָדוֹן	20	בֵּין	37	דָּם	54	חֶרֶב
4	אֲדָמָה	21	בַּיִת	38	דֶּרֶךְ	55	חֶרְפָּה
5	אוֹר	22	בֵּן	39	הֵיכָל	56	חֹשֶׁךְ
6	אָח	23	בֹּקֶר	40	הִנֵּה	57	טוֹב
7	אֶחָד	24	בְּרִית	41	הַר	58	טָמֵא
8	אָדָם	25	בְּרָכָה	42	זָהָב	59	יָד
9	אִי	26	בַּת	43	חַג	60	יוֹם
10	אִישׁ	27	גִּבּוֹר	44	חוֹמָה	61	יַיִן
11	אֵל	28	גָּדוֹל	45	חוּץ	62	יֶלֶד
12	אֱלֹהִים	29	גּוֹי	46	חָכְמָה	63	יָם
13	אֵם	30	גַּם	47	חֲלוֹם	64	יְשׁוּעָה
14	אַף	31	גָּמָל	48	חָמָס	65	כֹּהֵן
15	אֶרֶץ	32	גַּן	49	חָמֵשׁ	66	כּוֹכָב
16	אֵשׁ	33	גֵּר	50	חֵן	67	כֹּחַ
17	אִשָּׁה	34	דָּבָר	51	חֶסֶד	68	כִּי

#		#		#		#	
131	רֵאשִׁית	111	עֵץ	90	מָקוֹם	69	כֹּל
132	רַב	112	עֵצָה	91	מָשִׁיחַ	70	כָּנָף
133	רֶגֶל	113	עֵת	92	מָשָׁל	71	כִּסֵּא
134	רוּחַ	114	עַתָּה	93	מִשְׁפָּט	72	כֶּרֶם
135	רֶכֶב	115	פֶּה	94	נָבִיא	73	לֵב
136	רַע	116	פֶּן	95	נָהָר	74	לֶחֶם
137	שָׂדֶה	117	פָּנִים	96	נַחֲלָה	75	לַיְלָה
138	שַׂר	118	פְּרִי	97	נַעַר	76	לָשׁוֹן
139	שַׁבָּת	119	צֹאן	98	סוּס	77	מְאֹד
140	שׁוֹפָר	120	צֶדֶק	99	סֵפֶר	78	מֵאָה
141	שׁוֹר	121	צְדָקָה	100	עֶבֶד	79	מָאוֹר
142	שִׁיר	122	קָדוֹשׁ	101	עָנָן	80	מִגְדָּל
143	שָׁלוֹם	123	קוֹל	102	עֵד	81	מָגֵן
144	שֵׁם	124	קִיר	103	עֵדָה	82	מוֹעֵד
145	שְׁמֹנָה	125	קָטוֹן	104	עוֹד	83	מִזְבֵּחַ
146	שָׁנָה	126	קֵץ	105	עַיִן	84	מִזְמוֹר
147	תֵּבָה	127	קָצִיר	106	עִיר	85	מַלְכָּה
148	תּוֹרָה	128	קָרוֹב	107	עַל	86	מֶלֶךְ
149	תָּמִים	129	קֶרֶן	108	עַם	87	מִנְחָה
150	תְּפִלָּה	130	רֹאשׁ	109	עִם	88	מַעֲשֶׂה
				110	עָפָר	89	מִצְוָה

WORD LIST (TRANSLATION)

(See page 179)

VERBS

1. Love	31. Sacrifice
2. Eat	32. Remember
3. Say	33. Be old
4. Gather	34. Cease
5. Curse	35. Sin
6. Deal treacherously	36. Be gracious
7. Choose	37. Think, impute
8. Trust	38. Thank
9. Weep	39. Know
10. Build	40. Go out
11. Consume	41. Be afraid
12. Cleave, split	42. Go down
13. Seek	43. Sit, dwell
14. Create	44. Wash
15. Bless	45. Complete
16. Boil	46. Conceal
17. Redeem	47. Cover
18. Steal	48. Cut
19. Be strong, prevail	49. Stumble
20. Be great	50. Write
21. Reveal	51. Clothe, put on
22. Roll	52. Fight
23. Drive out	53. Capture
24. Cleave, cling	54. Learn
25. Speak	55. Take
26. Tread, seek	56. Refuse
27. Praise	57. Measure
28. Walk, go	58. Hasten
29. Overturn	59. Rain
30. Kill	60. Sell

61. Be full
62. Escape
63. Reign
64. Find
65. Anoint
66. Rule
67. Look
68. Make known
69. Touch
70. Approach
71. Inherit
72. Stretch out
73. Plant
74. Depart
75. Fall
76. Deliver, snatch
77. Lift up
78. Give
79. Surround
80. Shut, close
81. Sustain
82. Mourn
83. Number
84. Conceal
85. Serve
86. Pass over
87. Abandon
88. Assist
89. Stand
90. Arrange
91. Redeem
92. Pray
93. Visit
94. Separate
95. Rebel
96. Be righteous

97. Command
98. Be thirsty
99. Bury
100. Be holy
101. Be small
102. Be light
103. Call, meet
104. Draw near
105. See
106. Tremble
107. Pursue
108. Have mercy
109. Sing, cry aloud
110. Feed, tend
111. Heal
112. Be wise
113. Hate
114. Burn
115. Ask
116. Swear
117. Break in pieces
118. Rest, cease
119. Slaughter
120. Overflow
121. Sing
122. Lie down
123. Dwell
124. Rise early
125. Send
126. Cast, throw
127. Hear
128. Keep
129. Judge
130. Seize
131. Be complete
132. Strike

WORD LIST (TRANSLATION)
(See page 181)

SUBSTANTIVES

1. Father	29. Nation
2. Stone	30. Also
3. Master, Lord	31. Camel
4. Ground	32. Garden
5. Light	33. Sojourner
6. Brother	34. Word, thing
7. One	35. Honey
8. Man	36. Generation
9. Where	37. Blood
10. Man	38. Way
11. God	39. Temple
12. God	40. Behold
13. Mother	41. Mountain
14. Anger	42. Gold
15. Earth	43. Feast, festival
16. Fire	44. Wall
17. Woman	45. Abroad
18. Thou	46. Wisdom
19. Cattle, beast	47. Dream
20. Between	48. Violence
21. House	49. Five
22. Son	50. Favor
23. Morning	51. Kindness
24. Covenant	52. Arrow
25. Blessing	53. Statute
26. Daughter	54. Sword
27. Hero	55. Reproach
28. Great	56. Darkness

185

57. Good	93. Judgment
58. Unclean	94. Prophet
59. Hand	95. River
60. Day	96. Inheritance
61. Wine	97. Boy, servant
62. Child	98. Horse
63. Sea	99. Book
64. Salvation	100. Servant
65. Priest	101. Cloud
66. Star	102. Witness
67. Strength	103. Congregation
68. For, because	104. Again
69. All, every	105. Eye
70. Wing	106. City
71. Throne	107. Upon
72. Vineyard	108. People
73. Heart	109. With
74. Bread	110. Dust
75. Night	111. Tree
76. Tongue	112. Counsel
77. Exceedingly	113. Time
78. Hundred	114. Now
79. Luminary	115. Mouth
80. Tower	116. Lest
81. Shield	117. Faces
82. Season	118. Fruit
83. Altar	119. Flock
84. Psalm	120. Righteousness
85. Queen	121. Righteousness
86. King	122. Holy
87. Offering	123. Voice
88. Deed, work	124. Wall
89. Command	125. Small
90. Place	126. End
91. Anointed	127. Harvest
92. Proverb	128. Near

129. Horn		140. Trumpet
130. Head		141. Ox
131. Beginning		142. Song
132. Many, much		143. Peace
133. Foot		144. Name
134. Spirit		145. Eight
135. Chariot		146. Year
136. Bad, evil		147. Ark
137. Field		148. Law, instruction
138. Prince		149. Perfect
139. Sabbath		150. Prayer

TRANSLATIONS

These three stories prepared and translated by
PROF. J. WASH WATTS, PH. D.

A Story Concerning the Covenant with Israel
See page 70 for the Hebrew

Yahweh taught Israel in the wilderness. And he spake to him according to these words, Just as I spake to Abraham thy father so I am speaking to thee. I am cutting a covenant with thee. Remember the commandments of Yahweh thy God to keep them and *I* will magnify thee. Sanctify thyself and honor thy God. Thou shalt learn these words and thou shalt bind them for a sign upon thy hands and thou shalt write them upon the door posts of thy house and upon thy gates. Also thou shalt indeed teach them to thy children. Thus thou shalt indeed make wise thy children.

Therefore the children of Israel said, It is good for us to be taught by Yahweh. "The judgments of Yahweh are truth . . . Also thy servant is warned by them: in the keeping of them is great reward." (Ps. 19:10b, 12). "Yahweh will reign forever and ever." (Ex. 15:18).

A Story Concerning the Crossing of the Jordan
See page 82 for the Hebrew

Joshua said unto the children of Israel, This day we shall pass over the Jordan. The priests will pass over before the people and they will stand in the midst of the Jordan until all the people have passed over. Yahweh is sending us in this way and we shall indeed hearken to his voice. I am confident that all of us are trusting in him. He is causing us to trust. We shall say, Yahweh is with us and we shall not perish.

191

And Joshua spake again, saying, Carry ye over with you twelve stones and set them up in your lodging place. Your children will ask in the future saying, What are these stones to you? and ye shall say to them, The waters of the Jordan were cut off before the ark of the covenant of Yahweh, the children of Israel did not refuse to pass over according to the word of Yahweh and they were not rejected as their fathers were rejected in the wilderness; therefore these stones are for a memorial to the children of Israel forever.

A STORY CONCERNING THE CROSSING OF THE JORDAN (Continued)
See page 90 for the Hebrew

Yahweh said unto Joshua, This day I shall begin the magnifying of thee in the eyes of all Israel that they may know that just as I was with Moses I will be with thee. Say thou to them, By this ye should know that there is a living god in your midst and he will certainly dispossess for your sake the nations which are dwelling in the land. When the soles of the feet of the priests rest in the waters of the Jordan, the waters going down from above will be cut off and they will stand as one heap and the waters going down upon The Sea of The Salt will be exhausted until all the people will have finished passing over. This Yahweh will do for the sake of the understanding of all the peoples of the earth the hand of Yahweh that mighty it is and for the sake of the putting of the fear of Yahweh in your hearts.

And in that day Yahweh indeed began to magnify Joshua. The priests were standing in the midst of the Jordan until the completion of all the word which Yahweh had commanded Joshua. And it came to pass just as the priests finished passing over, the waters began to return to their place. And the children of Israel said in their hearts, Lovingkindness will encompass all those trusting in Yahweh as it is encompassing Joshua to-day; hallelujah!; praise ye the name of Yahweh.

A Story Concerning the Crossing of the Jordan (Continued)
See page 100 for the Hebrew

And Joshua spake unto the children of Israel again, saying, Just as the ark shall journey from its place then ye shall journey from your place. However, when the priests stand upon the banks of the river, ye shall stand also ye. I shall make known to thee when to journey again, saying, This is the time to draw near, take all that is yours, and carry your baggage. In that time we shall give encouragement each to his fellow. We shall call each to his fellow, saying, Let us not be afraid. Thus we shall be distinguished. Our children will say to us in the future, Ye called to us and we passed over without fear. A son will say to his father, Thou didst call to me in that day; a daughter to her mother, Thou didst indeed call to me. Thus Yahweh will make wonderful this day.

And the children of Israel did according to the word of Yahweh. Joshua said, Sanctify yourselves for Yahweh will perform wonders in your midst; and so they did. And the officers commanded them to do just as Yahweh commanded in everything; and so they did. And when the people went up unto the dry ground, they said, Yahweh is doing according to his word. It is good for us to do all which he is commanding.

PARADIGMS

		Qal	Qal (Middle O)	Qal (Middle E)	Niph'al
Perfect	3 m. s.	קָטַל	קָטֹן	כָּבֵד	נִקְטַל
	3 f. s.	קָטְלָה	קָטְנָה	כָּבְדָה	נִקְטְלָה
	2 m. s.	קָטַלְתָּ	קָטֹנְתָּ	כָּבַדְתָּ	נִקְטַלְתָּ
	2 f. s.	קָטַלְתְּ	קָטֹנְתְּ	כָּבַדְתְּ	נִקְטַלְתְּ
	1 c. s.	קָטַלְתִּי	קָטֹנְתִּי	כָּבַדְתִּי	נִקְטַלְתִּי
	3 c. p.	קָטְלוּ	קָטְנוּ	כָּבְדוּ	נִקְטְלוּ
	2 m. p.	קְטַלְתֶּם	קְטָנְתֶּם	כְּבַדְתֶּם	נִקְטַלְתֶּם
	2 f. p.	קְטַלְתֶּן	קְטָנְתֶּן	כְּבַדְתֶּן	נִקְטַלְתֶּן
	1 c. p.	קָטַלְנוּ	קָטֹנּוּ	כָּבַדְנוּ	נִקְטַלְנוּ
Imperfect	3 m. s.	יִקְטֹל	יִקְטַן	יִכְבַּד	יִקָּטֵל
	3 f. s.	תִּקְטֹל	תִּקְטַן	תִּכְבַּד	תִּקָּטֵל
	2 m. s.	תִּקְטֹל	תִּקְטַן	תִּכְבַּד	תִּקָּטֵל
	2 f. s.	תִּקְטְלִי	תִּקְטְנִי	תִּכְבְּדִי	תִּקָּטְלִי
	1 c. s.	אֶקְטֹל	אֶקְטַן	אֶכְבַּד	אֶקָּטֵל
	3 m. p.	יִקְטְלוּ	יִקְטְנוּ	יִכְבְּדוּ	יִקָּטְלוּ
	3 f. p.	תִּקְטֹלְנָה	תִּקְטַנָּה	תִּכְבַּדְנָה	תִּקָּטַלְנָה
	2 m. p.	תִּקְטְלוּ	תִּקְטְנוּ	תִּכְבְּדוּ	תִּקָּטְלוּ
	2 f. p.	תִּקְטֹלְנָה	תִּקְטַנָּה	תִּכְבַּדְנָה	תִּקָּטַלְנָה
	1 c. p.	נִקְטֹל	נִקְטַן	נִכְבַּד	נִקָּטֵל
Impv.	2 m. s.	קְטֹל	קְטַן	כְּבַד	הִקָּטֵל
	2 f. s.	קִטְלִי	קְטְנִי	כִּבְדִי	הִקָּטְלִי
	2 m. p.	קִטְלוּ	קְטְנוּ	כִּבְדוּ	הִקָּטְלוּ
	2 f. p.	קְטֹלְנָה	קְטַנָּה	כְּבַדְנָה	הִקָּטַלְנָה
Inf.	Absol.	קָטוֹל	קָטוֹן	כָּבוֹד	הִקָּטֵל (נִקְטֹל)
	Const.	קְטֹל	קְטֹן	כְּבֹד, כְּבַד	הִקָּטֵל
Part.	Active	קֹטֵל		כָּבֵד	
	Passive	קָטוּל			נִקְטָל

Pi'el	Pu'al	Hithpa'el	Hiph'il	Hoph'al
קִטֵּל	קֻטַּל	הִתְקַטֵּל	הִקְטִיל	הָקְטַל
קִטְּלָה	קֻטְּלָה	הִתְקַטְּלָה	הִקְטִילָה	הָקְטְלָה
קִטַּלְתָּ	קֻטַּלְתָּ	הִתְקַטַּלְתָּ	הִקְטַלְתָּ	הָקְטַלְתָּ
קִטַּלְתְּ	קֻטַּלְתְּ	הִתְקַטַּלְתְּ	הִקְטַלְתְּ	הָקְטַלְתְּ
קִטַּלְתִּי	קֻטַּלְתִּי	הִתְקַטַּלְתִּי	הִקְטַלְתִּי	הָקְטַלְתִּי
קִטְּלוּ	קֻטְּלוּ	הִתְקַטְּלוּ	הִקְטִילוּ	הָקְטְלוּ
קִטַּלְתֶּם	קֻטַּלְתֶּם	הִתְקַטַּלְתֶּם	הִקְטַלְתֶּם	הָקְטַלְתֶּם
קִטַּלְתֶּן	קֻטַּלְתֶּן	הִתְקַטַּלְתֶּן	הִקְטַלְתֶּן	הָקְטַלְתֶּן
קִטַּלְנוּ	קֻטַּלְנוּ	הִתְקַטַּלְנוּ	הִקְטַלְנוּ	הָקְטַלְנוּ
יְקַטֵּל	יְקֻטַּל	יִתְקַטֵּל	יַקְטִיל	יָקְטַל
תְּקַטֵּל	תְּקֻטַּל	תִּתְקַטֵּל	תַּקְטִיל	תָּקְטַל
תְּקַטֵּל	תְּקֻטַּל	תִּתְקַטֵּל	תַּקְטִיל	תָּקְטַל
תְּקַטְּלִי	תְּקֻטְּלִי	תִּתְקַטְּלִי	תַּקְטִילִי	תָּקְטְלִי
אֲקַטֵּל	אֲקֻטַּל	אֶתְקַטֵּל	אַקְטִיל	אָקְטַל
יְקַטְּלוּ	יְקֻטְּלוּ	יִתְקַטְּלוּ	יַקְטִילוּ	יָקְטְלוּ
תְּקַטֵּלְנָה	תְּקֻטַּלְנָה	תִּתְקַטֵּלְנָה	תַּקְטֵלְנָה	תָּקְטַלְנָה
תְּקַטְּלוּ	תְּקֻטְּלוּ	תִּתְקַטְּלוּ	תַּקְטִילוּ	תָּקְטְלוּ
תְּקַטֵּלְנָה	תְּקֻטַּלְנָה	תִּתְקַטֵּלְנָה	תַּקְטֵלְנָה	תָּקְטַלְנָה
נְקַטֵּל	נְקֻטַּל	נִתְקַטֵּל	נַקְטִיל	נָקְטַל
קַטֵּל		הִתְקַטֵּל	הַקְטֵל	
קַטְּלִי	NONE	הִתְקַטְּלִי	הַקְטִילִי	NONE
קַטְּלוּ		הִתְקַטְּלוּ	הַקְטִילוּ	
קַטֵּלְנָה		הִתְקַטֵּלְנָה	הַקְטֵלְנָה	
קַטֹּל (קַטֵּל)	קֻטֹּל	(הִתְקַטֹּל)	הַקְטֵל	הָקְטֵל
קַטֵּל	(קֻטַּל)	הִתְקַטֵּל	הַקְטִיל	הָקְטֵל
מְקַטֵּל		מִתְקַטֵּל	מַקְטִיל	
	מְקֻטָּל			מָקְטָל

		Qal		Niph'al	Pi'el
Perfect	3 m. s.		עָטַל	נֶעְטַל	עִטֵּל
	3 f. s.		עָטְלָה	נֶעְטְלָה	עִטְּלָה
	2 m. s.		עָטַלְתָּ	נֶעְטַלְתָּ	עִטַּלְתָּ
	2 f. s.		עָטַלְתְּ	נֶעְטַלְתְּ	עִטַּלְתְּ
	1 c. s.		עָטַלְתִּי	נֶעְטַלְתִּי	עִטַּלְתִּי
	3 c. p.		עָטְלוּ	נֶעְטְלוּ	עִטְּלוּ
	2 m. p.		עֲטַלְתֶּם	נֶעְטַלְתֶּם	עִטַּלְתֶּם
	2 f. p.		עֲטַלְתֶּן	נֶעְטַלְתֶּן	עִטַּלְתֶּן
	1 c. p.		עָטַלְנוּ	נֶעְטַלְנוּ	עִטַּלְנוּ
Imperfect	3 m. s.	יֶעֱטַל	יַעֲטֹל	יֵעָטֵל	יְעַטֵּל
	3 f. s.	תֶּעֱטַל	תַּעֲטֹל	תֵּעָטֵל	תְּעַטֵּל
	2 m. s.	תֶּעֱטַל	תַּעֲטֹל	תֵּעָטֵל	תְּעַטֵּל
	2. f. s.	תֶּעֶטְלִי	תַּעַטְלִי	תֵּעָטְלִי	תְּעַטְּלִי
	1 c. s.	אֶעֱטַל	אֶעֱטֹל	אֵעָטֵל	אֲעַטֵּל
	3 m. p.	יֶעֶטְלוּ	יַעַטְלוּ	יֵעָטְלוּ	יְעַטְּלוּ
	3 f. p.	תֶּעֱטַלְנָה	תַּעֲטֹלְנָה	תֵּעָטַלְנָה	תְּעַטֵּלְנָה
	2 m. p.	תֶּעֶטְלוּ	תַּעַטְלוּ	תֵּעָטְלוּ	תְּעַטְּלוּ
	2 f. p.	תֶּעֱטַלְנָה	תַּעֲטֹלְנָה	תֵּעָטַלְנָה	תְּעַטֵּלְנָה
	1 c. p.	נֶעֱטַל	נַעֲטֹל	נֵעָטֵל	נְעַטֵּל
Impv.	2 m. s.	עֱטַל	עֲטֹל	הֵעָטֵל	עַטֵּל
	2 f. s.	עֶטְלִי	עִטְלִי	הֵעָטְלִי	עַטְּלִי
	2 m. p.	עֶטְלוּ	עִטְלוּ	הֵעָטְלוּ	עַטְּלוּ
	2 f. p.	עֱטַלְנָה	עֲטֹלְנָה	הֵעָטַלְנָה	עַטֵּלְנָה
Inf.	Absol.		עָטוֹל	נַעֲטוֹל	עַטֹּל
	Const.		עֲטֹל	הֵעָטֵל	עַטֵּל
Part.	Active		עֹטֵל		מְעַטֵּל
	Passive		עָטוּל	נַעֲטָל	

Pu'al	Hithpa'el	Hiph'il	Hoph'al
עָטַּל	הִתְעַטֵּל	הֶעֱטִיל	הָעֳטַל
עָטְּלָה	הִתְעַטְּלָה	הֶעֱטִילָה	הָעֳטְלָה
עָטַּלְתָּ	הִתְעַטַּלְתָּ	הֶעֱטַלְתָּ	הָעֳטַלְתָּ
עָטַּלְתְּ	הִתְעַטַּלְתְּ	הֶעֱטַלְתְּ	הָעֳטַלְתְּ
עָטַּלְתִּי	הִתְעַטַּלְתִּי	הֶעֱטַלְתִּי	הָעֳטַלְתִּי
עָטְּלוּ	הִתְעַטְּלוּ	הֶעֱטִילוּ	הָעֳטְלוּ
עָטַּלְתֶּם	הִתְעַטַּלְתֶּם	הֶעֱטַלְתֶּם	הָעֳטַלְתֶּם
עָטַּלְתֶּן	הִתְעַטַּלְתֶּן	הֶעֱטַלְתֶּן	הָעֳטַלְתֶּן
עָטַּלְנוּ	הִתְעַטַּלְנוּ	הֶעֱטַלְנוּ	הָעֳטַלְנוּ
יְעֻטַּל	יִתְעַטֵּל	יַעֲטִיל	יָעֳטַל
תְּעֻטַּל	תִּתְעַטֵּל	תַּעֲטִיל	תָּעֳטַל
תְּעֻטַּל	תִּתְעַטֵּל	תַּעֲטִיל	תָּעֳטַל
תְּעֻטְּלִי	תִּתְעַטְּלִי	תַּעֲטִילִי	תָּעֳטְלִי
אֲעֻטַּל	אֶתְעַטֵּל	אַעֲטִיל	אָעֳטַל
יְעֻטְּלוּ	יִתְעַטְּלוּ	יַעֲטִילוּ	יָעֳטְלוּ
תְּעֻטַּלְנָה	תִּתְעַטַּלְנָה	תַּעֲטֵלְנָה	תָּעֳטַלְנָה
תְּעֻטְּלוּ	תִּתְעַטְּלוּ	תַּעֲטִילוּ	תָּעֳטְלוּ
תְּעֻטַּלְנָה	תִּתְעַטַּלְנָה	תַּעֲטֵלְנָה	תָּעֳטַלְנָה
נְעֻטַּל	נִתְעַטֵּל	נַעֲטִיל	נָעֳטַל
NONE	הִתְעַטֵּל	הַעֲטֵל	NONE
	הִתְעַטְּלִי	הַעֲטִילִי	
	הִתְעַטְּלוּ	הַעֲטִילוּ	
	הִתְעַטֵּלְנָה	הַעֲטֵלְנָה	
עֻטֹּל	(הִתְעַטֹּל)	הַעֲטֵל	הָעֳטֵל
(עֻטַּל)	הִתְעַטֵּל	הַעֲטִיל	הָעֳטַל
	מִתְעַטֵּל	מַעֲטִיל	
מְעֻטָּל			מָעֳטָל

		Qal	Niph'al	Pi'el
Perfect	3 m. s.	קָאַל	נִקְאַל	קֵאַל
	3 f. s.	קָאֲלָה	נִקְאֲלָה	קֵאֲלָה
	2 m. s.	קָאַלְתָּ	נִקְאַלְתָּ	קֵאַלְתָּ
	2 f. s.	קָאַלְתְּ	נִקְאַלְתְּ	קֵאַלְתְּ
	1 c. s.	קָאַלְתִּי	נִקְאַלְתִּי	קֵאַלְתִּי
	3 c. p.	קָאֲלוּ	נִקְאֲלוּ	קֵאֲלוּ
	2 m. p.	קָאַלְתֶּם	נִקְאַלְתֶּם	קֵאַלְתֶּם
	2 f. p.	קָאַלְתֶּן	נִקְאַלְתֶּן	קֵאַלְתֶּן
	1 c. p.	קָאַלְנוּ	נִקְאַלְנוּ	קֵאַלְנוּ
Imperfect	3 m. s.	יִקְאַל	יִקָּאַל	יְקָאַל
	3 f. s.	תִּקְאַל	תִּקָּאַל	תְּקָאַל
	2 m. s.	תִּקְאַל	תִּקָּאַל	תְּקָאַל
	2 f. s.	תִּקְאֲלִי	תִּקָּאֲלִי	תְּקָאֲלִי
	1 c. s.	אֶקְאַל	אֶקָּאַל	אֲקָאַל
	3 m. p.	יִקְאֲלוּ	יִקָּאֲלוּ	יְקָאֲלוּ
	3 f. p.	תִּקְאַלְנָה	תִּקָּאַלְנָה	תְּקָאַלְנָה
	2 m. p.	תִּקְאֲלוּ	תִּקָּאֲלוּ	תְּקָאֲלוּ
	2 f. p.	תִּקְאַלְנָה	תִּקָּאַלְנָה	תְּקָאַלְנָה
	1 c. p.	נִקְאַל	נִקָּאַל	נְקָאַל
Impv.	2 m. s.	קְאַל	הִקָּאַל	קֵאַל
	2 f. s.	קְאֲלִי	הִקָּאֲלִי	קֵאֲלִי
	2 m. p.	קְאֲלוּ	הִקָּאֲלוּ	קֵאֲלוּ
	2 f. p.	קְאַלְנָה	הִקָּאַלְנָה	קָאֵלְנָה
Inf.	Absol.	קָאוֹל	נִקְאוֹל	קָאֵל
	Const.	קְאֹל	הִקָּאֵל	קָאֵל
Part.	Active	קֹאֵל		מְקָאֵל
	Passive	קָאוּל	נִקְאָל	

Pu'al	Hithpa'el	Hiph'il	Hoph'al
קֻאַל	הִתְקָאֵל	הִקְאִיל	הָקְאַל
קֻאֲלָה	הִתְקָאֲלָה	הִקְאִילָה	הָקְאֲלָה
קֻאַלְתָּ	הִתְקָאַלְתָּ	הִקְאַלְתָּ	הָקְאַלְתָּ
קֻאַלְתְּ	הִתְקָאַלְתְּ	הִקְאַלְתְּ	הָקְאַלְתְּ
קֻאַלְתִּי	הִתְקָאַלְתִּי	הִקְאַלְתִּי	הָקְאַלְתִּי
קֻאֲלוּ	הִתְקָאֲלוּ	הִקְאִילוּ	הָקְאֲלוּ
קֻאַלְתֶּם	הִתְקָאַלְתֶּם	הִקְאַלְתֶּם	הָקְאַלְתֶּם
קֻאַלְתֶּן	הִתְקָאַלְתֶּן	הִקְאַלְתֶּן	הָקְאַלְתֶּן
קֻאַלְנוּ	הִתְקָאַלְנוּ	הִקְאַלְנוּ	הָקְאַלְנוּ
יְקֻאַל	יִתְקָאֵל	יַקְאִיל	יָקְאַל
תְּקֻאַל	תִּתְקָאֵל	תַּקְאִיל	תָּקְאַל
תְּקֻאַל	תִּתְקָאֵל	תַּקְאִיל	תָּקְאַל
תְּקֻאֲלִי	תִּתְקָאֲלִי	תַּקְאִילִי	תָּקְאֲלִי
אֲקֻאַל	אֶתְקָאֵל	אַקְאִיל	אָקְאַל
יְקֻאֲלוּ	יִתְקָאֲלוּ	יַקְאִילוּ	יָקְאֲלוּ
תְּקֻאַלְנָה	תִּתְקָאַלְנָה	תַּקְאַלְנָה	תָּקְאַלְנָה
תְּקֻאֲלוּ	תִּתְקָאֲלוּ	תַּקְאִילוּ	תָּקְאֲלוּ
תְּקֻאַלְנָה	תִּתְקָאַלְנָה	תַּקְאַלְנָה	תָּקְאַלְנָה
נְקֻאַל	נִתְקָאֵל	נַקְאִיל	נָקְאַל
NONE	הִתְקָאֵל	הַקְאֵל	NONE
	הִתְקָאֲלִי	הַקְאִילִי	
	הִתְקָאֲלוּ	הַקְאִילוּ	
	הִתְקָאַלְנָה	הַקְאֵלְנָה	
		הַקְאֵל	הָקְאֵל
קֻאֵל	הִתְקָאֵל	הַקְאִיל	הָקְאֵל
	מִתְקָאֵל	מַקְאִיל	
מְקֻאָל			מָקְאָל

		Qal	Niphʻal	Pʻiel
Perfect	3 m. s.	קָטַח	נִקְטַח	קִטַּח
	3 f. s.	קֶטְחָה	נִקְטְחָה	קִטְּחָה
	2 m. s.	קָטַחְתָּ	נִקְטַחְתָּ	קִטַּחְתָּ
	2 f. s.	קָטַחְתְּ	נִקְטַחַתְּ	קִטַּחַתְּ
	1 c. s.	קָטַחְתִּי	נִקְטַחְתִּי	קִטַּחְתִּי
	3 c. p.	קֶטְחוּ	נִקְטְחוּ	קִטְּחוּ
	2 m. p.	קְטַחְתֶּם	נִקְטַחְתֶּם	קִטַּחְתֶּם
	2 f. p.	קְטַחְתֶּן	נִקְטַחְתֶּן	קִטַּחְתֶּן
	1 c. p.	קָטַחְנוּ	נִקְטַחְנוּ	קִטַּחְנוּ
Imperfect	3 m. s.	יִקְטַח	יִקָּטַח	יְקַטַּח
	3 f. s.	תִּקְטַח	תִּקָּטַח	תְּקַטַּח
	2 m. s.	תִּקְטַח	תִּקָּטַח	תְּקַטַּח
	2 f. s.	תִּקְטְחִי	תִּקָּטְחִי	תְּקַטְּחִי
	1 c. s.	אֶקְטַח	אֶקָּטַח	אֲקַטַּח
	3 m. p.	יִקְטְחוּ	יִקָּטְחוּ	יְקַטְּחוּ
	3 f. p.	תִּקְטַחְנָה	תִּקָּטַחְנָה	תְּקַטַּחְנָה
	2 m. p.	תִּקְטְחוּ	תִּקָּטְחוּ	תְּקַטְּחוּ
	2 f. p.	תִּקְטַחְנָה	תִּקָּטַחְנָה	תְּקַטַּחְנָה
	1 c. p.	נִקְטַח	נִקָּטַח	נְקַטַּח
Impv.	2 m. s.	קְטַח	הִקָּטַח	קַטַּח
	2 f. s.	קִטְחִי	הִקָּטְחִי	קַטְּחִי
	2 m. p.	קִטְחוּ	הִקָּטְחוּ	קַטְּחוּ
	2 f. p.	קְטַחְנָה	הִקָּטַחְנָה	קַטַּחְנָה
Inf.	Absol.	קָטוֹחַ	נִקְטֹחַ	קַטֹּחַ
	Const.	קְטֹחַ	הִקָּטַח	קַטַּח
Part.	Active	קֹטֵחַ		מְקַטֵּחַ
	Passive	קָטוּחַ	נִקְטָח	

Pu'al	Hithpa'el	Hiph'il	Hoph'al
קֻטַּח	הִתְקַטַּח	הִקְטִיחַ	הָקְטַח
קֻטְּחָה	הִתְקַטְּחָה	הִקְטִיחָה	הָקְטְחָה
קֻטַּחְתָּ	הִתְקַטַּחְתָּ	הִקְטַחְתָּ	הָקְטַחְתָּ
קֻטַּחַתְּ	הִתְקַטַּחַתְּ	הִקְטַחַתְּ	הָקְטַחַתְּ
קֻטַּחְתִּי	הִתְקַטַּחְתִּי	הִקְטַחְתִּי	הָקְטַחְתִּי
קֻטְּחוּ	הִתְקַטְּחוּ	הִקְטִיחוּ	הָקְטְחוּ
קֻטַּחְתֶּם	הִתְקַטַּחְתֶּם	הִקְטַחְתֶּם	הָקְטַחְתֶּם
קֻטַּחְתֶּן	הִתְקַטַּחְתֶּן	הִקְטַחְתֶּן	הָקְטַחְתֶּן
קֻטַּחְנוּ	הִתְקַטַּחְנוּ	הִקְטַחְנוּ	הָקְטַחְנוּ
יְקֻטַּח	יִתְקַטַּח	יַקְטִיחַ	יָקְטַח
תְּקֻטַּח	תִּתְקַטַּח	תַּקְטִיחַ	תָּקְטַח
תְּקֻטַּח	תִּתְקַטַּח	תַּקְטִיחַ	תָּקְטַח
תְּקֻטְּחִי	תִּתְקַטְּחִי	תַּקְטִיחִי	תָּקְטְחִי
אֲקֻטַּח	אֶתְקַטַּח	אַקְטִיחַ	אָקְטַח
יְקֻטְּחוּ	יִתְקַטְּחוּ	יַקְטִיחוּ	יָקְטְחוּ
תְּקֻטַּחְנָה	תִּתְקַטַּחְנָה	תַּקְטֵחְנָה	תָּקְטַחְנָה
תְּקֻטְּחוּ	תִּתְקַטְּחוּ	תַּקְטִיחוּ	תָּקְטְחוּ
תְּקֻטַּחְנָה	תִּתְקַטַּחְנָה	תַּקְטֵחְנָה	תָּקְטַחְנָה
נְקֻטַּח	נִתְקַטַּח	נַקְטִיחַ	נָקְטַח
	הִתְקַטַּח	הַקְטַח	
NONE	הִתְקַטְּחִי	הַקְטִיחִי	NONE
	הִתְקַטְּחוּ	הַקְטִיחוּ	
	הִתְקַטַּחְנָה	הַקְטֵחְנָה	
קֻטֹּחַ		הַקְטֵחַ	הָקְטֵחַ
קֻטַּח	הִתְקַטַּח	הַקְטִיחַ	הָקְטַח
	מִתְקַטֵּחַ	מַקְטִיחַ	
מְקֻטָּח			מָקְטָח

		Qal		Niph'al	Pi'el
Perfect	3 m. s.		נָטַל	נִטַּל	נִטֵּל
	3 f. s.		נָטְלָה	נִטְּלָה	נִטְּלָה
	2 m. s.		נָטַלְתָּ	נִטַּלְתָּ	נִטַּלְתָּ
	2 f. s.		נָטַלְתְּ	נִטַּלְתְּ	נִטַּלְתְּ
	1 c. s.		נָטַלְתִּי	נִטַּלְתִּי	נִטַּלְתִּי
	3 c. p.		נָטְלוּ	נִטְּלוּ	נִטְּלוּ
	2 m. p.		נְטַלְתֶּם	נִטַּלְתֶּם	נִטַּלְתֶּם
	2 f. p.		נְטַלְתֶּן	נִטַּלְתֶּן	נִטַּלְתֶּן
	1 c. p.		נָטַלְנוּ	נִטַּלְנוּ	נִטַּלְנוּ
Imperfect	3 m. s.	יִטֹּל	יֵטַל	יִנָּטֵל	יְנַטֵּל
	3 f. s.	תִּטֹּל	תֵּטַל	תִּנָּטֵל	תְּנַטֵּל
	2 m. s.	תִּטֹּל	תֵּטַל	תִּנָּטֵל	תְּנַטֵּל
	2 f. s.	תִּטְּלִי	תֵּטְלִי	תִּנָּטְלִי	תְּנַטְּלִי
	1 c. s.	אֶטֹּל	אֵטַל	אֶנָּטֵל	אֲנַטֵּל
	3 m. p.	יִטְּלוּ	יֵטְלוּ	יִנָּטְלוּ	יְנַטְּלוּ
	3 f. p.	תִּטֹּלְנָה	תֵּטַלְנָה	תִּנָּטַלְנָה	תְּנַטֵּלְנָה
	2 m. p.	תִּטְּלוּ	תֵּטְלוּ	תִּנָּטְלוּ	תְּנַטְּלוּ
	2 f. p.	תִּטֹּלְנָה	תֵּטַלְנָה	תִּנָּטַלְנָה	תְּנַטֵּלְנָה
	1 c. p.	נִטֹּל	נֵטַל	נִנָּטֵל	נְנַטֵּל
Impv.	2 m. s.	נְטֹל	טַל	הִנָּטֵל	נַטֵּל
	2 f. s.	נִטְלִי	טְלִי	הִנָּטְלִי	נַטְּלִי
	2 m. p.	נִטְלוּ	טְלוּ	הִנָּטְלוּ	נַטְּלוּ
	2 f. p.	נְטֹלְנָה	טַלְנָה	הִנָּטַלְנָה	נַטֵּלְנָה
Inf.	Absol.	נָטֹל	נָטוֹל	הִנָּטֹל	נַטֵּל
	Const.	נְטֹל	טֶלֶת	הִנָּטֵל	נַטֵּל
Part.	Active		נֹטֵל		מְנַטֵּל
	Passive		נָטוּל	נִטָּל	

Pu‘al	Hithpa‘el	Hiph‘il	Hoph‘al
נֻטַּל	הִתְנַטֵּל	הִטִּיל	הֻטַּל
נֻטְּלָה	הִתְנַטְּלָה	הִטִּילָה	הֻטְּלָה
נֻטַּלְתָּ	הִתְנַטַּלְתָּ	הִטַּלְתָּ	הֻטַּלְתָּ
נֻטַּלְתְּ	הִתְנַטַּלְתְּ	הִטַּלְתְּ	הֻטַּלְתְּ
נֻטַּלְתִּי	הִתְנַטַּלְתִּי	הִטַּלְתִּי	הֻטַּלְתִּי
נֻטְּלוּ	הִתְנַטְּלוּ	הִטִּילוּ	הֻטְּלוּ
נֻטַּלְתֶּם	הִתְנַטַּלְתֶּם	הִטַּלְתֶּם	הֻטַּלְתֶּם
נֻטַּלְתֶּן	הִתְנַטַּלְתֶּן	הִטַּלְתֶּן	הֻטַּלְתֶּן
נֻטַּלְנוּ	הִתְנַטַּלְנוּ	הִטַּלְנוּ	הֻטַּלְנוּ
יְנֻטַּל	יִתְנַטֵּל	יַטִּיל	יֻטַּל
תְּנֻטַּל	תִּתְנַטֵּל	תַּטִּיל	תֻּטַּל
תְּנֻטַּל	תִּתְנַטֵּל	תַּטִּיל	תֻּטַּל
תְּנֻטְּלִי	תִּתְנַטְּלִי	תַּטִּילִי	תֻּטְּלִי
אֲנֻטַּל	אֶתְנַטֵּל	אַטִּיל	אֻטַּל
יְנֻטְּלוּ	יִתְנַטְּלוּ	יַטִּילוּ	יֻטְּלוּ
תְּנֻטַּלְנָה	תִּתְנַטֵּלְנָה	תַּטֵּלְנָה	תֻּטַּלְנָה
תְּנֻטְּלוּ	תִּתְנַטְּלוּ	תַּטִּילוּ	תֻּטְּלוּ
תְּנֻטַּלְנָה	תִּתְנַטֵּלְנָה	תַּטֵּלְנָה	תֻּטַּלְנָה
נְנֻטַּל	נִתְנַטֵּל	נַטִּיל	נֻטַּל
	הִתְנַטֵּל	הַטֵּל	
	הִתְנַטְּלִי	הַטִּילִי	
NONE	הִתְנַטְּלוּ	הַטִּילוּ	NONE
	הִתְנַטֵּלְנָה	הַטֵּלְנָה	
נֻטֹּל	(הִתְנַטֹּל)	הַטֵּל	הֻטֵּל
(נֻטַּל)	הִתְנַטֵּל	הַטִּיל	
	מִתְנַטֵּל	מַטִּיל	
מְנֻטָּל			מֻטָּל

		Qal	Niph'al	Pi'el
Perfect	3 m. s.	קָטָא	נִקְטָא	קִטֵּא
	3 f. s.	קָטְאָה	נִקְטְאָה	קִטְּאָה
	2 m. s.	קָטָאתָ	נִקְטֵאתָ	קִטֵּאתָ
	2 f. s.	קָטָאת	נִקְטֵאת	קִטֵּאת
	1 c. s.	קָטָאתִי	נִקְטֵאתִי	קִטֵּאתִי
	3 c. p.	קָטְאוּ	נִקְטְאוּ	קִטְּאוּ
	2 m. p.	קְטָאתֶם	נִקְטֵאתֶם	קִטֵּאתֶם
	2 f. p.	קְטָאתֶן	נִקְטֵאתֶן	קִטֵּאתֶן
	1 c. p.	קָטָאנוּ	נִקְטֵאנוּ	קִטֵּאנוּ
Imperfect	3 m. s.	יִקְטָא	יִקָּטֵא	יְקַטֵּא
	3 f. s.	תִּקְטָא	תִּקָּטֵא	תְּקַטֵּא
	2 m. s.	תִּקְטָא	תִּקָּטֵא	תְּקַטֵּא
	2 f. s.	תִּקְטְאִי	תִּקָּטְאִי	תְּקַטְּאִי
	1 c. s.	אֶקְטָא	אֶקָּטֵא	אֲקַטֵּא
	3 m. p.	יִקְטְאוּ	יִקָּטְאוּ	יְקַטְּאוּ
	3 f. p.	תִּקְטֶאנָה	תִּקָּטֶאנָה	תְּקַטֶּאנָה
	2 m. p.	תִּקְטְאוּ	תִּקָּטְאוּ	תְּקַטְּאוּ
	2 f. p.	תִּקְטֶאנָה	תִּקָּטֶאנָה	תְּקַטֶּאנָה
	1 c. p.	נִקְטָא	נִקָּטֵא	נְקַטֵּא
Impv.	2 m. s.	קְטָא	הִקָּטֵא	קַטֵּא
	2 f. s.	קִטְאִי	הִקָּטְאִי	קַטְּאִי
	2 m. p.	קִטְאוּ	הִקָּטְאוּ	קַטְּאוּ
	2 f. p.	קְטֶאנָה	הִקָּטֶאנָה	קַטֶּאנָה
Inf.	Absol.	קָטוֹא	נִקְטֹא	קַטֹּא
	Const.	קְטֹא	הִקָּטֵא	קַטֵּא
Part.	Active	קֹטֵא		מְקַטֵּא
	Passive	קָטוּא	נִקְטָא	

Pu'al	Hithpa'el	Hiph'il	Hoph'al
קֻטָּא	הִתְקַטָּא	הִקְטִיא	הָקְטָא
קֻטָּאָה	הִתְקַטָּאָה	הִקְטִיאָה	הָקְטָאָה
קֻטֵּאתָ	הִתְקַטֵּאתָ	הִקְטֵאתָ	הָקְטֵאתָ
קֻטֵּאת	הִתְקַטֵּאת	הִקְטֵאת	הָקְטֵאת
קֻטֵּאתִי	הִתְקַטֵּאתִי	הִקְטֵאתִי	הָקְטֵאתִי
קֻטְּאוּ	הִתְקַטְּאוּ	הִקְטִיאוּ	הָקְטְאוּ
קֻטֵּאתֶם	הִתְקַטֵּאתֶם	הִקְטֵאתֶם	הָקְטֵאתֶם
קֻטֵּאתֶן	הִתְקַטֵּאתֶן	הִקְטֵאתֶן	הָקְטֵאתֶן
קֻטֵּאנוּ	הִתְקַטֵּאנוּ	הִקְטֵאנוּ	הָקְטֵאנוּ
יְקֻטָּא	יִתְקַטָּא	יַקְטִיא	יָקְטָא
תְּקֻטָּא	תִּתְקַטָּא	תַּקְטִיא	תָּקְטָא
תְּקֻטָּא	תִּתְקַטָּא	תַּקְטִיא	תָּקְטָא
תְּקֻטְּאִי	תִּתְקַטְּאִי	תַּקְטִיאִי	תָּקְטְאִי
אֲקֻטָּא	אֶתְקַטָּא	אַקְטִיא	אָקְטָא
יְקֻטְּאוּ	יִתְקַטְּאוּ	יַקְטִיאוּ	יָקְטְאוּ
תְּקֻטֶּאנָה	תִּתְקַטֶּאנָה	תַּקְטֶאנָה	תָּקְטֶאנָה
תְּקֻטְּאוּ	תִּתְקַטְּאוּ	תַּקְטִיאוּ	תָּקְטְאוּ
תְּקֻטֶּאנָה	תִּתְקַטֶּאנָה	תַּקְטֶאנָה	תָּקְטֶאנָה
נְקֻטָּא	נִתְקַטָּא	נַקְטִיא	נָקְטָא
NONE	הִתְקַטָּא	הַקְטֵא	NONE
	הִתְקַטְּאִי	הַקְטִיאִי	
	הִתְקַטְּאוּ	הַקְטִיאוּ	
	הִתְקַטֶּאנָה	הַקְטֶאנָה	
——		הַקְטֵא	——
——	הִתְקַטֵּא	הַקְטִיא	——
	מִתְקַטֵּא	מַקְטִיא	
מְקֻטָּא			מָקְטָא

		Qal	Niph'al	Pi'el
Perfect	3 m. s.	קָטָה	נִקְטָה	קִטָּה
	3 f. s.	קָטְתָה	נִקְטְתָה	קִטְּתָה
	2 m. s.	קָטִיתָ	נִקְטֵיתָ	קִטִּיתָ
	2 f. s.	קָטִית	נִקְטֵית	קִטִּית
	1 c. s.	קָטִיתִי	נִקְטֵיתִי	קִטִּיתִי
	3 c. p.	קָטוּ	נִקְטוּ	קִטּוּ
	2 m. p.	קְטִיתֶם	נִקְטֵיתֶם	קִטִּיתֶם
	2 f. p.	קְטִיתֶן	נִקְטֵיתֶן	קִטִּיתֶן
	1 c. p.	קָטִינוּ	נִקְטֵינוּ	קִטִּינוּ
Imperfect	3 m. s.	יָקְטֶה	יָקָטֶה	יְקַטֶּה
	3 f. s.	תִּקְטֶה	תִּקָּטֶה	תְּקַטֶּה
	2 m. s.	תִּקְטֶה	תִּקָּטֶה	תְּקַטֶּה
	2 f. s.	תִּקְטִי	תִּקָּטִי	תְּקַטִּי
	1 c. s.	אֶקְטֶה	אֶקָּטֶה	אֲקַטֶּה
	3 m. p.	יִקְטוּ	יִקָּטוּ	יְקַטּוּ
	3 f. p.	תִּקְטֶינָה	תִּקָּטֶינָה	תְּקַטֶּינָה
	2 m. p.	תִּקְטוּ	תִּקָּטוּ	תְּקַטּוּ
	2 f. p.	תִּקְטֶינָה	תִּקָּטֶינָה	תְּקַטֶּינָה
	1 c. p.	נִקְטֶה	נִקָּטֶה	נְקַטֶּה
Impv.	2 m. s.	קְטֵה	הִקָּטֵה	קַטֵּה
	2 f. s.	קְטִי	הִקָּטִי	קַטִּי
	2 m. p.	קְטוּ	הִקָּטוּ	קַטּוּ
	2 f. p.	קְטֶינָה	הִקָּטֶינָה	קַטֶּינָה
Inf.	Absol.	קָטֹה	נִקְטֹה	קַטֹּה (קַטֵּה)
	Const.	קְטוֹת	הִקָּטוֹת	קַטּוֹת
Part.	Active	קֹטֶה		מְקַטֶּה
	Passive	קָטוּי	נִקְטֶה	

Pu'al	Hithpa'el	Hiph'il	Hoph'al
קֻטָּה	הִתְקַטָּה	הִקְטָה	הָקְטָה
קֻטְּתָה	הִתְקַטְּתָה	הִקְטְתָה	הָקְטְתָה
קֻטֵּיתָ	הִתְקַטֵּיתָ	הִקְטֵיתָ	הָקְטֵיתָ
קֻטֵּית	הִתְקַטֵּית	הִקְטֵית	הָקְטֵית
קֻטֵּיתִי	הִתְקַטֵּיתִי	הִקְטֵיתִי	הָקְטֵיתִי
קֻטּוּ	הִתְקַטּוּ	הִקְטוּ	הָקְטוּ
קֻטֵּיתֶם	הִתְקַטֵּיתֶם	הִקְטִיתֶם	הָקְטֵיתֶם
קֻטֵּיתֶן	הִתְקַטֵּיתֶן	הִקְטִיתֶן	הָקְטֵיתֶן
קֻטֵּינוּ	הִתְקַטֵּינוּ	הִקְטֵינוּ	הָקְטֵינוּ
יְקֻטֶּה	יִתְקַטֶּה	יַקְטֶה	יָקְטֶה
תְּקֻטֶּה	תִּתְקַטֶּה	תַּקְטֶה	תָּקְטֶה
תְּקֻטֶּה	תִּתְקַטֶּה	תַּקְטֶה	תָּקְטֶה
תְּקֻטִּי	תִּתְקַטִּי	תַּקְטִי	תָּקְטִי
אֲקֻטֶּה	אֶתְקַטֶּה	אַקְטֶה	אָקְטֶה
יְקֻטּוּ	יִתְקַטּוּ	יַקְטוּ	יָקְטוּ
תְּקֻטֶּינָה	תִּתְקַטֶּינָה	תַּקְטֶינָה	תָּקְטֶינָה
תְּקֻטּוּ	תִּתְקַטּוּ	תַּקְטוּ	תָּקְטוּ
תְּקֻטֶּינָה	תִּתְקַטֶּינָה	תַּקְטֶינָה	תָּקְטֶינָה
נְקֻטֶּה	נִתְקַטֶּה	נַקְטֶה	נָקְטֶה
	הִתְקַטֵּה	הַקְטֵה	
NONE	הִתְקַטִּי	הַקְטִי	NONE
	הִתְקַטּוּ	הַקְטוּ	
	הִתְקַטֵּינָה	הַקְטֶינָה	
קֻטֹּה	הִתְקַטֹּה	הַקְטֵה	הָקְטֵה
קֻטּוֹת	הִתְקַטּוֹת	הַקְטוֹת	הָקְטוֹת
	מִתְקַטֶּה	מַקְטֶה	
מְקֻטֶּה			מָקְטֶה

		Qal		Niph'al	Po'el
Perfect	3 m. s	קַט		נָקַט	קוֹטֵט
	3 f. s.	קַטָּה		נָקַטָּ ה	קוֹטְטָה
	2 m. s.	קַטּוֹתָ		נְקַטּוֹתָ	קוֹטַטְתָּ
	2 f. s.	קַטּוֹת		נְקַטּוֹת	קוֹטַטְתְּ
	1 c. s.	קַטּוֹתִי		נְקַטּוֹתִי	קוֹטַטְתִּי
	3 c. p.	קַטּוּ		נָקַטּ וּ	קוֹטְטוּ
	2 m. p.	קַטּוֹתֶם		נְקַטּוֹתֶם	קוֹטַטְתֶּם
	2 f. p.	קַטּוֹתֶן		נְקַטּוֹתֶן	קוֹטַטְתֶּן
	1 c. p.	קַטּוֹנוּ		נְקַטּוֹנוּ	קוֹטַטְנוּ
Imperfect	3 m. s.	יָקֹט	יִקֹּט	יִקַּט	יְקוֹטֵט
	3 f. s.	תָּקֹט	תִּקֹּט	תִּקַּט	תְּקוֹטֵט
	2 m. s.	תָּקֹט	תִּקֹּט	תִּקַּט	תְּקוֹטֵט
	2 f. s.	תָּקֹטִי	תִּקְּטִי	תִּקַּטִי	תְּקוֹטְטִי
	1 c. s.	אָקֹט	אֶקֹּט	אֶקַּט	אֲקוֹטֵט
	3 m. p.	יָקֹטּוּ	יִקְּטוּ	יִקַּטּ וּ	יְקוֹטְטוּ
	3 f. p.	תְּקֻטֶּינָה	תִּקֹּטְנָה	תִּקַּטֶּינָה	תְּקוֹטֵטְנָה
	2 m. p.	תָּקֹטּוּ	תִּקְּטוּ	תִּקַּטּ וּ	תְּקוֹטְטוּ
	2 f. p.	תְּקֻטֶּינָה	תִּקֹּטְנָה	תִּקַּטֶּינָה	תְּקוֹטֵטְנָה
	1 c. p.	נָקֹט	נִקֹּט	נִקַּט	נְקוֹטֵט
Impv.	2 m. s.	קֹט		הִקַּט	קוֹטֵט
	2 f. s.	קֹטִּי		הִקַּטִי	קוֹטְטִי
	2 m. p.	קֹטּ וּ		הִקַּטּ וּ	קוֹטְטוּ
	2 f. p.	קֹטֶּינָה		הִקַּטֶּינָה	קוֹטֵטְנָה
Inf.	Absol.	קָטוֹט		הִקּוֹט	קוֹטֵט
	Const.	קֹט		הִקַּט	קוֹטֵט
Part.	Active	קֹטֵט			מְקוֹטֵט
	Passive	קָטוּט		נָקֹט	

Po'al	Hithpa'el	Hiph'il	Hoph'al
קוֹטַט	הִתְקוֹטֵט	הֵקֵט	הוּקַט
קוֹטְטָה	הִתְקוֹטְטָה	הֵקַטָּ ה	הוּקַטָּ ה
קוֹטַטְתָּ	הִתְקוֹטַטְתָּ	הֲקֵטּוֹתָ	הוּקַטּוֹתָ
קוֹטַטְתְּ	הִתְקוֹטַטְתְּ	הֲקֵטּוֹת	הוּקַטּוֹת
קוֹטַטְתִּי	הִתְקוֹטַטְתִּי	הֲקֵטּוֹתִי	הוּקַטּוֹתִי
קוֹטְטוּ	הִתְקוֹטְטוּ	הֵקֵטּוּ	הוּקַטּוּ
קוֹטַטְתֶּם	הִתְקוֹטַטְתֶּם	הֲקֵטוֹתֶם	הוּקַטּוֹתֶם
קוֹטַטְתֶּן	הִתְקוֹטַטְתֶּן	הֲקֵטוֹתֶן	הוּקַטּוֹתֶן
קוֹטַטְנוּ	הִתְקוֹטַטְנוּ	הֲקֵטּוֹנוּ	הוּקַטּוֹנוּ
יְקוֹטֵט	יִתְקוֹטֵט	יָקֵט	יוּקַט (יָקַט)
תְּקוֹטֵט	תִּתְקוֹטֵט	תָּקֵט	תּוּקַט
תְּקוֹטֵט	תִּתְקוֹטֵט	תָּקֵט	תּוּקַט
תְּקוֹטְטִי	תִּתְקוֹטְטִי	תָּקֵטִּ י	תּוּקַטִּ י
אֲקוֹטֵט	אֶתְקוֹטֵט	אָקֵט	אוּקַט
יְקוֹטְטוּ	יִתְקוֹטְטוּ	יָקֵטּ וּ	יוּקַטּ וּ
תְּקוֹטֵטְנָה	תִּתְקוֹטֵטְנָה	תְּקֵטֶּינָה	תּוּקַטֶּינָה
תְּקוֹטְטוּ	תִּתְקוֹטְטוּ	תָּקֵטּוּ	תּוּקַטּ וּ
תְּקוֹטֵטְנָה	תִּתְקוֹטֵטְנָה	תְּקֵטֶּינָה	תּוּקַטֶּינָה
נְקוֹטֵט	נִתְקוֹטֵט	נָקֵט	נוּקַט
	הִתְקוֹטֵט	הָקֵט	
	הִתְקוֹטְטִי	הָקֵטִּ י	
NONE	הִתְקוֹטְטוּ	הָקֵטּ וּ	NONE
	הִתְקוֹטֵטְנָה	הָקֵטֶּינָה	
	הִתְקוֹטֵט	הָקֵט	
קוֹטֵט		הָקֵט	הוּקַט
	מִתְקוֹטֵט	מֵקֵט	
מְקוֹטָט			מוּקָט

		Qal (ע"ו)	Qal (ע"ו)	Qal (ע"ו)	Qal (ע"י)
Perfect	3 m. s.	קָל	מֵת	בּוֹשׁ	קָל
	3 f. s.	קָלָה	מֵתָה	בּוֹשָׁה	קָלָה
	2 m. s.	קַלְתָּ	מַתָּה	בֹּשְׁתָּ	קַלְתָּ
	2 f. s.	קַלְתְּ	מַתְּ	בֹּשְׁתְּ	קַלְתְּ
	1 c. s.	קַלְתִּי	מַתִּי	בֹּשְׁתִּי	קַלְתִּי
	3 c. p.	קָלוּ	מֵתוּ	בּוֹשׁוּ	קָלוּ
	2 m. p.	קַלְתֶּם	מַתֶּם	בָּשְׁתֶּם	קַלְתֶּם
	2 f. p.	קַלְתֶּן	מַתֶּן	בָּשְׁתֶּן	קַלְתֶּן
	1 c. p.	קַלְנוּ	מַתְנוּ	בֹּשְׁנוּ	קַלְנוּ
Imperfect	3 m. s.	יָקוּל	יָמוּת	יֵבוֹשׁ	יָקִיל
	3 f. s.	תָּקוּל	תָּמוּת	תֵּבוֹשׁ	תָּקִיל
	2 m. s.	תָּקוּל	תָּמוּת	תֵּבוֹשׁ	תָּקִיל
	2 f. s.	תָּקוּלִי	תָּמוּתִי	תֵּבוֹשִׁי	תָּקִילִי
	1 c. s.	אָקוּל	אָמוּת	אֵבוֹשׁ	אָקִיל
	3 m. p.	יָקוּלוּ	יָמוּתוּ	יֵבוֹשׁוּ	יָקִילוּ
	3 f. p.	תְּקוּלֶינָה	תְּמוּתֶינָה	תֵּבַשְׁנָה	תְּקִילֶינָה
	2 m. p.	תָּקוּלוּ	תָּמוּתוּ	תֵּבוֹשׁוּ	תָּקִילוּ
	2 f. p.	תְּקוּלֶינָה	תְּמוּתֶינָה	תֵּבַשְׁנָה	תְּקִילֶינָה
	1 c. p.	נָקוּל	נָמוּת	נֵבוֹשׁ	נָקִיל
Impv.	2 m. s.	קוּל	מוּת	בּוֹשׁ	קִיל
	2 f. s.	קוּלִי	מוּתִי	בּוֹשִׁי	קִילִי
	2 m. p.	קוּלוּ	מוּתוּ	בּוֹשׁוּ	קִילוּ
	2 f. p.	קֹלְנָה	מֹתְנָה	בֹּשְׁנָה	———
Inf. {	Absol.	קוֹל	מוֹת	בּוֹשׁ	קוֹל
	Const.	קוּל	מוּת	בּוֹשׁ	קִיל
Part. {	Active	קָל	מֵת	בּוֹשׁ	קָל
	Passive	קוּל			קוּל קִיל

Niph'al	Polel	Polal	Hiph'il	Hoph'al
נָקוֹל	קוֹלֵל	קוֹלַל	הֵקִיל	הוּקַל
נָקוֹלָה	קוֹלְלָה	קוֹלְלָה	הֵקִילָה	הוּקְלָה
נְקוּלֹוֹתָ	קוֹלַלְתָּ	etc.	הֲקִילֹוֹתָ	הוּגַקְלְתָּ
נְקוּלֹות	קוֹלַלְתְּ		הֲקִילות	הוּקַלְתְּ
נְקוּלֹוֹתִי	קוֹלַלְתִּי		הֲקִילֹוֹתִי	הוּגַקְלְתִּי
נָקוֹלוּ	קוֹלְלוּ		הֵקִילוּ	הוּקְלוּ
נְקוֹלוֹתֶם	קוֹלַלְתֶּם		הֲקִילוֹתֶם	הוּקַלְתֶּם
נְקוֹלוֹתֶן	קוֹלַלְתֶּן		הֲקִילוֹתֶן	הוּקַלְתֶּן
נְקוּלֹונוּ	קוֹלַלְנוּ		הֲקִילֹונוּ	הוּגַקְלְנוּ
יָקוֹל	יְקוֹלֵל	יְקוֹלַל	יָקִיל	יוּקַל
תִּקּוֹל	תְּקוֹלֵל	תְּקוֹלַל	תָּקִיל	תּוּקַל
תִּקּוֹל	תְּקוֹלֵל	etc.	תָּקִיל	תּוּקַל
תִּקּוֹלִי	תְּקוֹלְלִי		תָּקִילִי	תּוּקְלִי
אָקוֹל	אֲקוֹלֵל		אָקִיל	אוּקַל
יִקּוֹלוּ	יְקוֹלְלוּ		יָקִילוּ	יוּקְלוּ
תִּקּוֹלֶלְנָה	תְּקוֹלֵלְנָה		תְּקַלְנָה	תּוּגַקְלְנָה
תִּקּוֹלוּ	תְּקוֹלְלוּ		תָּקִילוּ	תּוּקְלוּ
תִּקּוֹלֶלְנָה	תְּקוֹלֵלְנָה		תְּקַלְנָה	תּוּגַקְלְנָה
נִקּוֹל	נְקוֹלֵל		נָקִיל	נוּקַל
הִקּוֹל	קוֹלֵל		הָקֵל	
הִקּוֹלִי	קוֹלְלִי	NONE	הָקִילִי	NONE
הִקּוֹלוּ	קוֹלְלוּ		הָקִילוּ	
הִקּוֹלֶלְנָה	קוֹלֵלְנָה		הֲקֵלְנָה	
הִקּוֹל	קוֹלֵל		הָקֵל	
הִקּוֹל	—		הָקִיל	
—	מְקוֹלֵל	—	מֵקִיל	
נָקוֹל	—	מְקוֹלָל	—	מוּקָל

	Qal	Niph'al	Qal (prop. פ"י)	Hiph'il (prop. פ"י)
Perfect 3 m. s.	אָטַל	נֶאֱטַל	יָטַל	הֵיטִיל
3 f. s.	etc.	etc.	etc.	הֵיטִילָה
2 m. s.	same as	same as	Regular	הֵיטַלְתָּ
2 f. s.	Pe Guttural	Pe Guttural		הֵיטַלְתְּ
1 c. s.				הֵיטַלְתִּי
3 c. p.				הֵיטִילוּ
2 m. p.				הֵיטַלְתֶּם
2 f. p.				הֵיטַלְתֶּן
1 c. p.				הֵיטַלְנוּ
Imperfect 3 m. s.	יֹאטַל (יֵאטַל)	same as	יִיטַל	יֵיטִיל
3 f. s.	תֹּאטַל	Pe Guttural	תִּיטַל	תֵּיטִיל
2 m. s.	תֹּאטַל		תִּיטַל	תֵּיטִיל
2 f. s.	תֹּאטְלִי		תִּיטְלִי	תֵּיטִילִי
1 c. s.	אֹטַל		אִיטַל	אִיטִיל
3 m. p.	יֹאטְלוּ		יִיטְלוּ	יֵיטִילוּ
3 f. p.	תֹּאטַלְנָה		תִּיטַלְנָה	תֵּיטִילְנָה
2 m. p.	תֹּאטְלוּ		תִּיטְלוּ	תֵּיטִילוּ
2 f. p.	תֹּאטַלְנָה		תִּיטַלְנָה	תֵּיטִילְנָה
1 c. p.	נֹאטַל		נִיטַל	נֵיטִיל
Impv. 2 m. s.	אֱטֹל	same as	יְטַל	הֵיטֵל
2 f. s.	אִטְלִי	Pe Guttural	יִטְלִי	הֵיטִילִי
2 m. p.	אִטְלוּ		יִטְלוּ	הֵיטִילוּ
2 f. p.	אֱטֹלְנָה		יְטַלְנָה	הֵיטֵלְנָה
Inf. Absol.	אָטוֹל	same as	יָטוֹל	הֵיטֵל
Const.	אֱטֹל	Pe Guttural	יְטֹל	הֵיטִיל
Part. Active	אֹטֵל	same as	יֹטֵל	מֵיטִיל
Passive	אָטוּל	Pe Guttural	יָטוּל	

	Qal	Niph'al	Hiph'il	Hoph'al
	יָטַל	נוֹטַל	הוֹטִיל	הוּטַל
	etc.	נוֹטְלָה	הוֹטִילָה	הוּטְלָה
	Regular	נוֹטַלְתָּ	הוֹטַלְתָּ	הוּטַלְתָּ
		נוֹטַלְתְּ	הוֹטַלְתְּ	הוּטַלְתְּ
		נוֹטַלְתִּי	הוֹטַלְתִּי	הוּטַלְתִּי
		נוֹטְלוּ	הוֹטִילוּ	הוּטְלוּ
		נוֹטַלְתֶּם	הוֹטַלְתֶּם	הוּטַלְתֶּם
		נוֹטַלְתֶּן	הוֹטַלְתֶּן	הוּטַלְתֶּן
		נוֹטַלְנוּ	הוֹטַלְנוּ	הוּטַלְנוּ
יֵטַל	יִיטַל	יִנָּטֵל	יוֹטִיל	יוּטַל
תֵּטַל	תִּיטַל	etc.	תּוֹטִיל	תּוּטַל
תֵּטַל	תִּיטַל	Regular	תּוֹטִיל	תּוּטַל
תֵּטְלִי	תִּיטְלִי		תּוֹטִילִי	תּוּטְלִי
אֵטֵל	אִיטַל		אוֹטִיל	אוּטַל
יֵטְלוּ	יִיטְלוּ		יוֹטִילוּ	יוּטְלוּ
תֵּטַלְנָה	תִּיטַלְנָה		תּוֹטֵלְנָה	תּוּטַלְנָה
תֵּטְלוּ	תִּיטְלוּ		תּוֹטִילוּ	תּוּטְלוּ
תֵּטַלְנָה	תִּיטַלְנָה		תּוֹטֵלְנָה	תּוּטַלְנָה
נֵטַל	נִיטַל		נוֹטִיל	נוּטַל
טַל	יְטַל	הִוָּטֵל	הוֹטֵל	
טְלִי	יְטְלִי	הִוָּטְלִי	הוֹטִילִי	NONE
טְלוּ	יְטְלוּ	הִוָּטְלוּ	הוֹטִילוּ	
טֵלְנָה	יְטַלְנָה	הִוָּטַלְנָה	הוֹטֵלְנָה	
יְטוֹל	יָטוֹל	הִוָּטֵל	הוֹטֵל	———
טֵלֶת	יְטַל	הִוָּטֵל	הוֹטִיל	———
יֵטַל			מוֹטִיל	
יָטוּל		נוֹטַל		מוּטַל

		1 c. s.	2 m. s.	2 f. s.	3 m. s.	3 f. s.
Perfect	3 m. s.	קְטָלַנִי	קְטָלְךָ (‑ְךָ)	קְטָלֵךְ	קְטָלָהוּ / קְטָלוֹ	קְטָלָהּ
	3 f. s.	קְטָלַתְנִי	קְטָלָתֶךָ	קְטָלָתֶךְ	קְטָלָתְהוּ / קְטָלָתוּ	קְטָלָתָּה
	2 m. s.	קְטַלְתַּנִי / קְטַלְתָּנִי	———	———	קְטַלְתָּהוּ / קְטַלְתּוֹ	קְטַלְתָּהּ
	2 f. s.	קְטַלְתִּינִי	———	———	קְטַלְתִּיהוּ / קְטַלְתִּיו	קְטַלְתִּיהָ
	1 c. s.	———	קְטַלְתִּיךָ	קְטַלְתִּיךְ	קְטַלְתִּיו	קְטַלְתִּיהָ
	3 c. p.	קְטָלוּנִי	קְטָלוּךָ	קְטָלוּךְ	קְטָלוּהוּ	קְטָלוּהָ
	2 m. p.	קְטַלְתּוּנִי			קְטַלְתּוּהוּ	(קְטַלְתּוּהָ)
	1 c. p.	———	קְטַלְנוּךָ	קְטַלְנוּךְ	קְטַלְנוּהוּ	קְטַלְנוּהָ
Perf. { Mid. E. 3 m. s.		קְטֵלַנִי	קְטֵלְךָ	קְטֵלֵךְ	קְטֵלוֹ	קְטֵלָהּ
Imperfect	3 m. s.	יִקְטְלַנִי	יִקְטָלְךָ	יִקְטְלֵךְ	יִקְטְלֵהוּ	יִקְטְלֶהָ / יִקְטְלָהּ
	With Nun Ep.	יִקְטְלַנִּי	יִקְטָלֶךָּ	———	יִקְטְלֶנּוּ	יִקְטְלֶנָּה
	3 m. p.	יִקְטְלוּנִי	יִקְטְלוּךָ	יִקְטְלוּךְ	יִקְטְלוּהוּ	יִקְטְלוּהָ
	2 f. p.	תִּקְטְלוּנִי	———	———	תִּקְטְלוּהוּ	תִּקְטְלוּהָ
Impv. { 2 m. s.		קָטְלֵנִי	———	———	קָטְלֵהוּ	קָטְלֶהָ / קָטְלָהּ
Inf. { Const.		קָטְלִי / קָטְלֵנִי	קָטְלְךָ / קָטְלֶךָ	קָטְלֵךְ	קָטְלוֹ	קָטְלָהּ

1 c. p.	2 m. p.	2 f. p.	3 m. p.	3 f. p.
קְטָלָנוּ	קְטַלְכָם	(קְטַלְכָן)	קְטָלָם	קְטָלָן
קְטַלְתָּנוּ	――	――	קְטָלָתַם	(קְטָלָתַן)
קְטַלְתָּנוּ	――	――	קְטַלְתָּם	(קְטַלְתָּן)
קְטַלְתִּינוּ	――	――	קְטַלְתִּים	(קְטַלְתִּין)
――	קְטַלְתִּיכָם	(קְטַלְתִּיכָן)	קְטַלְתִּים	קְטַלְתִּין
קְטָלוּנוּ	――	――	קְטָלוּם	קְטָלוּן
קְטַלְתּוּנוּ	――	――	(קְטַלְתּוּם)	(קְטַלְתּוּן)
――	קְטָלְנוּכֶם	(קְטָלְנוּכֶן)	קְטָלְנוּם	(קְטָלְנוּן)
קְטֶלָנוּ	קְטֶלְכֶם	(קְטֶלְכֶן)	קְטֶלָם	קְטֶלָן
יִקְטְלֵנוּ	יִקְטָלְכֶם	(יִקְטָלְכֶן)	יִקְטְלֵם	(יִקְטְלֵן)
יִקְטְלֵנוּ	יִקְטְלוּכֶם	(יִקְטְלוּכֶן)	יִקְטְלוּם	(יִקְטְלוּן)
יִקְטְלוּנוּ	――	――	תִּקְטְלוּם	תִּקְטְלוּן
תִּקְטְלוּנוּ				
קָטְלֵנוּ	――	――	קָטְלֵם	――
קָטְלֵנוּ	קָטְלְכֶם / קָטְלְכֶם	קָטְלְכֶן / קָטְלְכֶן	קָטְלָם	קָטְלָן

		Strong Verb	Pe Guttural	Ayin Guttural	Lamedh Guttural	Pe Nun	Lamedh Aleph	Lamedh He	Doubled Ayin	Middle Vowel	Pe Waw — Pe Yodh
Qal	Perf.	קָטַל	עָמַד	שָׁאַל	שָׁלַח	נָגַשׁ	מָצָא	גָּלָה	סָבַב	קָם, מֵת	יָשַׁב, יָטַב
	Impf.	יִקְטֹל	יַעֲמֹד	יִשְׁאַל	יִשְׁלַח	יִגַּשׁ, יִתֵּן	יִמְצָא	יִגְלֶה	יָסֹב, יִסֹּב	יָקוּם, יָמוּת	יֵשֵׁב, יִיטַב
	Impv.	קְטֹל	עֲמֹד	שְׁאַל	שְׁלַח	גַּשׁ, נְגַשׁ	מְצָא	גְּלֵה	סֹב	קוּם	שֵׁב
	Inf. A.	קָטוֹל	עָמוֹד	שָׁאוֹל	שָׁלוֹחַ	נָגוֹשׁ	מָצוֹא	גָּלֹה	סָבוֹב	קוֹם	יָשׁוֹב
	Inf. C.	קְטֹל	עֲמֹד	שְׁאֹל	שְׁלֹחַ	גֶּשֶׁת	מְצֹא	גְּלוֹת	סֹב	קוּם	שֶׁבֶת
	Ptc. A.	קֹטֵל	עֹמֵד	שֹׁאֵל	שֹׁלֵחַ	נֹגֵשׁ	מֹצֵא	גֹּלֶה	סֹבֵב	קָם	יֹשֵׁב
	Ptc. P.	קָטוּל	עָמוּד	שָׁאוּל	שָׁלוּחַ	נָגוּשׁ	מָצוּא	גָּלוּי	סָבוּב		יָשׁוּב
Niph'al	Perf.	נִקְטַל	נֶעֱמַד	נִשְׁאַל	נִשְׁלַח	נִגַּשׁ	נִמְצָא	נִגְלָה	נָסַב	נָקוֹם	נוֹשַׁב
	Impf.	יִקָּטֵל	יֵעָמֵד	יִשָּׁאֵל	יִשָּׁלַח	יִנָּגֵשׁ	יִמָּצֵא	יִגָּלֶה	יִסַּב	יִקּוֹם	יִוָּשֵׁב
	Impv.	הִקָּטֵל	הֵעָמֵד	הִשָּׁאֵל	הִשָּׁלַח	הִנָּגֵשׁ	הִמָּצֵא	הִגָּלֵה	הִסַּב	הִקּוֹם	הִוָּשֵׁב
	Inf. A.	הִקָּטֹל	הֵעָמֹד	הִשָּׁאֹל	הִשָּׁלֹחַ	הִנָּגֹשׁ	הִמָּצֹא	הִגָּלֹה	הִסּוֹב	הִקּוֹם	הִוָּשֹׁב
	Inf. C.	הִקָּטֵל	הֵעָמֵד	הִשָּׁאֵל	הִשָּׁלַח	הִנָּגֵשׁ	הִמָּצֵא	הִגָּלוֹת	הִסַּב	הִקּוֹם	הִוָּשֵׁב
	Part.	נִקְטָל	נֶעֱמָד	נִשְׁאָל	נִשְׁלָח	נִגָּשׁ	נִמְצָא	נִגְלֶה	נָסָב	נָקוֹם	נוֹשָׁב
Pi'el	Perf.	קִטֵּל	עִמֵּד		שִׁלַּח		מִצֵּא	גִּלָּה		קִיֵּם	יִשֵּׁב
	Impf.	יְקַטֵּל	יְעַמֵּד		יְשַׁלַּח		יְמַצֵּא	יְגַלֶּה		יְקַיֵּם	יְיַשֵּׁב
	Impv.	קַטֵּל	עַמֵּד		שַׁלַּח		מַצֵּא	גַּלֵּה		קַיֵּם	יַשֵּׁב
	Inf. A.	קַטֹּל	עַמֵּד		שַׁלֵּחַ		מַצֵּא	גַּלֹּה		קַיֵּם	יַשֵּׁב

Hoph'al					Hiph'il						Pu'al				Pi'el	
Part.	Inf. C.	Inf. A.	Impf.	Perf.	Part.	Inf. C.	Inf. A.	Impv.	Impf.	Perf.	Part.	Inf. A. / —	Impf.	Perf.	Inf. C.	Part.
מָקְטָל	הָקְטֵל	הָקְטֵל	יָקְטַל	הָקְטַל	מַקְטִיל	הַקְטִיל	הַקְטֵל	הַקְטֵל	יַקְטִיל	הִקְטִיל	מְקֻטָּל	—	יְקֻטַּל	קֻטַּל	קַטֵּל	מְקַטֵּל
מָעֳמַד	הָעֳמֵד	הָעֳמֵד	יָעֳמַד	הָעֳמַד	מַעֲמִיד	הַעֲמִיד	הַעֲמֵד	הַעֲמֵד	יַעֲמִיד	הֶעֱמִיד	מְעֻמָּד	—	יְעֻמַּד	עֻמַּד	עַמֵּד	מְעַמֵּד
מָמְצָא	הָמְצֵא	הַמְצֵא	יָמְצָא	הָמְצָא	מַמְצִיא	הַמְצִיא	הַמְצֵא	הַמְצֵא	יַמְצִיא	הִמְצִיא	מְמֻצָּא	—	יְמֻצָּא	מֻצָּא	מַצֵּא	מְמַצֵּא
מָשְׁלַחַת	הָשְׁלֵחַ	הָשְׁלֵחַ	יָשְׁלַח	הָשְׁלַח	מַשְׁלֵחַ	הַשְׁלִיחַ	הַשְׁלֵחַ	הַשְׁלַח	יַשְׁלִיחַ	הִשְׁלִיחַ	מְשֻׁלָּח	—	יְשֻׁלַּח	שֻׁלַּח	שַׁלֵּחַ	מְשַׁלֵּחַ
מָסֵב	הוּסַב	הוּסֵב	יוּסַב	הוּסַב	מֵסֵב	הָסֵב	הָסֵב	הָסֵב	יָסֵב	הֵסֵב	מְסֻבָּב	—	יְסֻבַּב	סֻבַּב	סַבֵּב	מְסַבֵּב
מָצָא	הֻמְצָא	הֻמְצֵא	יֻמְצָא	הֻמְצָא	מַמְצִיא	הַמְצִיא	הַמְצֵא	הַמְצֵא	יַמְצִיא	הִמְצִיא	מְמֻצָּא	—	יְמֻצָּא	מֻצָּא	מַצֵּא	מְמַצֵּא
מָקְטֶלֶת	הֻקְטֵל	הֻקְטֵל	יֻקְטַל	הֻקְטַל	מַקְטֶלֶת	הַקְטִיל	הַקְטֵל	הַקְטֵל	יַקְטִיל	הִקְטִיל	מְקֻטֶּלֶת	—	יְקֻטַּל	קֻטְּלָה	קַטֵּל	מְקַטֶּלֶת
מָקָם	הוּקַם	הוּקֵם	יוּקַם	הוּקַם	מֵקִים	הָקִים	הָקֵם	הָקֵם	יָקִים	הֵקִים	מְקוֹמָם	—	יְקוֹמַם	קוֹמַם	קוֹמֵם	מְקוֹמֵם
מָגְלֶה	הֻגְלָה	הֻגְלֵה	יֻגְלֶה	הֻגְלָה	מַגְלֶה	הַגְלוֹת	הַגְלֵה	הַגְלֵה	יַגְלֶה	הִגְלָה	מְגֻלֶּה	—	יְגֻלֶּה	גֻּלָּה	גַּלּוֹת	מְגַלֶּה
מוּשַׁל	—	—	יוּשַׁל	הוּשַׁל	מַשִּׁיל	הַשִּׁיל	הַשֵּׁל	הַשֵּׁל	יַשִּׁיל	הִשִּׁיל	מְשֻׁלָּל	—	יְשֻׁלַּל	שֻׁלַּל	שַׁלֵּל	מְשַׁלֵּל

vocalisare: (3FS) הָקְטְלָה ...

(all others are
consonantal)   (3MP) קָטְלוּ   הָקְטְלוּ ...

Qal Pf.   examples of rules below

1. קָטַל (3MS) קָטְלָה (3FS) [not קָטַלָה] — הִקְטִיל הִקְטִילָה (3FS) [not הִקְטִיל...] ᴴⁱᵖʰⁱˡ

2. (2MS) קָטַלְתָ (always) — קָטַל

   Pf. Qal
   3MS   קָטַל Qal Pf.   Impf. Passive (Niph.) הָקַטֵל הִקָטְלִי הִקָטְלוּ   all others
              קָטְלוּ   הָקַטֵל ...

           (3FP) תִּקְטֹלְנָה תִּ...
                 (Piel)   הָקַטֵל הִקַטְלוּ (Piel)
           (3FP) הִ ...

3. Impf. is   Niphal Impf. is:
   (1FS) תִּקְטְלִי — (the הִ) being dropped   (2FS) תִּקָּטֵל ...   (הִ replaced ...)
   (2MS) תִּקְטֹל — (note הִ is raised to הֹ   (2MS) תִּקָּטֵל ...   in 2FS & 2MS
                    before long ending)

4. Inf. cst. קְטֹל but Hiphil is הַקְטִיל   תִּקָּטֵל ...
   Inf. abs. קָטוֹל but Hophal is הָקְטֵל   הִקָּטֵל ...

Rules for Identification of forms

1. In adding a vocalic ending the vowel of the original ultima is reduced to sh'wa everywhere (i.e.) except in the Hiph'il where it is retained and accented.

2. In adding consonantal ending in the perfect the vowel of the 2nd radical is everywhere pattah (—). In the Imperfect it is holem for qal, pattah in passive stems, and tsere elsewhere.

┌───┐
│ ONE MUST LEARN THE SEVEN 2 M S Imperfect STEMS │
└───┘

3. The Inur. is formed by taking 2 ms Imrpf. and dropping the preformative (תִ); In the Niph'al, Hiph'il, and Hithpa'el, the תִ appears

4. The Infinitive cst. is same as imperative, except in Hiph'il where the original long vowel (—) is retained. Imperf. ibid. is always holem save in Hiph'il and Hoph'al where it is tsere

5.